HELPING
RELATIONSHIPS

HELPING RELATIONSHIPS

BASIC CONCEPTS FOR THE HELPING PROFESSIONS

THIRD EDITION

Arthur W. Combs
PRIVATE PRACTICE
GREELEY, COLORADO

Donald L. Avila
UNIVERSITY OF FLORIDA

ALLYN AND BACON, INC.
Boston • London • Sydney • Toronto

Series Editor: Jeffery W. Johnston
Production Coordinator: Helyn Pultz

Library of Congress Cataloging in Publication Data

Combs, Arthur Wright.
  Helping relationships.

  Bibliography: p.
  Includes index.
  1. Counseling. 2. Helping behavior. I. Avila, Donald L. II. Title.
BF637.C6C48 1985   158′.3   84-12437
ISBN 0-205-08250-5

Printed in the United States of America

10 9 8 7 6 5 4 3 2 1   89 88 87 86 85 84

CONTENTS

PREFACE

In earlier editions we stated that the goal of *Helping Relationships* was an attempt to explore two basic questions: (1) What ideas about human behavior have special value for understanding helping relationships? and (2) What do these ideas imply for effective practice in the helping professions? The response to that effort has been deeply satisfying to us and to our publisher. But time does not stand still, especially in such rapidly growing fields as the helping professions. It is time for a new edition to bring things up to date.

For some time we have been in the midst of an "information explosion." Some of the new information corroborates prior understandings; some points the way to exciting new concepts or practices; and some contradicts what has gone before, so that we must constantly revise what we believe about human beings and how we may go about helping them.

A number of basic concepts about helping relationships have stood the test of time and provide effective guidelines for practice in all the helping professions. We have maintained these concepts as the foundation for this edition. We have also tried to incorporate the most recent research; remove outdated material; streamline the presentation; delete elements considered repetitious by readers of previous editions; provide fresh perspectives; and bring the book in line with the most recent thinking about the helping professions.

We believe three features, especially, make this edition an improvement over previous ones. First, the material has been reorganized, with many changes in titles and subtitles that make the book clearer and easier to follow and better reflect the content of chapters and sections.

Second, a new first chapter has been added that sets the tone and intent of the book and lends a much needed reality factor (previous editions have been criticized for being "too idealistic"). Chapter One also gives a brief history and evaluation of the helping professions that should be particularly helpful to young people who are making career decisions in a time when such decisions seem more difficult than ever to make.

Third, we have adopted a more convenient, less confusing referencing style than that used in previous editions.

Another important change is a shift in author responsibility. For the first two editions Arthur Combs served as senior author. In this volume Donald Avila has assumed the leadership role, with Art Combs serving as editor-consultant, and William Purkey has moved on to other interests.

Two problems have proved particularly difficult for us to solve in this volume. One has to do with the definition of a professional helper. Being a helper is more a matter of people's perceptions than of title. The number of individuals who might be considered helpers is enormous, including such persons as police officers, military personnel, salespersons, funeral directors, sanitation engineers, secretaries, and merchants. Almost anyone who performs a service that improves the quality of the lives of others can, in some frame of reference, be considered a helper. To ease this literary burden, we have limited our reference to helpers to those who are more typically labeled so, such as teachers, counselors, psychologists, physicians, lawyers, and clergy.

The second problem has to do with gender. There is not yet an adequate convention to escape the awkwardness and chauvinism of "his" or "man" references. We have tried to solve the problem in three ways: (1) by alternating the use of "he" and "she," "himself" and "herself"; (2) by using "them" and "they" when appropriate; and (3) by avoiding stereotyped occupational identifications. If, on occasion, this has violated the structure of language, so be it. We believe the violation is justified in order to strike a blow for sexual equality.

We express our thanks to the many people who have made this book possible; to the numerous authors and researchers whose work we have incorporated; to the students, clients, and patients with whom we have worked and from whom we have learned so much; and to the readers of previous editions who have made many fine suggestions as to how the book could be improved. Special thanks go to Carol Springer, who not only typed the manuscript but also corrected errors and suggested ways to make the book more readable.

A reviewer who read the manuscript described this edition as being "clearer," "an improvement in style," "cleaner," and "more realistic, accurate" and as dealing with the "issues of concern to professions in the '80s." We hope the reviewer is right, for that was our intent.

A.W.C.
D.L.A.

ONE

THE NATURE OF THE HELPING PROFESSIONS

If Dickens's was the best and worst of times, ours must surely be the most confusing. We are surrounded by conflict and controversy. There are few, if any, "truths" we can be certain of. Everything seems relative, and we have to dig deep into ourselves to find values and beliefs to guide our behavior, for not much is "out there" to help. Good things and bad things are happening all around us, and it is hard to determine whether there is more good than bad. It is as if humankind were in a race with itself to reach the millennium or self-destruct, and no one can be sure which impulse will win out.

One thing we *can* be sure of: Whether times get better or worse, they are going to get more complex, and the helping professions will be in the thick of things. As life becomes more complex, people find it harder to cope. When coping becomes more difficult, helpers are sought after in greater numbers. All we have to do to affirm this is briefly examine the recent development of the helping professions.

For most of human history the major problems that people faced revolved around control of the environment—finding ways to extract from their surroundings the food, clothing, shelter, and security from danger that were necessary for the well-being of self and loved ones. About a hundred years ago a major change began to take place. With the coming of science, industrial technology, and, most recently, the exploitation of energy sources, little by little we gained control of our environment to such an extent that today we have the know-how and the techniques available to feed, clothe, and shelter everyone on earth—if we don't first do ourselves in. We have gained the capabilities to solve our ancient physical problems only to find ourselves confronted with a new set: the people problems.

EXPANDING NEEDS FOR THE HELPING PROFESSIONS

The most pressing problems people face today are human ones—how to grow satisfactorily as individuals, on one hand, and how to interact successfully with others in an ever-shrinking world, on the other. We live in the most interdependent, cooperative society the world has ever known. We depend on the goodwill and cooperation of millions of other people. We have created a world in which few of us could live for longer than a few days if we were totally out of touch with others. We are so dependent on one another that one person making an error (crashing a plane, pushing the wrong buttons in a nuclear power plant) or running amok (holding people hostage, shooting a great leader) can jeopardize thousands. Some of the greatest problems we face as a society are those of population growth, pollution, poverty, war and peace, civil and ethnic rights, social security, mental and physical health, and distribution of goods and services. All these are essentially human problems. Even the dreaded nuclear bomb is a human problem; it is not the bomb that we need to fear but rather those who might use it. Likewise, some of the greatest problems we face as individuals are those of human relationships at home, school, and work or as we are caught up in the dynamic forces of our complex social order.

The social sciences—psychology, sociology, anthropology, and political science—came into being in response to people's need to cope with the pressing new problems of the human condition. The helping professions in turn were invented to apply the new understandings of the social sciences to the practical problems of human welfare. We are living in the midst of a great revolution, as we move out of the era of the physical sciences and into the era of the social sciences. Predicting the future in such times of rapid change is a risky business, but this much seems certain: With each technological advance supplied by science and industry we become more dependent on one another. Consequently, futurists agree that the world into which we are moving will be characterized by an ever-increasing interdependence and the need for cooperative, responsible citizens who are knowledgeable about themselves and human interrelationships and who are ready, willing, and able to put such knowledge to work.

The same forces that make us more interdependent also set folks free to seek personal fulfillment. Abraham Maslow pointed out that human needs exist in a kind of hierarchy, ranging from the very basic needs for air, water, and food; through needs for comfort and security, love, self-esteem, and social acceptance; to high-level needs for self-actualization and personal fulfillment.[1] Generally, people whose low-order needs go unsatisfied cannot spend much energy seeking fulfillment at higher levels. It is hard, for example, to think nice thoughts about democracy on an empty stomach. On the other hand, satisfying one's basic needs has the effect of setting one free to seek personal fulfillment. We have succeeded in creating a more affluent society, and this may be a prime cause for the surge of interest in personal health, consciousness-expanding activities, and the search for personal meaning and actualization. Such movements often have been described as selfish manifestations of the "me generation." Some may, indeed, be self-indulgent. But such phenomena may also have deeper roots in the more positive strivings of people for personal fulfillment.

With every technological advance that provides the goods and services to fulfill our basic needs, we are at the same time increasingly free to seek the fulfillment of higher needs. Therefore, the successes of science and industry may make us more dependent on one another, but they also set us free to seek for ever-higher levels of personal fulfillment. All this seems certain to increase enormously the need for professional helpers in the foreseeable future.

THE EXPANDING ROLE OF PROFESSIONAL HELPERS

With the possible exception of teaching, most helping professions began as rehabilitative services. They were designed to pick up, patch up, and restart those who were seriously injured by life or who could not adjust to the predicaments in which they found themselves. This rehabilitative phase of the helping professions was mostly a one-on-one relationship, generally carried out in a setting psychologically removed from the client's customary life-style. Later, the role of professional helpers was expanded to serve a preventive function, to diagnose people's strengths and weaknesses, and to forestall their getting into difficulties. This shift in the task of helping greatly increases the number of potential clients. It also moves the function of helping much closer to the mainstream of daily life. Most recently we have seen a third shift in the role of professional helpers toward facilitating the processes of self-actualization for the sick and well, in trouble or out, whatever their age or condition. Because every human being has a need for self-actualization, this increases the potential clients for the helping professions to all human beings everywhere and calls for the application of helping processes wherever people are growing and interacting.

The expansion of clientele for the helping professions is already far advanced in a number of areas. In education, for example, more and more teachers, supervisors, and administrators are becoming involved in various approaches to "humanistic education," the application of helping thought and practice in the public schools. Counseling and guidance are no longer seen as ancillary functions for a comparative few. Instead, these functions are moving into classroom, laboratory, and extracurricular activities. Helping practices that were developed originally for psychotherapeutic purposes are increasingly being applied in the classroom. Concern for "affective education," helping relationships, and the introduction of group processes to the classroom are becoming more commonplace in the public schools. Indicative of this thrust is the fact that recently an entire issue of *Educational Leadership* was devoted to affective education, pointing out how important it is in the education process.[2]

At the same time the need for continuing education in a rapidly changing world has made formal learning opportunities available to people of all ages and for every conceivable interest. The growth of junior colleges and adult education has made it possible for people to be instructed in almost anything if enough students can be brought together to make up a class. Much of this instruction has been deeply influenced by the helping professions, especially in the application of group-process thinking and techniques.

In the field of health a new interest in physical and mental well-being has sprung to life. Since the early 1970s there has been an enormous increase in the number of people engaged in "in-tune-with" physical activities like running, jogging, gymnastics, skiing, hiking, sailing, cycling, skating, swimming, climbing, soaring, surfing, and camping, as opposed to "conquering" sports like off-road biking, auto racing, snowmobiling, and drag racing. The medical profession now speaks of high-level wellness and the unitary character of physical and mental health.

Many people have become deeply interested in personal growth, self-awareness, consciousness-expanding activities, transcendent experiences, meditation, and relaxation. In the social area the use of groups to improve sensitivity, to increase awareness of self and others, and to bring together people with common problems of a thousand varieties for personal exploration and growth has become commonplace. Increasing numbers of professional helpers are being employed in industry as managers discover that helping processes pay "on the bottom line." Some industries, like the auto industry, are also discovering that such changes in thinking are necessary if they are to compete successfully with foreign manufacturers. All these expanded areas of interest in helping processes are already in place and growing by leaps and bounds.

NEW AND EXPANDING AREAS OF RESEARCH

All sorts of experiments looking into every aspect of human growth and experience are currently going on. Some bid fair to change our concepts about the very nature of the human organism. As a result of modern research, for example, we are changing our conception of the human brain as a kind of storehouse–switchboard to a conception of the brain as a marvelous organ that is continuously searching the world for meaning or "fit." Such conceptions are much more in tune with humanistic psychology and humanistic approaches to teaching, counseling, social work, and most other helping professions. Research on relaxation, transcendent experiences, and meditation is providing us with new understanding about what it means to be fully alive and in touch with ourselves. All kinds of research are being conducted in the field of group experience, as workers seek to determine the dynamics of these processes, to discover the guiding principles for action and the selection of facilitating practices. Even industry, long notorious for authoritarian control and management orientation, is beginning to seek more human approaches to administration, worker participation in decision making, and the application of humanistically oriented concepts of motivation and group structure to problems of production.

New Concepts of Health

Perhaps one of the most exciting areas of research is the shift in thinking about what it means to be healthy or well adjusted. For years we have lived with the concept of adjustment dictated by the good old normal curve in which the well adjusted sat proudly astride the mean, with the poorly adjusted at either end of the distribution. Such a concept made human adjustment synonymous with average, an idea not very useful to educators, counselors, or social workers. Today, workers in all the social sciences, as well as in medicine and theology, are turning their attention to the question, What does it mean to be truly healthy in the fullest sense of the word? This search has brought us new concepts of human fulfillment that are expressed in such terms as high-level wellness, self-actualization, self-fulfillment, transcendent being, and even "the beautiful and noble person." Such research and thinking have vast implications for all the helping professions and for society itself. Whatever we decide is the truly healthy, maximally fulfilling person must automatically become the goal not only of the helping professions but also of society and its institutions.

THE EXPANDING NEEDS OF SOCIETY FOR HELPING PROCESSES

The mix of conceptions of health and fulfillment, new psychologies concentrating on human experience, and the ferment of thought and exploration in the helping professions is exciting and promising. We have hardly scratched the surface of the changes all this is likely to bring to our ways of thinking and being in the near future. A movement has already started. One can see its origins in such areas as the following:

In the steady growth of the humanist movement in our public schools
In new concepts and practices in industrial management and the relationship of management and labor
In new role definitions in family life and alternative arrangements for family living
In governmental concerns for human welfare, expressed in such efforts as social security, civil rights, employment, voting rights, and a hundred more
In the introduction of group dynamics in churches, synagogues, mosques, and temples, to say nothing of new concepts of religious experience and the formation of structures for their facilitation
In new conceptions of role and scope for medicine and psychiatry and the concept of high-level wellness

In new conceptions of law and the applications of helping processes in prisons, courts, and many kinds of legal disputes

In improvements in international communication and cooperation as understanding of the dynamics of the threat and challenge seeps into diplomatic thinking and international relationships.

All this, and more, is only the beginning of what must be inevitable trends brought on by a shrinking world and our ever-increasing dependence on one another. The helping professions were born of such needs, and what we discover about the nature of human beings and how their growth and development can be facilitated is fundamental to the structures and processes we invent for human welfare. Understanding the nature and processes of helping is a primary tool for the construction of a truly humanitarian world. In the years to come professional helpers are going to be involved in a great revolution in human events. Being a part of that revolution is sustaining and exciting for the professional helper. At the same time, as a member of and contributor to the helping professions, one will have the satisfaction of feeling that he or she is making a significant contribution to human affairs.

HAZARDS AND HEADACHES OF HELPING

As exciting as these prospects are, helping is far from being all fun and games. There are problems enough to discourage many individuals from becoming helpers and to cause others to drop out of the helping professions. Some of the larger problems should be considered by every prospective helper.

The Highs and the Lows

Support for the helping professions is cyclical. Sometimes social and financial support is strong, as in the 1960s, and sometimes it is not, as in the 1970s and so far in the 1980s. Being a professional helper is much easier when support is high. Things get done and all the professions move forward. It can be exasperating when support is low. Programs get cut and there just don't seem to be enough people or money to do things right. Most of the helping professions, such as teaching, counseling, mental health clinics, and hospitals, fall under public services. When times are hard, as they are now, public services suffer, and the professional helper suffers as well. But times change, and if one holds on awhile, things will improve. Over the long haul public service moves forward.

You'll Never Get Rich

Professional helpers, with the exception of those who are self-employed or on executive levels in business and industry, need not expect to make a lot of money. Most members of the helping professions are public servants in one way or another, and public servants are usually paid at the lowest going rate. Furthermore, it is a strange phenomena, but the closer a helper is to the front line, the less she or he is likely to make. Secondary and elementary teachers make less than counselors; counselors in turn make less than school psychologists; and they all make less than public school administrators. College professors who spend the bulk of their time teaching and counseling students make less than those who spend most of their time publishing and doing research. Nurses *notoriously* make less than physicians. If money is high on your list of things that are important in life, and you have no aspirations of becoming a physician or a lawyer, the helping professions are not for you.

Helping Can Be Hazardous

High pay, however, may not be all that it's cracked up to be. A case can be made for placing high salaries low on one's list of priorities. Evidence suggests that the more a professional helper makes, the more he or she is in danger. Currently, suicide rates are quite high in the helping professions and, with the exception of nurses, are related to a helper's income. Of *all* professionals the highest rates of suicide occur, in order, among (1) nurses, (2) dentists, (3) physicians, and (4) psychologists.[3]

The helping professions are, indeed, tough careers to go into for those who are not strong. Working day after day with other human beings, visiting the dark and painful places in their lives, is not easy. As the suicide rates suggest, a person cannot carry that burden without a special effort, a certain kind of personality, and a great deal of internal strength.

Professional helpers must be able to find joy in bringing people through these dark places, rather than take on their clients' problems as their own and suffer with them. Helpers must learn to grow and increase their strength through wrestling with the pain of others rather than let that pain drag them down too.

Why nurses are at the top of the suicide list and do not follow the general pattern is not clear. Maybe it is because they shoulder such tremendous responsibility, often of a life-and-death nature, and yet do not receive nearly the financial or social status they deserve.

The plight of attendants in psychiatric hospitals is probably the most blatant example of injustice. Psychiatric attendants have high suicide rates and many other problems as well, including rampant alcohol and drug addiction. This is true partly because they are regarded as being at the bottom of the medical staff totem pole, are paid pitiful sums, and are treated poorly, despite the fact that they probably have a greater effect on and are more immediately responsible for the patients' well-being than any other staff members. Psychiatrists usually meet briefly with most patients two or three times a week and with some patients not at all. The attendants are with the patients twenty-four hours a day.

No Finished Products Here

If you are the kind of person who has an overpowering need to see the final fruit of your efforts, you will want to choose a particular branch of the helping professions carefully. Physical changes usually take place faster than psychological ones. For example, a dentist or a physician can, in most cases, minister to a patient and see results immediately. One person has dental problems and the dentist fixes them. Another individual is sick or injured and the physician can often help cure the sickness or heal the injury quickly. However, for those members of the helping professions who deal with mental, moral, and social aspects of development, there are no "quick fixes."

Growth, change, and improvement take time. Consequently, helpers like teachers, counselors, psychotherapists, and persons of the cloth often may not be able to do more than launch their helpees into new ways of being, assist them to *begin* to see new possibilities in their lives. Seldom will helpers dealing with problems of growth and change be able to experience the kind of satisfying end that a lawyer "closing a case" or a nurse escorting a patient from a hospital does. Many aspiring helpers have turned to painting or working with computers because they were totally frustrated by this aspect of helping. Helping can be a terribly frustrating experience, especially in some public agencies in which, because of the large number of persons that *must* be assisted, helpees are passed through the system more quickly than the helpers would like, and nothing resembling a sense of closure is ever achieved.

Most helpers discover that sometimes they cannot travel down the road of life with a particular helpee as long as they would like or feel the need to. At such times they must simply "keep the faith" and believe that what they did made a difference.

Helpers Are Flaky

One problem often encountered in the helping professions is that of generalization. In disciplines as young, ambiguous, and poorly defined as are many of the helping professions, a great deal of exuberant activity and experimentation is always going on. With few concrete answers available to them, helpers are forever seeking, searching, trying one thing and another in an attempt to find more successful methods, techniques, and processes. Of course, with all this ferment and experimentation there are bound to be offbeat and even, as in the case of experiments with drugs, potentially deadly activities that are zealously espoused by enthusiastic experimenters in one field or another. Many of the experiments are bound to be shocking or unacceptable to the general public and to result in ridicule or condemnation of some helping process.

Such condemnation can spill over to the whole area of exploration, as has happened with group process. Group-process experiments run the gamut from taking a friend to lunch at one extreme to marathon encounters at the other. However, the question usually asked by people whose sensibilities have been outraged by some experiments is, "Are you for or against group process?" Such undeserved spread of criticism to whole movements are a great pity but also probably inevitable. Whenever people confront exciting new ideas, experimentation is likely to take place "all across the board," as understandings of new concepts and practices are sought. Eventually, the extremes get dropped and the kernel of truth in the movement remains. In the helping professions we can therefore expect to be the victims of ridicule, misunderstandings, and condemnation from some quarters while the experiments run their courses. Over time, however, the problem of guilt by association proves to be a small price to pay for the understandings and accomplishments we are likely to reap from the probing.

It's Tough to Be Yourself

The flip side of being rejected as flaky is finding that people do not know how to deal with a professional helper as a person. When the helper encounters society simply as a person in a social, nonprofessional way, two problems may develop.

First, helpers are like everyone else. They enjoy relaxing, socializing, and playing. When they do these things, they want to shed their professional cloaks and forget how they make their living. That is what fun time is all about— getting away from the routine of daily work, no matter how much one might enjoy it. Sometimes the public can make it difficult for helpers to do this.

Some people will always try to take advantage of a helper. When they find out that a person is a physician, a nurse, a psychologist, a lawyer, or a social worker, they will try to get free services. Giving free service is not the problem. Helpers, for the most part, are a pretty gracious and generous lot, often donating their time for one good cause or another. But when helpers are relaxing at social gatherings, they are not in the mood to diagnose a disorder, give legal advice, or explain the dynamics of an emotional disease. Helpers find it hard to say no, even when they are off duty, but sometimes they must, if they intend to maintain their own mental health.

A second problem develops because some people have the strangest ideas about what helpers are really like. This probably comes from the distorted pictures of members of the helping profession that are projected in the mass media—for example, the Dr. Kildares and the dedicated nurses and physicians of "General Hospital"—helpers who are so immersed in their professions that they never quit being professionals, even in social situations. Consequently, the professional person frequently encounters individuals who are defensive or on guard when they discover what the helper does. This is particularly true of those professionals who are engaged in occupations that are concerned with the emotional aspects of helping, such as counselors, psychiatrists, and psychologists. The term "head shrinker," for example, has a negative connotation and strikes fear in the hearts of many. They see a therapist as someone who goes around analyzing everyone he or she meets, ferreting out a person's deepest and darkest secrets.

One of us was at a party recently, having a very nice conversation with a young woman. The woman did not know that she was talking with a psychologist and was being warm and open about herself. Each was enjoying the interaction. Eventually the young woman asked her companion what he did for a living. When he told her, she literally stiffened in her chair, brought her hand to her face, and said, "O my god, what have I said?" She was afraid she had revealed some aspect of herself that she had no intention of revealing, something possibly embarrassing, shameful, or demeaning.

The young woman's response is common. Many a helper's good times have been ruined because people who are outside the helping professions think that helpers cannot drop their professional roles and just be themselves. To the contrary! When helpers are relaxing the last thing they want to do is engage in those very behaviors from which they *are* relaxing!

What Am I?

A constant complication for those who are engaged in the helping professions is related to what they are and what they do. Defining the helping professions in such fashion as to make the practice of helping the exclusive prerogative of any particular group is difficult. People have been helping one another for generations and the skills and techniques that are used lie in the public domain. Listening, advising, caring, confronting, supporting, reflecting, respecting, interpreting, or being empathic are things everyone does on occasion. Consequently, the helping professions cannot be defined unquestionably in terms of particular functions. About the best that can be done is to demand that those who call themselves teachers, counselors, social workers, or whatever, must demonstrate that they have successfully completed an acceptable period of training and internship.

What Can I Believe?

The physical sciences are fairly precise. There are some open ends and many unanswered questions, and mistakes are made. But for the most part, when a discovery is made, a principle elucidated, or a law established, it stays that way. Not so in the helping professions. The research data on which these professions are based are full of ifs, maybes, buts, and possibilities. The ambiguity of the social sciences is enough to drive a hard-nosed physicist or engineer crazy. To make the point, let us look at just a few of the changes in beliefs about human beings that have taken place in the past few years. Some of them are not just changes, but 180-degree turnabouts!

Beliefs of the 1950s and 1960s	Beliefs of the 1970s and 1980s
Working Mothers[4]: If a mother works, her children suffer many psychological problems.	*Working Mothers*[5]: There is no difference in the physical and mental health between children whose mothers work and those whose mothers do not work.
Only Children: Only children suffer in personal and social development.	*Only Children*[6]: Only children are brighter and physically and mentally healthier than children from larger families.
Neonates: Newborn babies are blank tablets of buzzing confusion.	*Neonates*[7]: Newborn babies have many well-established response patterns.
Intelligence: Intelligence fades with age.	*Intelligence*[8]: A few specific skills deteriorate with age, but mostly intelligence increases over the years.
Parents: Parents are the greatest and most important influence in a child's life.	*Parents*[9]: Parents are only one influence on the development of the child. Many other factors contribute to this growth.
Children: Children are egocentric.	*Children*[10]: Piaget's tasks were inappropriate for the children he used; thus he was unable to detect their ability to decenter and attend to the feelings of others.
Dreams: Dreams are symbolic representations of repressed desires.	*Dreams*[11]: Dreams are not symbolic, but are the result of physiological processes.

The above "facts" should give you an idea of the problem we are dealing with. On what should professional helpers base their judgments and what data source should determine the techniques they use? The only answer that can be given is that a helper must first be aware of the best and newest data available and then proceed on the basis of his or her own good sense, integrity, and intuition. One simply does not have the kind of hard, cold, relatively stable source of data available to the physical scientist. Research in the helping professions is simply one's best guess about the nature of things at any given moment, and if you can't live with that ambiguity you may not want to get involved.

There is an apocryphal story that circulates about the dean of the medical school where one of us works. As the story goes, this particular dean is said to greet each new medical class, in part, with this statement:

Ladies and gentlemen, as you advance through our program, you may find many occasions to question the validity of what you are being taught. This feeling is not without justification, for, by the time you graduate, half of what you have learned will have proven to be false information. Our only problem is, we don't know which half.

The Burdens I Carry

Perhaps the one thing that is most likely to drive an individual out of helping is the sharing of clients', students', or patients' problems. Walking through the private passages of another person's life, sharing the pain and sorrow of human beings in need of help, hour after hour, day after day, is not easy. Many people cannot carry this burden. Successful helpers find ways to deal with it; others, the exceptional helpers, are even able to gain something positive from the experience. A dear friend of ours, Fred Richards, puts it this way:

> Many persons have asked me, "How can you listen to all those troubles and still care?" The fact is, my life has been enlarged ten-fold by the clients who have become part of my history, my being, and my experience. Yes, I'm often tired, sometimes exhausted at the end of a day, but with few exceptions I have known that my humanity has been deepened and enriched by what I do.[12]

Admittedly, it is difficult to develop this attitude, but if you develop it, you know that by entering the helping professions you have made the right decision.

WHY BOTHER?

At this point you may be asking, "If things are so bad in the helping professions, why bother?" For us, two people who have collectively spent more than fifty years at the business of helping, answering that question really isn't difficult. Believe it or not, there are some good reasons why someone might wish to enter one of the helping professions. The first and perhaps the only reason one might need for helping is a rather heavy one. It has to do with finding meaning in one's life.

A Purpose in Life

In present times, people are having difficulty finding meaning or purpose for their lives. One constantly hears complaints from friends, relatives, and loved ones: "I'm bored"; "I'm not getting any fun out of life"; "There doesn't seem to be any purpose in what I'm doing"; "I hate my job!" Studs Turkel did a classic study of how people feel about the work they do.[13] The majority of those he sampled saw what they did as simply a way to make a living, and because of that, something they were able to tolerate. Many others saw their jobs as a major source of aggravation and stress but didn't believe they could do anything else. Few derived pleasure from their work.

Finding pleasure and meaning in what one does often comes easier for members of the helping professions. Helping other human beings can be one of the most satisfying and rewarding experiences. Seeing people come through sorrow and pain, change directions in their lives, grow, bloom, come alive again, and knowing that you have been part of it all is truly thrilling. Men and women who devote their lives to the welfare of others don't have to ask whether they are making a contribution or whether what they do has a purpose. The answers may be seen in the joy and appreciation of those they help.

Personal Satisfaction

A person who sees meaning in what he or she does will experience a great deal of personal satisfaction for the effort. The teacher watching young folks grow, the nurse seeing people get well, and the counselor saving a marriage all experience deep satisfaction. Even if they cannot see the fruition of most of their efforts, *knowing* that they have been responsible for major positive changes in the lives of even a small number of people is a joy that can sustain them for a long time. When helping is your thing, life can just be more pleasant.

A Certain Respect

Many people feel guilty and defensive about what they do. They have to fight social stereotypes. Think about the images conjured up when occupations like used-car or insurance salesperson, politician, or dog catcher are mentioned. The people who are engaged in these occupations may be quite honorable. That doesn't matter, for the labels conjure up negative images nonetheless. The titles of teacher, nurse, social worker, pastor, and doctor, however, generate much different impulses.

A Practical Aspect

Helping also has a practical aspect. Humans are so dependent on one another that one troubled person can have a tremendous effect on the lives of others. Troubled people are seldom problems only to themselves and almost always cause difficulties for those around them. Our lives can be snuffed out by total strangers, and for no reason other than that we happened to be in the wrong place at the wrong time. A single assassin can change the course of history and affect all our lives. Helpers are needed. Think of what an incredible difference it would make if every professional helper were responsible for preventing just one potentially dangerous person from committing an act of violence. On the other hand, think what it would be like if *no one* out there were *trying*. The life a helper saves may be his or her own!

You Are Unique

When a person commits herself or himself to the helping professions, she or he becomes a member of a rapidly diminishing, but unique, group of people, a group distinguished by the attitude that the pursuit of humanitarian purposes is more important than money! One of us recently heard the report of an interview survey of young people in southern California. When asked what their main goal in life was, a large number of these young folks responded: "To make enough money to buy a Porsche." The majority of professional helpers may never own Porsches, but they will sleep better at night not worrying about it.

Notes and References

1. A. H. Maslow, *Motivation and Personality*, 2d ed. (New York: Harper & Row, 1970).
2. *Educational Leadership: Affective Education Pays Off.* Association for Supervision and Curriculum Development 39, no. 7 (April 1982).
3. *Gainesville Sun*, 2 April 1982, p. 1C.
4. Sometimes prevailing social attitudes are what primarily determine the outcome of research, as these examples suggest. When the social attitude was that women shouldn't work and an only child was a bad position to be in, the research supported these beliefs. But now that the attitudes have changed, with many women working and many parents having only one child or none, the research has changed also.
5. S. W. Olds, "When Mommy Goes to Work," in N. Jackson, ed., *Personal Growth and Behavior* (Guilford, Conn: Dushkin, 1982), pp. 142–144.
6. D. Moore, "The Only Child Phenomenon," in T. H. Carr and H. E. Fitzgerald, eds., *Psychology 82/83* (Guilford, Conn: Dushkin, 1982), pp. 148–152.
7. A. Macfarlane, "What a Baby Knows," in H. E. Fitzgerald and T. H. Carr, eds., *Human Development* (Guilford, Conn: Dushkin, 1982), pp. 88–93.
8. J. E. Rodgers, "Our Insatiable Brain," in Carr and Fitzgerald, eds., *Psychology 82/83*, pp. 111–113.
9. A. Skolnick, "The Myth of the Vulnerable Child," *Psychology Today* 11 (1978): 56–65.
10. J. K. Black, "Are Young Children Really Egocentric?" *Young Children*, September 1981, 51–55.
11. E. Kiester, "Images of the Night," in Carr and Fitzgerald, eds., *Psychology 82/83*, pp. 64–68.
12. F. Richards, "Psychotherapy: A Loving Relationship." Unpublished manuscript, 1983.
13. S. Turkel, *Working* (New York: Pantheon Books, 1972).

TWO

WHAT MAKES A GOOD HELPER?

Since the 1960s the authors have been closely associated with a series of research designed to explore the question, What makes the difference between good helpers and poor ones in the helping professions? Among the professionals examined in these studies are public school teachers, counselors, nurses, supervisors, Episcopal priests, professors, and public officials.[1] These explorations and our own attempts to apply the results to the professional preparation of helpers have led us to new understandings about what makes a good helper.

KNOWLEDGE AND METHODS

Two characteristics are generally assumed to distinguish between good helpers and poor ones; these are knowledge and methods. One cannot tell the difference between good helpers and poor helpers on the basis of what they know. Each of us is familiar with this fact from personal experience. Who has not suffered at the hands of a brilliant scholar who knew her subject but could not teach? In similar fashion, the possession of knowledge about human behavior is no guarantee that a helper will be good at any of the other helping professions.

Neither can one find reliable differences between good and poor practitioners on the basis of methods. There seems to be no such thing as a good or right method of helping that can be shown to be definitely associated with either good or bad practice. Hundreds of researchers, hoping to demonstrate that this or that particular method is correct, have been frustrated by ambiguous results, and we remain unable to specify with any degree of certainty good or right methods for the helping professions.

Yet everyone knows that there are good helpers and poor ones. If the difference is not in the knowledge they possess or in the methods they use, where is it? We are convinced that the crucial distinction lies in *the belief systems* of the helpers. Here is why we think this is so.

HELPER BELIEFS ARE CRUCIAL

For several generations the prevailing mode of psychology used to understand human beings has concentrated on behavior. Accordingly, our attempts to explore the nature of good and poor helpers have concentrated on studies of their traits, methods, and behavior. Behavior, however, is not cause; it is result or symptom. The behavior of a person at any moment is only a symptom of what is going on inside as the person interacts with the observable events in his or her environment. Preoccupation with symptoms in understanding the helping professions is likely to be no more satisfying than consulting a physician who does nothing but deal with a patient's symptoms. In the field of counseling it is notorious that any method or behavior—even the most extreme or bizarre—will sometimes get results with some clients some times.

The behavior of a person at any moment must be understood as the outcome or result of what is going on inside the person at that moment. Applying this understanding to the process of helping, it becomes apparent that the dynamics of helping can be grasped adequately only in terms of the inner life of the helper and the helpee. In particular, one needs to understand what the helper is trying to do and what message is being received by the client, student, or patient. An outside observer viewing the helping situation may actually get a distorted picture of events. To illustrate this point, let us take an example from a study on good teaching conducted by Marie Hughes.[2] Dr. Hughes sought to determine the characteristics of good teachers by stationing observers in the classroom to record teacher behavior from moment to moment. The results showed that a large portion of the behavior of these good teachers fell into a category called "controlling and directing behaviors." If this is true, what must be done to prepare good teachers? Obviously, student teachers must be taught to control and direct. But behavior is only symptom, and when these good teachers are examined in terms of the teacher's purposes and the child's perceptions, the view is entirely different. For example, a teacher who is walking about the room comes to a child who is having difficulty with a problem. The teacher says to the child, "Not like that, son. Try it like this. I think it will go better." This behavior is recorded by the observer as "controlling and directing." From the teacher's point of view, it was nothing of the sort; it was helping and facilitating. From the child's point of view, it was also not controlling and directing; to him, it may have meant "My teacher likes me," "My teacher helps me," "Gee, but I'm dumb!" or any of a number of other perceptions. It becomes apparent that the dynamics of helping can be fully understood only in terms of the perceptions of helpers and helpees.

Helping professions require instantaneous responses from helpers. When clients say something, counselors must respond; when children ask questions, teachers must answer; when parishioners ask for advice, pastors must reply. Effective helping is an immediate, creative, problem-solving activity of great complexity. To help explain its dynamics we might draw an analogy to a giant computer. A computer takes in vast quantities of information from outside, combines the information with that already stored in its memory bank, and produces appropriate answers with dazzling speed. This is very much like the situation of the helper absorbing information from clients or outsiders and combining it with information already possessed from personal experience and understanding. The answers supplied by the computer, of course, are determined by the program that is placed in the machine—usually a mathematical formula. In a human being the formula that determines the outcome is not a mathematical equation, but rather the individual's personal meanings or perceptions, especially those we call beliefs.

In the research mentioned earlier in this chapter, clear differences between a good and poor helper are found when attention is focused on the perceptual organization or belief systems of the helper. People behave in terms of their beliefs. The beliefs we hold determine the goals we seek, the events we attend to, and the choices of behavior we make to accomplish these ends. Just so, the belief systems of the helper act like personal theories or guidelines that determine the thinking and behavior of the helper at every moment in the course of professional relationships. We are only beginning to understand the full significance of this way of thinking about helpers and their relationships, but researchers to date suggest at least five major areas of helper belief or perceptual organization that are significantly related to effective practice.

Area 1. Sensitivity, Empathy, or the Phenomenological View

The first of these major areas has to do with what the helper believes is the essential data from which to work. The fundamental purpose of the helping professions is to assist students, patients, or clients to find more satisfying, fulfilling ways of being and behaving. People behave or misbehave in terms of their perceptions of themselves and their worlds, including attitudes, beliefs, likes, dislikes, loves, hates, hopes, fears, and aspirations. Because people behave in terms of their perceptions, effective helping requires awareness of the students', patients', or clients' perceptual fields. To understand helpees, it is necessary to see through their eyes, to walk in their shoes, to perceive the world from their points of view. Not only is such awareness important for understanding and communicating, but it also provides necessary data for determining the helper's choice of goals and behavior and for predicting the probable outcomes of helper acts. The capacity of the helper to place herself or himself in the helpee's shoes and perceive as the helpee does, is called sensitivity, or empathy.

In all our studies good helpers were perceptually or phenomenologically oriented. That is, good helpers were always concerned with how things looked from the point of view of the client. Poor helpers were concerned mostly with how things looked to themselves. If the goal of helping is to produce some change in personal meanings, then helpee perceptions are the primary data with which the helper must work. Preoccupation with "facts" or how things seem to outsiders concentrates attention on matters tangential to the dynamics of helpee growth.

Years ago one of the authors saw an example of such preoccupation in a psychological clinic in which he worked with several colleagues. In the beginning, when a mother first brought her child to the clinic, standard procedure was to hold a case conference, make a diagnosis, and develop a plan of action. We would study the child, the mother, and anyone else in the family who would cooperate. Then we would hold a case conference and decide what was wrong and what the mother needed to do. After that, we would assign someone from the staff to tell the mother what to do. *Rarely* was this treatment successful! These anxious mothers could not do successfully what they were already trying. When we added more things for them to do, we simply added to their frustration. Later, we learned that a better way to help the mothers was by trying to get them to see themselves and their children differently. When that was accomplished they could find their own best ways of coping. Take the case of the mother with a very difficult child. His behavior shocked and offended her. When she brought him to the clinic her entire orientation was, "That's got to stop!" Believing that is the problem, what kinds of behavior are called for? Clearly, some form of force, coercion, wheedling, bribing—*something* to produce a change in behavior. Unfortunately, such techniques are rarely effective.

We learned how to help the mother see her child differently. As she began to see her child differently, she found her own ways of behaving in a more adequate fashion, and the ways she found were nearly always more effective than those we thought of. We would say, for example, "When we were working with Jimmy back there in the playroom, Mrs. Smith, we noticed that he seems to feel that people don't like him very much." That's a new idea for the mother, and it calls for a different approach to her child than the one she has been using. A mother who understands that her little boy feels as though "people don't like him very much" selects entirely different patterns of action from those called for when the problem is seen as "That's got to stop!" Therapy that concentrates on client meanings requires counselors who regard such meanings as the crucial data with which they must work.

Failure to understand how things seem to the other party is probably the most important single cause for the breakdown of communication, whether we are talking about individuals, groups, or nations. In our research, good helpers were characterized by continuous concern for the "people" question—immediate understandings about how things seem to the person involved. Poor helpers were preoccupied with "things" questions—external matters, pressures, power, possessions, and the historical details of how matters came to the present state. Sensitivity or empathy in the helping professions is not just a nice idea or device to facilitate the helping process; it is the helper's key to the essential data with which helpers deal—the perceptual world of the client, student, or patient.

Area 2. Beliefs about People

The second major area of difference between good helpers and poor ones has to do with the helpers' belief about people. Effective helpers typically possess positive views of human beings; poor helpers have grave doubts about people. Good helpers believe that people are able, that they have the capacity to deal effectively with their own lives. Poor helpers, on the other hand, have little confidence in human capacity; they are not at all sure that people are able to achieve their own salvation. It makes a big difference whether you believe that people are able or unable. For one thing, if you do not believe that they can do this, you do not dare let them do anything! You must save them in spite of themselves.

A positive view of clients shows up in other ways in our research. Good helpers believe that people are basically dependable, worthy, friendly, and helpful. Poor ones see others as hostile, apathetic, and unworthy and as hinderers. Good helpers believe that the human organism is essentially trustworthy; poor ones approach their clients or students with suspicion. Good helpers believe that their clients are people of dignity and integrity; poor ones feel free to violate the dignity and integrity of others. A basic principle of democracy is the belief that when people are free they can find their own best ways. Good helpers believe that. Poor ones say, "Yes, I believe that is true—when people are free they can find their own best ways." Then they add, "But not in this case!"

This perceptual difference between good and poor helpers might explain why we cannot tell the difference between good ones and poor ones on the basis of the methods they use. Let us take the categories *able* and *unable* as examples and use teachers as typical helpers. Two teachers believe that people are fundamentally able. One teacher makes students work hard and sees to it that they adhere to high standards. The message conveyed by this behavior is, "My teacher thinks I can and expects me to." The other teacher behaves in a nondirective, permissive fashion, saying to a student, "That's an interesting idea. Why don't you take the rest of the day to explore it by yourself?" These are two vastly different methods of teaching, but the same message is delivered in each case: "My teacher thinks I can." The significance of methods lies not in the techniques but in the messages they convey.

Many recent studies have clearly demonstrated that people tend to live up to the expectations of those who are significant in their lives. Positive beliefs about clients, students, or patients are not only good for establishing relationships, but they are also therapeutic in strengthening helpees' feelings about themselves. A major characteristic of well-adjusted, self-actualizing people is a positive view of self. The helper who has such a positive view about humanity in general and the helpee in particular automatically contributes to personal strength without conscious effort. Our beliefs have a way of showing themselves whether we will it or not.

Area 3. The Helper's Feeling about Self

One of the most significant areas of psychological exploration that has been dealt with since the 1960s, is that of self-concept. We now know that what a person believes about self is perhaps the most important single factor in determining every behavior. Evidence suggests that self-concept can also have an important effect on intelligence, mental health, delinquency, crime, and success in school or professional work as well as in the achievement of self-actualization and fulfillment. This is as true of persons in the helping professions as of anyone else. What the helper perceives about self is likely to be crucial in determining effectiveness or ineffectiveness. The person who has positive feelings about self is far more likely to be an effective worker than is the person who does not. Positive feelings give the individual an air of confidence and assurance that goes a long way toward facilitating effective practice.

In our research the helper's self-concept is a clearly distinguishable factor in effective and ineffective practice. Good helpers see themselves in positive ways. They see themselves as "enough"—as liked, wanted, accepted, able people of dignity and integrity. Poor helpers, on the other hand, see themselves in negative ways—as unliked, unwanted, unacceptable people. One of the important effects of positive views of self is the feeling of personal security such belief systems provide. Positive views of self provide a sturdy platform from which one can deal with the world. Like going sailing in a stout ship, one can move with assurance and sail far from shore. A leaky vessel, on the other hand, makes it necessary to proceed tentatively, to play it safe and stay close to harbor. With positive views of self, helpers provide an image of strength and security that in itself contributes much to their success.

Area 4. Helper Purposes

The fourth major area of difference between effective and ineffective practitioners has to do with helper purposes. Earlier we stated the belief that the dynamics of the counseling process can be understood only in terms of the perceptions of the counselor and the client. One needs to understand what the counselor is trying to do and what the client thinks has happened. As Freud pointed out long ago, we all do only what we would rather. All of us behave in terms of our purposes, and these are revealed to others in spite of ourselves. Some time ago one of us had to speak before an audience that he was certain would be hostile to what was said. He was afraid when he delivered the speech, not at all sure that he could make his point successfully. Actually, the speech turned out rather well, and he was happy to have survived. Later, while making his way through the auditorium, he met three friends. The first one said, "Don't you just love it when you are up there and the spotlight is on you and there you are?" For a moment the author looked at his friend in astonishment. That was not at all how he felt. He had honestly felt afraid. The author then realized that his friend Bill was talking to him in terms of his own purposes; that is why *he* likes to make speeches. A little further on the author met his friend Charles, who said, "You really had them! Right there!" And he made a fist and pounded it up and down. Charles too was seeing the author in terms of his own purposes. He likes the feeling of power. The third encounter was with the author's friend Paul. Paul said, 'Very adroit, very adroit!" To Paul, the author's speech was a neat intellectual trick, a clever manipulation. But that is Paul. That is his purpose and his lifestyle. Whatever our purposes, it is almost impossible to keep them from other people, no matter how skillfully we try.

To this point our research has not been able to investigate a wide assortment of helper purposes. The few that have been explored, however, clearly distinguish between good and poor helpers and seem to be very crucial. Good helpers' purposes, for example, tend to be freeing purposes, rather than controlling ones. That is, good helpers are continuously concerned with freeing their clients, opening perceptions, broadening horizons, setting students or patients free. Consequently, the very words they use in speaking about their practices convey their beliefs. Good helpers say, "I am trying to help my student or client see or do such and such." One hears them use words like "aid," "assist," "facilitate," "encourage." Poor helpers, on the other hand, typically say such things as, "If I can just make my patient or client see so and so." They frequently use such words as "arrange," "convince," "persuade," or a phrase such as "get my client to . . ." They are preoccupied with directing and controlling. They seek to manipulate themselves, their practices, and their clients.

Good helpers' goals and purposes tend to be large rather than small. Poor helpers tend to state their purposes in precise, atomistic, or picayune objectives. Good helpers, on the other hand, are more concerned with holistic, global considerations. Because everyone behaves in terms of purposes, helpers' purposes show. They also create expectations for helpees, who generally believe that their helpers know what they are doing.

We are convinced that a major cause for the breakdown of helping activities lies in the failure of helpers to determine what is important. Good helpers seem to have clear, well-established ideas about what is truly significant. Without such beliefs one's behavior is likely to be uncertain, tentative, and perhaps even fearful. Helpers who are not certain about what is really important ride a carousel, familiar, we are sure, to almost anyone. When we don't know what is important, then everything is important. When everything is important, then we must do everything. People see us doing everything and assume that we *should* be doing everything. They expect us to do everything. This keeps us so busy that we don't have time to think about what is important! This kind of endless cycle is responsible for innumerable failures, not only in the helping professions but in administration and managerial occupations as well.

Although there is no research to corroborate other aspects of helper purposes, we feel sure that in time clear differences will be found between good and poor helpers with respect to additional purposes; for example, what helpers believe is the purpose of their particular brand of helping, of the goal of helping, of the place of helping professions in the social order, and of the personal goals for wanting to be helpers in the first place. Purposes like these have deeply affected our own practices, and we feel sure they must be equally significant for others.

Area 5. Authenticity and Methods

Most schools of thought about professional helping grow up around some method or technique. A helper discovers that some method used either accidentally or on purpose produced good results. After several more trials with positive results, the helper comes to the conclusion that he or she has an important new approach to the profession. Other helpers try the method and perhaps they get good results too. The next thing you know there is a new school of counseling, or social work, or nursing, or teaching that is primarily oriented around a certain method or technique. To date, however, research has been unable to find any method or practice that can be clearly associated with either good or poor helpers. Apparently, there is no such thing as a good or bad technique.

Methods are never simple; they are always complex and personal. The methods used by good helpers are creative, problem-solving techniques that are determined by a multitude of factors in the helper's awareness. They are products of the helper's purposes, beliefs about self, personal philosophy, beliefs about people in general and about a particular helpee. They are also determined by the time, place, and surroundings in which the encounter takes place, including whether the method is used early or late in the relationship or at the beginning or end of a particular helping hour. Methods must also be adapted to the nature and condition of the client, to his or her needs, understandings, cultural background, habits, and perceptions of self and the world.

Methods are like the clothes we wear. The authors would not look good in your clothes and you would not look good in ours. We each must wear what becomes us. We have tried to use other people's methods without success, and others have tried to use ours with disastrous results. Methods are unique and are related to the circumstances in which they are used. This explains why we have been unsuccessful in finding "right" methods. The search for a common uniqueness is, by definition, an exercise in futility.

A method is only a behavior, and behavior, as pointed out earlier, is only a symptom. Methods are not good or right in themselves but only in terms of the messages they convey. Whatever method a helper uses carries some message to the student, patient, or client, whether the helper is aware of the message or not. Even the same method at different points in time may have quite different meanings to the helpee. For example, in counseling, early in the process, when a client does not know the counselor very well but has great respect for her prestige and authority, a simple statement like, "Do you think that was wise?" may be seen by a client as disapproval or condemnation or as pointing the way to a "right" thing he should do. Later in the counseling relationship, when the client and counselor understand each other better and the client sees the counselor as a helper and facilitator rather than as an authority figure, the same statement may be accepted by the client as a suggestion to examine his position. He may even be able to reject or ignore the statement because the counselor–client relationship is more secure.

The results of our research show that the most significant factor with respect to the helper's methods is not which ones are used but the authenticity of whatever the helper does in the relationship. Good helpers are self-revealing. That is, they are willing and able to share themselves with their clients. Their sincerity, honesty, and clarity of purpose are communicated no matter which method they use. Poor helpers, on the other hand, tend to be self-concealing. They *act* their roles, obscure their purposes, and hold themselves aloof from the relationship.

Communicating with others when we do not know where they stand, what they believe, or what they are trying to do is difficult or impossible. It is like trying to find someone in the dark. Effective helpers make themselves visible. They are authentic, willing, and able to share themselves and their understanding with other people.

THE PERSON-CENTERED HELPER

Carl Rogers refers to his helping approach as being person-centered.[3] Helpers who hold the kinds of beliefs we have been discussing may be called person-centered helpers. Their main concern is the welfare of the helpee, and they see themselves as facilitators rather than as authorities, controllers, or manipulators. Rogers says that this kind of helper is "a leader or a person who is sufficiently secure within herself and in her relationship to others that she experiences an essential trust in the capacity of others to think for themselves, to learn for themselves, and regards human beings as trustworthy organisms."[4]

The Aspy and Roebuck Studies

Promoting the person-centered approach has been an uphill struggle. In education particularly, this approach has been regarded as too soft, frilly, a waste of time. It has been considered antithetical to the important things that pupils are supposed to learn. Champions of the back-to-basics movement have no tolerance for it. However, in light of some recent research, detractors of the approach are going to find it more difficult to defend their criticisms.

Since the mid-1960s Dave Aspy and Flora Roebuck have been doing research on the person-centered helper in education. Their work is monumental, bound to become classic, and may be one of the most important pieces of work ever carried out in the helping professions. Of the Aspy and Roebuck studies Carl Rogers says, "They cannot be dismissed as inconclusive."[5]

Aspy and Roebuck were instrumental in establishing the National Consortium for Humanizing Education. Their main purposes were to ask such questions as, "Are person-centered classes different from other classes, and if so, what are those differences?" Person-centered classes were defined as classes in which teachers manifested high levels of empathy, congruence, positive regard, caring, and understanding. When such classes were compared with teacher- and subject matter–centered classes, the results were overwhelming.

In person-centered classes, as opposed to more traditional kinds of education, students missed fewer days of school, increased their self-concept and IQ scores and scores on measures of creativity, made greater academic gains in all areas, had fewer discipline problems, and committed fewer acts of vandalism.

Probably the most exciting aspect of these studies is that the researchers demonstrated that they could enter a school, train the faculty in the person-centered mode, and bring about the kind of changes just mentioned. This was true even in the schools with the worst records and reputations.

In a study of alternative schools, Daniel Duke and Cheryl Perry found much the same kind of things as did Aspy and Roebuck.[6] The students in the alternative schools studied were making greater gains in all areas than were the students in traditional schools, and the alternative schools were experiencing fewer problems, such as with discipline and vandalism. These schools were described as being flexible and informal and as having fewer rules than did traditional schools. The teachers were characterized as being sensitive, sincere, and spontaneous; as having a sense of humor; and as refraining from moralizing or making value judgments.

The advantages of a person-centered approach apparently go beyond helping relationships, and this attitude can have much value even very early in life. Arminta Jacobson reports on a series of studies of highly competent and less competent children designed to see whether any differences existed between the mothers of these two groups.[7] The characteristics and techniques of the mothers studied were distributed along a continuum ranging from child-centered to mother-centered. In each study the more child-centered a mother was, the more *competent* was the child. The child-centered mothers were described as being lovingly responsive to their children, attentive, accepting, and sensitive and as having a positive attitude toward life. The relationship between these mothers and their children involved more mother–infant interactions, interaction techniques that were facilitative in nature, more freedom, less restrictive techniques, and less punishment.

The consistency of the studies discussed in this chapter is amazing. Whether the person-centered approach is used by counselors, priests, nurses, teachers, or even parents, it holds up as one of the best ways to foster health and growth. Regardless of what kind of helping relationship is involved, the same characteristics are possessed by the helpers being examined—they are sensitive, caring, nonjudgmental, open, freeing, etc.; and even in a relationship that is seemingly remote from the helping professions, that between a mother and her child, this facilitative model appears to have its advantages.

Some General Implications

As a consequence of the research we have been discussing, we are convinced that effective helping is not only a question of learning how to teach, counsel, nurse, or whatever. It is not simply a question of learning and practicing skills and techniques. Rather, effective helping must be seen as the development of a kind of personal theory; a system of beliefs that serve as guidelines for the helper; a stable, trustworthy frame of reference for the long-term goals and moment-to-moment decisions that the helper is required to make.

Such a conception of the nature of effective helpers means at least six things:

1. If it is true that the dynamics of helping are a consequence of the perceptions of helper and helpee, then we need a perceptual–humanistic psychology to provide more adequate bases for understanding those processes. Other psychologies on which we have customarily based our thinking are no longer sufficient by themselves. We need, in addition, a psychology expressly designed for understanding the perceptual worlds of human beings and the dynamics by which these internal processes grow and change. A psychology capable of providing an experimental approach to learning is especially required to provide the helping professions with adequate guidelines for effective practice.

Note that we did not say we should give up other psychologies. This is not a matter of either/or. It is a question of adding another frame of reference that is capable of dealing with events that cannot be understood otherwise. Workers with several tools at their command are generally able to operate more effectively than are workers with only one tool. It is a question of choosing the psychology that is most appropriate for the problems we wish to consider.

2. If it is true that what happens in the helping process is determined by the perceptual experiences of helper and helpee, then helper and helpee behavior must be understood as symptoms, and research must be designed to explore what is happening experimentally for all parties involved. In particular, research on helping processes must concentrate on the exploration of helper and helpee perceptions and on the dynamics of perceptual change in the helping relationship. We believe our research has demonstrated that such studies are possible and that the results can be both profitable and exciting. Perhaps the most important contribution of the research cited here is that it

opened the door to this approach and demonstrated some promising techniques for perceptual exploration.

3. All helping professions are essentially learning processes—helping people learn to see and behave in more effective and satisfying ways. Because learning processes do not change with the various professions, it follows that all helping professions are fundmentally alike, and comparisons between teaching, counseling, social work, nursing, psychiatry, clinical psychology, and so on, are mischievous and divisive. There may be different expressions or different aspects of concentration in the tasks of particular professions, but generally they must operate from the same basic premises. Helping professions are far more alike than they are different. Full understanding of this fact can go a long way toward discouraging battles for turf. It can also open doors for communication and learning from one another in the various branches of the helping professions.

4. If the belief systems of helpers are as crucial to effective practice as research suggests, then the training of professional helpers must be approached as a process in personal becoming. The goal of training must be on the personal development of aspiring helpers' belief systems, including at the very least the development of sensitivity, a phenomenological approach to understanding human beings, clarification of personal and professional goals and purposes, acquisition of positive self-concepts, and high levels of personal authenticity. Programs must aid young helpers in the personal discovery of beliefs about themselves; about their students, patients, or clients; about the goals and purposes of professional help and of the world in which they live. Such goals call for important changes in the customary ways of thinking about the training of professional workers.

5. More emphasis will have to be placed on selection procedures. Measures must be developed that can identify people who have the kind of perception and personal beliefs we have been speaking of.

6. Finally, for those who are already professional helpers, these concepts mean that the process of becoming a helper is never complete. It is a continuous, lifelong, never-ending process of exploring and refining one's personal system of beliefs.[8]

We have barely begun to explore the full implications of helper belief systems for effective practice.[9] There is much to be done, but the promise of important new understandings of the helping professions is great indeed.

Notes and References

1.   A. W. Combs, ed., *Florida Studies in the Helping Professions,* Social Science Monograph no. 39 (Gainesville, Fla.: University of Florida Press, 1969).

2.   M. M. Hughes, *Development of the Means for Assessing the Quality of Teaching in Elementary Schools,* Cooperative Research Program no. 353 (Washington, D.C.: U.S. Office of Education, 1959).

3. C. R. Rogers, "The Foundations of the Person-Centered Approach," *Education* 100 (Winter 1979): 98–107.

4. C. R. Rogers, *Freedom to Learn: For the 80's* (Columbus, Ohio: Charles E. Merrill, 1983).

5. Ibid., pp. 197–198.

6. D. L. Duke and Cheryl Perry, "Can Alternative Schools Succeed Where Benjamin Spock, Spiro Agnew, and B. F. Skinner Have Failed?" *Adolescence* 13 (Fall 1978): 376–392.

7. A. L. Jacobson, "Infant Day Care: Toward a More Human Environment," *Young Children* 33 (July 1978): 14–23.

8. For a complete discussion of the relationship between a person's belief system and his or her role as a professional helper, see A. W. Combs, *A Personal Approach to Teaching: Beliefs That Make A Difference* (Boston: Allyn and Bacon, 1982).

9. For those who may wish to continue the exploration of the implication of helper belief systems for effective practice, the following list of studies on the subject may prove helpful:

Monograph

Combs, A. W. *Florida Studies in the Helping Professions.* Social Science Monograph no. 37. Gainesville, Fla.: University of Florida Press, 1969. Includes studies by Benton, Dickman, Gooding, Usher, Combs, and Soper.

Dissertations

Brown, Robert G. "A Study of the Perceptual Organization of Elementary and Secondary Outstanding Young Educators." University of Florida, 1970.

Choy, Chunghoon. "The Relationship of College Teacher Effectiveness to Conceptual Systems Orientation and Perceptual Orientation." University of Northern Colorado, 1969.

Dedrick, Charles Van Loan. "The Relationship Between Perceptual Characteristics and Effective Teaching at the Junior College Level." University of Florida, 1972.

Dellow, Donald A. "A Study of the Perceptual Organization of Teachers and Conditions of Empathy, Congruence, and Positive Regard." University of Florida, March 1971.

Doyle, Eunice J. "The Relationship Between College Teacher Effectiveness and Inferred Characteristics of the Adequate Personality." University of Northern Colorado, 1969.

Jennings, Gerald Douglas. "The Relationship Between Perceptual Characteristics and Effective Advising of University Housing Para-Professional Residence Assistants." University of Florida, 1973.

Koffman, R. G. "A Comparison of the Perceptual Organizations of Outstanding and Randomly Selected Teachers in Open and Traditional Classrooms." University of Massachusetts, 1975.

O'Roark, Anne. "A Comparison of Perceptual Characteristics of Elected Legislators and Public School Counselors Identified as Most and Least Effective." University of Florida, 1974.

Parker, James. "The Relationship of Self Report to Inferred Self Concept in Sixth Grade Children." University of Florida, 1964.

Swanson, John LeRoy. "The Relationship Between Perceptual Characteristics and Counselor Effectiveness Ratings of Counselor Trainees." University of Florida, 1975.

Vonk, Herman G. "The Relationship of Teacher Effectiveness to Perception of Self and Teaching Purposes." University of Florida, June 1970.

Wasicsko, M. W. "The Effect of Training and Perceptual Orientation on the Reliability of Perceptual Inferences for Selecting Effective Teachers." University of Florida, 1977.

THREE

PERCEPTION AND THE SELF

We have examined a set of beliefs that we think is necessary for effective helping. There is another set that is equally as important. This includes the beliefs the helper holds about such things as, "What is the basic nature of human beings? What are they like and what do they need?" What we believe about such matters determines what we do in the helping process and the goals we attempt to achieve. This chapter and Chapter Four address these questions.

PERCEPTUAL PSYCHOLOGY

What we are actually dealing with here is the helper's *theory* of human behavior. A helper may never think about it that way, but each of us—professional helper or not—has a theory about the basic nature of human beings. We may think of these things as values or beliefs, and they may range from being highly organized and formulated to being highly disorganized and informal, but these ideas do constitute a theory.

Having been involved in helping for so many years, and having thought about the matter so often, the authors have a highly organized and formulated theory of human behavior. It is not the only theory available; there are many (e.g., psychoanalytic, behaviorist, Adlerian, Gestaltist, and Jungian theory). Nor is the theory we favor sacred; none are. This particular theory, however, seems to make the most sense in light of the facts available and has been the most useful to us during our professional lives. The position is identified variously as perceptual psychology,[1] self-theory, and the humanistic approach.

The concepts of perceptual psychology help us to understand people through studying the processes of perception—how things seem to a person at the moment of action. It is a psychology that looks at people through the "eye of the beholder," from the perspective of the person's own experience.

Perceptual psychologists take the position that all behavior is a function of the perceptions that exist for an individual at the moment of behaving, especially the perceptions about self and world. The term "perception," as these psychologists use it, refers not only to "seeing" but also, more importantly, to "meaning"—the personal significance of an event for the person experiencing it. These meanings extend far beyond sensory experience to include such perceptions as beliefs, values, feelings, hopes, desires, and the personal ways in which people regard themselves and others. Behavior is understood in terms of the ways people see themselves and their world now, in the present, at this instant. For those in the helping professions, this concept is of great significance.

Most modern schools of psychotherapy are predicated on the belief that effective changes can be accomplished by helping clients directly in the present. The long, agonizing delving into the client's past that used to be considered essential for effective treatment is no longer so regarded. One can see many instances of this new psychotherapy in daily life. Nurses, for example, can help patients feel less depressed without knowing the facts of their lives outside the hospital. Businesspersons can help employees feel better about themselves and their jobs and still be unaware of their employees' lives outside the office. One of the authors has often noted, in his experience as a psychotherapist on a college campus, that clients who spend long hours exploring their pasts are, almost without exception, graduate students in psychology! From their studies they know that behavior is a function of the past. When they come for therapy, then, they set about exploring it in detail. Clients who have not learned so thoroughly that behavior is a function of the past spend little time digging into it. They begin at once to explore their present feelings and perceptions. Often they get well despite the fact that at the end of therapy their counselors may still not know how they became unhappy in the first place!

In the beginning the decision to ignore the past was based mainly on intuition, but subsequent research has clearly justified the change. A helper who is concerned with the past is depending on the memory of the helpee. Not only is this a grave error, but it may also send the helper so far afield that he wastes his time and that of the helpee, accomplishing nothing. In summarizing recent research, Carol Tavris concluded that "memory researchers now confirm the worst for all of us: Memory is, in a word, lousy. It is a traitor at worst, a mischief-maker at best. It gives us vivid recollections of events that could never have happened, and it obscures critical details of events that did."[2] Some source of data!

Because an immediate frame of reference does not impose on the helper the necessity to search, probe, diagnose, and analyze, the development of rapport and cooperative relationships is also facilitated. Working with a person's immediate perceptions means working on her own ground in a subject matter she knows and understands. Consequently, she is likely to feel much closer to the professional helper, more readily understood, and more willing to communicate.

It should not be supposed that we are denying the truth of the genetic principle that behavior is a product of the individual's past experience. Generally speaking, the more data we have about any problem, the more likely we are to arrive at correct solutions. Not all data, however, are of equal value in all situations. The helper's goals and method of reaching them determine which data are relevant.

From the perceptual frame of reference, an individual's behavior is understood to be the direct consequence of the total field of personal meanings existing at that instant (the perceptual field). At any moment a person's perceptual field contains some perceptions that clearly are differentiated from the rest and toward which behavior is directed. At the same time the person's field contains many other perceptions. These vary in degrees of awareness from those in very clear figure at the center of attention to those that are so vague and undifferentiated that the person could not report them if we were to ask about them. This sounds very much like the Freudian concept of conscious and unconscious awareness. In a sense it is, but perceptual psychologists prefer not to speak of "conscious" and "unconscious," because these constructs give the impression of two distinct conditions rather than of varying levels of awareness with different degrees of clarity.

At the core of each person's perceptual field are the perceptions about self. Although situations may change from moment to moment or place to place, the beliefs people have about themselves are always present factors in determining behavior. The self is the star of every performance, the central figure in every act. Because this is so, people working in the helping professions need clear understandings of the nature, origins, and functions of the self-concept.

WHAT IS THE SELF-CONCEPT?

The self-concept includes all the aspects of the perceptual field to which we refer when we say "I" or "me." It is the organization of perceptions about self that seems to the individual to be who he or she is. It is composed of thousands of perceptions that vary in clarity, precision, and importance in the person's peculiar economy. Taken altogether, this organization is called the self-concept.

We each have literally thousands of ideas or concepts about self: who we are, what we stand for, where we live, what we do or do not do, and the like. A particular person might see herself as Sally Blanton—mother, wife, lawyer, American, young, resident of Tampa, good swimmer, poor tennis player. These and many other perceptions or beliefs about herself make up the personal and unique self-concept of Sally Blanton. Not all concepts about self are equally important to her. Concepts like her age or residence may be recognized as transitory. Others, like her concept of herself as a woman or as a professional, are probably extremely important and difficult to change.

Descriptive perceptions like those of Sally Blanton distinguish her as unique from other selves. Self-description does not stop here, however, since we are seldom content with description alone.

The self-concept, it should be understood, is not a thing but an organization of ideas. It is an abstraction, a gestalt, a peculiar pattern of perceptions of self. To outsiders, the different parts may seem like only ideas, but for the owner they have the feeling of reality. In fact, to its owner, the self-concept is more important than the body in which it exists. According to Earl Kelley, the body is but "the meat house we live in," the vehicle in which the self resides.[3] We recognize the distinction between body and self when we complain that "the spirit is willing but the flesh is weak," or that "I would have come to the meeting, Joe, but my old body let me down, and I had to stay in bed with the flu."

The distinction between the self-concept and the physical self may be observed in other ways. For example, the self-concept may be defined in such a way as to include matters quite outside the skin. This often happens with respect to one's most cherished possessions. A woman may regard her desk as so much a part of her that she treats interference with it as a personal violation. Consequently, her reaction to a colleague who has intruded on her territory by disturbing things in or on her desk may be so angry and forceful as to be bewildering. The colleague exclaims to the other people in the office, "You'd think I'd wounded her or something!" In fact, he had. What seems to be only a piece of furniture to the colleague is an extension of self to the owner of the desk.

The extension of self is even more common with respect to people. Psychologists refer to this experience as "identification." By this they mean the feeling of oneness we have with those people or groups who are especially important to us. The feeling of oneness we have with those we love may sometimes be so strong that awareness of physical separation may be temporarily lost. A young mother describes this feeling with respect to her newborn infant:

> When they brought my baby to me I unwrapped her and lay for a while in awe, examining the marvelous way she was made. Then, after a while, I placed her on my stomach with her head between my breasts and lay there with a curious feeling of triumph and exquisite peace. Now and then I would raise the covers a little and peek down at her. As she lay there, I honestly couldn't tell where she began and I left off. I remember I wept a little because I was so happy. I'll never forget the moment as long as I live.

The expansion of self-concept also extends to feelings about groups. One reason members of a group come together in the first place is to have the experience of oneness. When an individual joins a group the self-concept is expanded to include the other members. Thereafter the individual begins to behave as though the members are an extension of self. He speaks of "my gang," "my school," "my friend," "my church," "my neighborhood," "my country." Depending on the strength of the identification, he may also behave with respect to other members as though they were part of self.

The Self: Personal Center of the Universe

The self-concept is the frame of reference from which observations are made. It is our personal reality, the vantage point from which all else is observed and comprehended. We speak of things as being right or left, near or far, and, of course, we mean from ourselves. The self is also used as a yardstick for making judgments. Others are regarded as taller, shorter, smarter, more unscrupulous, older, or younger than ourselves. As the self changes, the yardstick changes, and what we believe to be true changes with it. What is considered "old" is likely to be defined quite differently at ages six, sixteen, thirty-six, and sixty.

We generally feel at home with "what is me." Toward "what is not me" we are likely to be indifferent, even repelled. Gordon Allport points out, for example, that a person who cuts his finger may put it in his mouth and so drinks his own blood without the slightest concern.[4] Once the finger has been bandaged, however, a suggestion to lick blood from the bandage would likely be regarded with revulsion. Similarly, an individual is continuously engaged in swallowing the saliva that collects in her mouth. If the same saliva were collected in a glass and offered to the person to drink, it would be a very different matter!

Experiences consistent with the existing self-concept are readily accepted. They are treated as though they belong even when accepting them might be painful. A failing grade may not concern a student who thinks he is a failure; it only corroborates what he already believes. On the other hand, incongruous experiences may produce feelings of great discomfort. For example, one of us once counseled a young lady who, in tears and near hysteria, complained that she was flunking out of college. Taking what she said at face value, the listener began dealing with the problem as one would with a student who was failing. A great deal of time and effort was wasted before the author discovered that the student's perception of failing was based on the fact that, in three years of college, she had just gotten her first grade of C. All the others were As!

Doctors and nurses have trouble getting some patients who are newly diagnosed as diabetic to care for themselves properly. Such patients find it difficult to accept the new concept of self, the accompanying use of insulin, and the special dietary requirements. Assimilating new definitions of self takes time. The disturbing effect of inconsistent experiences will occur even if the new concept is something the person would like to believe. This can be observed in the embarrassment people feel when, after long periods of failure, they are told they have performed something very well.

SELF-CONCEPT DETERMINES BEHAVIOR

The importance of the self-concept in the economy of the individual goes far beyond providing the basis of reality. Its very existence determines what else the person may perceive. The self-concept has a selective effect on perceptions. People tend to perceive what is congruent with their existing concepts of self. Men perceive what they have been taught to perceive, whereas women see what they have been taught to perceive. So it happens that on the way home from a party, Mrs. Adams may say to her husband, "John, did you notice what Helen was wearing?" John is likely to reply, "No, I didn't notice that." But being a man, he did notice other things that almost certainly his wife would not think to ask him about—and probably would not want to hear about if she had!

Once established, the self-concept begins to mediate subsequent experience. For example, if a potential self-perception appears to the perceiving individual as congruent with those already present in the self-system, the perception is easily assimilated. If a potential idea about self is dissonant with ideas already incorporated, then it will probably be rejected. So the self-concept becomes a kind of personal gyrocompass, providing stability and direction for the interaction of self with the world. It provides a screen through which everything else is seen, heard, evaluated, and understood.

Psychological literature is overflowing with articles and research studies dealing with the effect of the self-concept on a variety of behaviors, including failure in school, levels of aspiration, athletic prowess, mental health, intelligence, delinquency, industrial productivity, and the behaviors of ethnic groups and the socially disadvantaged. The self-concept exerts its influence on every aspect of human endeavor. When we know how people see themselves, much of their behavior becomes clear to us, and often we can predict with great accuracy what they are likely to do next.

Circular Effect of the Self-Concept

The selective effect of the self-concept has another important consequence. It corroborates existing beliefs about self and therefore tends to maintain and reinforce its own existence. This circular characteristic of the self-concept may often be observed in the problems of children learning arithmetic, spelling, public speaking, physical education, history, music, or any other school subject. Let's look at reading, for example. Rarely these days does the child coming to the reading clinic have anything wrong with his or her eyes. With modern methods of assessing children's health, sight deficiencies are usually discovered routinely. Instead, youngsters who come to the reading clinic are much more likely to be handicapped because they *believe* they cannot read. Take the case of Jimmy Brown. Jimmy has developed the idea that he cannot read, and now he is caught in a vicious circle. Because he believes that he cannot read, he avoids it, thus avoiding the very activity that would help. Because he avoids reading, he doesn't get any practice and continues to be a poor reader. When his teacher asks him to read he reads poorly, and the teacher says, "My goodness, Jimmy, you don't read very well!" This, of course, is what he already believes! To make matters worse, a report card telling the parents how poorly the child reads is often sent home, and then the parents join in the act, confirming the child's belief that he is indeed a poor reader. In this way a poor reader is frequently surrounded by a veritable conspiracy in which all experience corroborates the deficiency. This conspiracy is, for the most part, produced by people whose intentions are excellent. They *want* the child to be a good reader, even though the net effect of their pressures is to prove that the child is not.

You may be one of the many people who believe they cannot do mathematics, make a speech, or spell. With such a belief, you may avoid those occasions that necessitate your using the particular skill. Many research studies show the effects of student beliefs on achievement in a wide variety of school subjects. Evidence even suggests that the self-concept may be a better predictor of a child's success in school than time-honored IQ scores are.

The self-perpetuating effect of the self-concept is by no means limited to success or failure in academic subjects. The same dynamics may be seen at work in all walks of life. Walter Reckless and his colleagues at Ohio State University carried out a series of studies on the self-concepts of delinquent and nondelinquent boys.[5] Among their findings are the following: The twelve-year-old "good" boy in a slum area perceives himself and his friends as staying out of trouble, himself as finishing school, and his family as being good. The mothers of the "good" boys also had favorable perceptions and prognostications of their sons. The so-called bad boy, spotted by his sixth-grade teacher as a dropout and troublemaker, has the opposite perception of himself. He perceives himself as being headed for trouble, his friends as being delinquents, and his family as being a "bum" family. The "bad" boy's mother echoed his perceptions. The results of a follow-up study conducted at the end of four years showed that the "good" boys had been practically free of delinquency, whereas forty percent of the "bad" boys had been in juvenile court one to seven times.

As this example shows, the circular effect of the self-concept operates in both positive and negative directions. People with positive self-concepts are likely to behave with confidence, causing others to react in corroborative fashion. People who believe they *can* are more likely to succeed. The very existence of such feelings about self creates conditions that are likely to make them so. The nurse who feels sure of himself behaves with dignity and certainty, expecting positive responses from other people. These expectations in turn call forth responses from his co-workers and patients that tend to confirm the beliefs he already holds. Therefore, the circular effect of the self-concept creates a kind of spiral in which "the rich get richer and the poor get poorer." This self-corroborating characteristic gives the self-concept a high degree of stability and makes changing it difficult once it has become firmly established.

Self-Concept and Social Problems

The self-perpetuating characteristic of the self-concept is of special concern in dealing with some of the great social problems of our time. Many people are caught in vicious circles in which their experiences always seem to confirm their unhappy or disastrous concepts of self. Having defined themselves in ways that preclude much hope of success, they remain forever victims of their own self-perceptions. Believing that they are only X much, that is all the much they do. Those who see them behave so label and treat them as "X much people," and this only confirms what they felt in the first place! How to help these desperate victims of their own perceptions off the treadmill of self-corroboration is one of the great problems faced by society.

The self-concept also plays its part in the social and philosophical problems posed by the great international dilemmas. People who see themselves as U.S. citizens behave like U.S. citizens, whereas people who see themselves as Russians, Chinese, Japanese, Germans, British, or Ghanians behave in ways that are appropriate to their conceptions of themselves. Sometimes diverse ways of seeing even create differences and misunderstandings where none would exist, were it possible to penetrate to the basic issues beneath the surface. U Thant, former Secretary-General of the United Nations, expresses this in a description of his own growth and philosophy, which had brought him to the point where he could see himself as a "person in the world" rather than as a representative of Burma, his native country. Feeling so, he says he could watch a wrestling match between a man from his own country and a man from another country and rejoice for whoever won. For most of us, such a citizen-of-the-world self-concept is still beyond our experience.

HOW THE SELF-CONCEPT IS LEARNED

The self-concept, we have said, is an organization of beliefs about the self. We acquire these concepts in the same way we acquire all other perceptions—as a consequence of experience. Before a child is born he has already begun to differentiate between self and the world. After birth the infant spends a large part of his waking hours in continuous exploration. Everything is smelled, felt, tasted, listened to, and looked at. At an early stage he begins to distinguish betwen "what is me" and "what is not me." With continued exploration, these perceptions become increasingly differentiated into more and more explicit definitions. As language use develops, giving "me" a name soon becomes possible, and the whole process of differentiation and concept formation accelerates. Before long the child possesses many perceptions about self and the world, and a sense of identity emerges. The child becomes aware of himself as a unique person of many qualities and values, which together contribute toward a feeling of personness. A new self-concept has come into being. Once established, this self-concept will exert its influence on every behavior for the rest of its owner's life.

Some of the things people learn about self are discovered by interaction with the physical world. From such experiences people learn how big or how little they are, how fast they can walk or swim, and where they are located in the space they live in. They also learn what they can lift or not lift, what they can control, which dangers they must avoid or protect themselves from, which things are good or enhancing, and thousands of other perceptions used for getting along in the physical world.

The Role of Significant Others

Of much more importance to the growth of the self are the concepts acquired from interaction with other human beings. People are primarily social animals, and they derive their most crucial self-concepts from experiences with other people. They learn who they are and what they are from the treatment they receive from the important people in their lives—sometimes called *significant others*. From these interactions, people learn that they are either liked or disliked, acceptable or unacceptable, successful or failures, respectable or of no account. We learn little from unimportant people, even if they are teachers, parents, social workers, counselors, priests, or rabbis. Only the people the individual considers significant have much effect on the self-concept.

Although the self-concept is primarily learned from experience with significant others, this is not simply a matter of what one is *told* by the important people in one's life. What people say to one another may, of course, have considerable importance, but not always. The effect of words does not lie in what is said but in how it is interpreted by the hearer. Understanding this fact is especially important for people in the helping professions because so much of their work depends on verbal interaction in one form or another. The belief that words are extremely important or that any problem can be solved by talk can result in making the helper ineffective. Talking is one of the most valuable tools we have for influencing the behavior of others, but its contribution is easily exaggerated. To be told that one is loved is not enough; one must *feel loved*—and by someone who matters. Speech is by no means infallible and is often vastly overrated. We need only remind ourselves of how seldom we take "good advice" from others.

A great deal of what we learn about ourselves is received through nonverbal communication. Everyone expresses feelings, attitudes, and beliefs through "body language": the ways we sit or stand, the gestures we use, our facial expressions, and a thousand other more or less subtle signs that convey our personal meanings. We become skillful in reading such signals so that we know what others think of us with not a word being spoken. Indeed, the fact that something was not said that should have been may itself be the most significant idea expressed between two people. Children learn about themselves, for example, from the atmosphere of the classroom, from the moods of teachers, and from the overt or covert indications of success or failure implied by approval or disapproval of teachers and classmates. This unplanned learning is likely to be much more significant and permanent than what the teacher "taught." The child in fifth grade who is reading at second-grade level has a daily diet of failure imposed by the rigidity of a system that insists on teaching all children at a given level as though they were alike. In the face of this daily experience, calling the child "a good girl or boy" is like dropping a spoonful of water onto a dry lake bed.

What is learned about self is a matter of the individual's own experience, not what some outsider thinks is happening. A parent who scolds a child for not doing well in school may do so with the best of intentions, hoping to motivate the child to greater effort. To the child, the meaning of this event may be only that he is stupid, unacceptable, and not much good. This kind of "incidental learning" is often more important in determining behavior than what the counselor or teacher or social worker expected to convey. A grasp of the crucial effects of significant others on self-concept is important to helpers not only for understanding the people they seek to help but also for guiding them as they strive to serve as significant others in the lives of their students, clients, and patients. In Chapter Ten we will examine some ways prospective helpers can learn to perceive the self-concepts of others.

Place of Trauma in the Growth of Self

Many believe that the self-concept is primarily a product of the dramatic events that happened to the child while she or he was growing up. The development of this idea is based on concepts introduced by Sigmund Freud and his students. As he listened to his patients retrace their development during psychoanalysis, Freud found them concentrating on shocking events from their pasts. Naturally, he assumed that these events had powerful influences on the formation of personality and the creation of the problems his patients carried into adulthood. This impression was further confirmed by the patients themselves, who frequently spoke of traumatic events as being critical. Yet we know that two persons can experience the same kind of tragedy and react quite differently. One person may lose an entire family in an auto accident and be destroyed psychologically, whereas another person may recover quickly from such an experience. A traumatic event may cause one person to suffer a total mental collapse, whereas the same experience may cause another to eventually become a stronger person than before.

We now understand that most important changes in the self-concept probably occur only as a consequence of many experiences repeated over long periods of time. The little day-to-day events that repeatedly chip away at an individual's feelings produce the most pervasive effects on the self. A child learns that she is acceptable or unacceptable not so much from dramatic events as from the thousands of everyday nuances of attitude and feeling that are picked up from those around her. Often these are so subtle and indistinct at the time they occur that the grown-up will find it impossible to distinguish the particular childhood event that produced a current feeling. Looking backward down the years of our growth, dramatic events provide the hooks on which we can hang accumulated meanings. Consequently, an adult may recall how shy he was as a child and how devastated he was in third grade on the day "when all the children laughed at me." What makes the difference in human personality is not the trauma itself but the complex of other experiences that hammered and molded a person's meanings to a state that is later triggered into explicit expression by some traumatic event.

Stability of the Self-Concept

We have described the self-concept as an organization of concepts that are of varying importance to the individual. We have also observed that, once established, the core of self-concept has a high degree of stability. Peripheral aspects of the self can often be acquired or changed fairly quickly. For example, a person can be taught to play tennis and come to think of himself as a "tennis player." By taking a person for a ride in an airplane, we may produce a change in her self-concept to "one who has been in a plane." These kinds of changes are comparatively simple to bring about, but they are seldom significant enough to produce important changes in personality. Important changes in self-concept, like those related to values, attitudes, or basic beliefs, occur much more slowly and sometimes only after long periods. Although this is often frustrating to those who would like to help people quickly or easily, we need to remind ourselves that this resistance to change is also our best guarantee against control by a demagogue. It is a good thing that people do not change easily.

Generally speaking, the more important the aspect of self is in the economy of the individual, the more experience will be required to establish it and the more difficult it will be to change. Fritz Redl illustrated this slow development of individual feelings about self in a lecture on juvenile delinquency. Delinquents, he pointed out, are not made by any one thing:

> It takes fourteen years to make a good delinquent. Before that you can't really be sure you have one. To make a good delinquent everything has to go wrong, not once, but over and over again. The home has to go wrong, the school has to go wrong, the church has to go wrong, the community has to go wrong, his friends have to let him down, not once, but over and over again. They have to make a habit of it! Then, after fourteen years of that you have a good delinquent.[6]

With fourteen years of this kind of experience, it is understandable why such a child's beliefs about self and the world are slow to change.

SELF-CONCEPT AND SELF-REPORT

If the self-concept plays as important a role in the determination of behavior as modern psychologists believe, then members of the helping professions must be sensitive to the self-concepts of their students, clients, or patients and skillful in helping them change concepts of self. At first glance, understanding someone's self-concept seems like an easy proposition. If you want to know how someone sees himself, why not just ask him? Unfortunately, it is not that simple. A person's self-perceptions are very private, and what the person can tell you about self will depend on his willingness to reveal self to you. Even if the person is willing, there is still a question as to whether he can accurately describe self to you on demand. Members of the helping professions should develop a clear understanding of the differences between a person's self-report and self-concept.[7]

The self-concept is what a person perceives herself to be; it is what she *believes* about self. The self-report, on the other hand, is what a person is willing or able to divulge, or what she can be induced into *saying* about self. The self-concept is a system of beliefs; the self-report is a behavior. These categories are not the same.

What people say about themselves may be accepted as interesting and informative data but not, without question, as a direct indication of the self-concept. The self-concept can, however, be understood indirectly through a process of inference from some form of observed behavior. The rationale is as follows: If it is true that behavior is a product of the individual's perceptual field, then it should be possible, by a process of reading behavior backward, to infer from observed behavior the nature of the perceptions that produced it. This is in fact what all of us do with people who are important to us. We deduce what they are thinking and feeling from the behavior we observe. The psychologist in research and the helper in the professional role do the same thing, although with greater control and precision than the general public does.

The question may legitimately be raised as to why inferences about the self-concept, made from observed behavior, are more acceptable indicators of the self-concept than is a person's self-report. First, the inferred self-concept is more accurate on theoretical grounds; it approaches the self-concept as an organization of *perceptions* that *produce* behavior rather than accepting the person's behavior as synonymous with self-perception. Second, it recognizes the existence of distorting factors in the self-report and attempts to eliminate as many of these as practicable. Making inferences about the self-concept, for example, can eliminate or reduce errors introduced by social expectancy, lack of cooperation of the subject, lack of adequate language, or the subject's feelings of threat. One may argue that inference procedures introduce other errors in the perceptions of the observer, but this is a problem in every human observation that scientists must deal with, no matter what the nature of the observations.

A person's *real* self, of course, is not measured by the inferred self-concept or the self-report. The question is, Which of these provides the closest approximation for the purposes we have in mind? Despite criticism of the self-report as a measure of self-concept, the self-report has value in its own right. What a person has to say about self is observable behavior. Because of its symbolic character and the uses the behaver makes of it for self-expression, it has more than ordinary value for helping us understand another person. Used as behavioral data, a self-report can provide valuable clues to the nature of the self-concept when subjected to processes of inference. Despite its distortions, the self-report may also provide sufficient data for the citizen operating in daily life. The scientist, student of behavior, or practitioner in the helping professions, however, will generally need descriptions of self that are more carefully and rigorously obtained.

SELF-CONCEPT AND SELF-ESTEEM

It may be helpful at this point to discuss briefly the construct of self-esteem. This is the value aspect of self-concept. People regard themselves not only as fathers and mothers but also as "good" or "bad" fathers and mothers. They see themselves not simply as persons but also as attractive or ugly, pleasant or unpleasant, fat or thin, happy or sad, adequate or inadequate.

Self-esteem can be considered with regard to some specific part of the self-concept or to self as a whole. We might say of ourselves, for example, "I'm really good at dancing, but I can't sing worth a damn." What we are really saying is that we have high self-esteem as a dancer but low self-esteem as a singer. It may also be said that this or that person has high or low self-esteem, meaning that he or she has high or low regard for the total self.

Many writers and researchers in the field prefer to speak about self-esteem rather than self-concept. This is because the instruments used in self-concept–related studies really deal with self-esteem and not self-concept. Subjects are asked to respond to such statements as:

I like myself.
I'm not as good a parent as I should be.
I am smart.
I like my body.

These kinds of statements are clearly evaluative and deal not with what a person is but with the value the person places on what she or he is. The term is also preferred because it is easier to change self-esteem than it is to change a self-concept. We prefer to speak mostly of the self-concept, for it *is* with self-concepts that we are concerned. That self-concepts are difficult to change, and our instruments aren't very effective in measuring them, do not change the focal point of our interest.

Changing Self-Concepts

The most important part of what professional helpers do is to positively affect the self-concepts of their clients, students, patients, or parishioners. William Fitts, a leader in self-concept research, has stated that importance as clearly and strongly as anyone:

> I have visualized the issue of self-concept change as central to all of our so-
> ciety. To me, this is the real issue underlying many others that plague us—

crime and delinquency, mental illness, racial conflict, alcoholism, drug abuse, marital misery, and many other people-related problems. In that sense, it is easy for me to view the institutions, agencies, and movements who deal with those problems as essentially concerned with self-concept change. I also have no difficulty in extending this view to other broad areas like education and religion.[8]

Strong stuff, to be sure. But we couldn't agree more. A better understanding of and the ability to change self-concepts may be the solution to most of society's biggest problems.

There is another, rather practical reason for focusing on the self-concept in helping relationships. A helpee may not be able to formulate her understanding of the helping relationship in the formal vocabulary of phenomenology, but she knows she should be the focus—her needs, problems, etc. are to be dealt with. She will judge the value of the experience from the point of view of self. If the helper continually misses this mark, sooner or later the helpee will conclude that the relationship is a waste of time and will physically or mentally depart the scene.

What, then, do we know about changing self-concepts? Not nearly as much as we would like. But neither are we totally ignorant.

First, because the self-concept is learned, it can be taught. This fact provides the theoretical basis on which the helping professions depend. The purpose of these occupations is to assist people in exploring and discovering more effective relationships between themselves and the world. To accomplish this objective, helpers need to understand the nature of the self-concept and how it changes. Generally speaking, the self of another person may be modified in two ways: (1) through confrontation with some experience calling for a different view of self, or (2) through evaluation of existing experience.

The first of these routes to change is familiar to all of us. This is the way we learned our identities, as a consequence of the ways we were treated by those who were around us while we were growing up. Helpers affect the self-concepts of students, clients, or patients by arranging appropriate experiences. Teachers help children feel able by providing success experience; counselors help clients feel able by treating them as though they were.

Whether they are aware of it or not, helpers engage in a subtle process of teaching. They cannot be nonentities. The helping relationship is an active one, and a completely passive helper will probably not teach a client anything but his or her own futility. The personality of the helper must play a vital part in any helping relationship.

The second way in which self changes is a consequence of new ways of seeing old experience. This kind of learning, often called "insight," occurs when the elements of perceptual organization are put together in a new pattern or gestalt. A person who is talking about concerns with a teacher or counselor may conclude that his original way of perceiving the matter was inaccurate or inappropriate and may change his point of view about the event and about self.

What we are saying is that helpers can bring about change in self-concepts primarily by helping clients gain new insights (changes of perception) into themselves or by providing or suggesting new experiences (changes in behavior). Some see conflict in this position, thinking that the factors of changes in perceptions and changes in behavior are an either/or relationship. They say that only one can be a cause and thus the other must be a result. What we end up with in that case is the fruitlessness of the which-came-first syndrome of the chicken and the egg. The authors believe that either can be cause or effect and that they have a transactional relationship. For example, from working with a skillful counselor a person might say, "Yes, you are right. I never looked at it quite like that before," and as a result bring about changes in his behavior. On the other hand, a person who never thought she would be good as a skier might, as the result of encouragement, take skiing lessons and discover she is great—the chicken or the egg?

Changing Self Takes Time

Changing important aspects of self is rarely accomplished quickly. A proper perspective of the limitations of these changes can forestall the helper from setting impractical goals and can contribute to the helper's own mental health and probabilities of successful practice. Generally speaking, the more fundamental or important the aspect of self we hope to change, the longer it is likely to take. A person who has been deeply deprived, for example, has a great void within that requires filling. Helping that person is like trying to help a person who has fallen deeply in debt. For a long time all the money he makes must go just to keep himself solvent from day to day. All efforts are spent in trying to balance the budget. Until that is done, little can be used to get ahead. The matter is made more difficult by interest charges or withdrawals to meet new emergencies. It may take a long time to help such a person recover to the point where he can take some positive action on his own. Helpers often have to believe that their efforts are worthwhile despite the lack of tangible evidence for a considerable period. For deeply deprived persons, a single experience is rarely enough to make much difference.

The impatient helper may begin the task intending to help and end by making the client worse. The following scenario with a tough delinquent is all too common:

Here he is—surly, angry, against the world, feeling as a result of his long experience, "Nobody likes me. Nobody wants me. Nobody cares about me. Well, I don't care about nobody neither!" Now the well-meaning social worker, with the best of intentions, says to him, "Eddie, I like you." Much to his dismay, his friendly words are met with a stream of profanity. The inexperienced social worker may be deeply hurt by this rejection and outraged by the violence of the child's reply. Why should the child behave in this way? He does so, because from his point of view, "you can't trust people who talk like that." All his past experience has taught him so. The social worker's words are a mockery to the child. They sound like outright lies or, worse still, like someone is making fun of him. Small wonder that he lashes out at his attacker and lets him have "what he deserves." Unless the social worker knows what he is about and possesses a great deal of patience, he may succumb to the "natural" thing and slap the youth across the mouth. This, of course, only proves what the youngster felt in the first place—"you can't trust people who talk like that!" What started out as an attempt to help becomes shipwrecked by the helper's own lack of perspective about the self-concept and confirms the child's beliefs more deeply than ever before. Worse still, the experience may increase the child's distrust of persons in the helping professions generally.

Helping Is Never in Vain

Despite the high degree of stability that is characteristic in its central aspects, the self-concept is always capable of change. Indeed, throughout life it is continually changing. Good examples are the changes in feeling about self that occur from childhood to adolescence, to maturity, and finally to old age. Even very old people sometimes make considerable changes in self-concept, albeit not so easily as they did in their youth. Change, to be sure, is more rapid in the peripheral and less important aspects of self. But learning goes on continuously and even the central aspects of the self-concept may change as a consequence of experience over the years.

Life is not reversible; every experience a person has is forever. One cannot *un*experience what has already happened! Every experience of significant interaction has an impact on those who were involved in it. Meaningful experiences provided by a helper may not be sufficient to produce the changes hoped for, but they are always important. The importance of the helper in the life of a client is never without meaning unless the helper makes it so.

Professional helpers often complain that they can do little because they do not have control over the outside lives of clients, students, or patients. They complain that their work is spoiled by the unhappy experiences visited on their clients by bosses, parents, or society in general. As a matter of fact, even a holding operation may make an important contribution. When everything in a child's life outside of school is teaching him that he is unliked, unwanted, and unable, a loving teacher who provides experiences of success may make a world of difference. A teacher may not be able to turn the tide completely, but if she does no more than help such a child keep afloat, the effort is surely not wasted. Teachers rarely get credit for this kind of help, but it probably occurs with far more frequency than any of us realize. Similarly, the social worker who helps a young delinquent stay only "as bad as he is" when everything else in his world is pushing him downhill can make a contribution of tremendous importance—even if the social worker does not succeed in making him over into a more socially acceptable image.

Helpers must not fall into the trap of thinking their efforts are futile. To do so may only contribute to the inadequacies of their clients or students.

After all, because a child is rejected at home is no good reason to reject him in school as well. What happens to an individual outside the helper's sphere of influence may operate in directions opposite to those sought by the helper. This does not mean that what the helper does is of no avail. Take the case of the teacher who exclaims, "What can you do with a child from a home like that?" It seems to him that all his hard-won gains are negated by what happens to the child in her family. Such an attitude is most unfortunate. It overlooks the fact that a family is a dynamic unit in which each person interacts with all the others. What happens to any one member must affect everyone else. Let us take the hypothetical case of George Anderson, who is driving his mother to distraction by his hostile behavior. Let us also suppose that this child is fortunate enough to have a teacher who provides some warmth, friendship, and experience of success. When George goes home from school these days he feels better than he did when school was an unhappier place. As a consequence, he doesn't upset his mother quite as much. Mr. Anderson, coming home tired from work, discovers that his wife is easier to live with and that his home is a more restful place. When Judith Anderson, George's little sister, claims her father's attention while he is trying to read the paper, instead of pushing her away gruffly, as he often does, he makes room for her to climb onto his lap, and Judith gains from her father a greater measure of the love and care she needs. Because she feels better, she feels less need to nag her brother George, as she usually does, and we have come full circle! Every good thing a helper does is forever. It may not be enough, but it is never futile. There is always the further possibility that someone else may contribute something elsewhere, and such cumulative experiences may in time be sufficient to bring about the changes hoped for.

The self-concept lies at the very heart of the helping process.[9] A proper knowledge of the self-concept and its dynamics can add immeasurably to understanding people in need of help. It can also provide the guidelines by which people in the helping professions may focus their practice more effectively and efficiently and therefore contribute greater certainty to the health and growth of clients.

Notes and References

1. The complete statement of this approach may be found in A. W. Combs, A. Richards, and F. Richards, *Perceptual Psychology: A Humanistic Approach to the Study of Persons* (New York: Harper & Row, 1976).

2. Carol Tavris, "The Freedom to Change," in T. H. Carr and H. E. Fitzgerald, eds., *Psychology 82/83* (Guilford, Conn.: Dushkin, 1982), pp. 14–19.

3. E. C. Kelley, *In Defense of Youth* (Englewood Cliffs, N.J.: Prentice-Hall, 1962).

4. G. W. Allport, *Becoming* (New Haven: Yale University Press, 1955).

5. W. C. Reckless, S. Dinity, and B. Kay, "Self-Component in Potential Delinquency," *American Sociological Review* 22 (1957):566–570.

6. From notes taken by A. W. Combs at Dr. Redl's lecture. Because Dr. Redl was speaking *ex tempore*, the accuracy of the quotation cannot be checked.

7. This matter is in great confusion in the psychological literature. Most of the studies pre-

sented as research on the self-concept turn out, on closer examination, to be studies of self-report. Purporting to be research on the self-concept, they used measures of the self-report as though these concepts were identical. Treating these terms as though they were synonymous has greatly complicated the literature, and serious students need to be aware of this in interpreting research findings.

8.   W. H. Fitts, "Issues Regarding Self-Concept Change," in M. D. Lynch et al., *Self Concept: Advances in Theory and Research* (Cambridge, Mass.: Ballinger, 1981), pp. 261–262.

9.   One of the first authors to introduce the construct of self-concept to American psychology was Victor Raimy. His doctoral dissertation proved to be a pioneering effort in self-theory and became so popular a source of information on the subject that Ohio State University, where it was written, published it as part of their university press series under the title of *The Self-Concept as a Factor in Counseling and Personality* (Columbus: Ohio State University Libraries, 1971).

FOUR

A PERSON-CENTERED VIEW OF MOTIVE

Next to our beliefs about ourselves, perhaps no others are more important than those we hold about what people are like and why they behave as they do. These beliefs provide the bases for every human interaction. What we do in dealing with other people is always predicated on some conception of what they are like and what we think they are trying to do. It makes a great difference in a person's behavior, for example, what she thinks the man who is running toward her wants to do—walk along with her, ask for directions, deliver a message, or rob her. For helpers, a clear understanding of human motivation is essential for successful practice.

TWO VIEWS OF MOTIVATION

Two ways of examining motivation are commonly used. One looks at motivation externally—from the point of view of an outsider seeking to influence another person's behavior. The other is an internal approach to motivation that is concerned with what people want, need, or are trying to do.

Underlying the external approach to motivation are several assumptions about the fundamental characteristics of the human organism. The more scientific of these conceptions sees human beings as objects, products at the end of a long chain of molding influences originating at conception. Other, less scientific views regard the human organism as essentially untrustworthy, likely to revert to its perverse original nature if something isn't done to assure its proper behavior. In either case, the external approach views motivation in terms of what one person does to another to cause the behavior that the motivator has in mind. This is essentially a matter of management, involving the application of stimuli to control behavior, generally through some form of reward or punishment. Control may be exerted by various forms of manipulation like directing, ordering, making, convincing, telling, exhorting, threatening, and coercing. Coercion can be subtle, with a velvet glove masquerading as "guidance." Control may also be exerted by carrot-on-a-stick techniques, with concrete rewards like cash, food, or presents, or by various kinds of seduction like, "Please," or "If you do this, I will love you," or "Macho men shave with _____."

Seen from the internal or person-centered view, motivation involves human needs, goals, and aspirations. These are internal matters arising from an understanding of human behavior as a consequence of a person's perceptions of self and the world. Helpers may sometimes find it useful to operate in terms of external approaches to motivation, but more often their efforts at helping will be directed toward facilitating change in the perceptual worlds of those they seek to help.

OLDER CONCEPTS OF THE NATURE OF PEOPLE

The Basically Evil Person

Throughout history, people have been intrigued by the problem of the "nature of man" and many explanations have been proposed. These ideas have had their effect on the generations that believed them, and many still influence modern thought. One of these concepts is the doctrine of original sin. This doctrine maintained that children entered the world innately evil. The purpose of life was to correct this evil and strive toward goodness. Because adults used their own behavior as the criteria for judging others, the child who did not conform to adult standards was considered "naughty" or "bad." And because most children who behaved in approved ways managed to develop into satisfactory adults, it seemed evident that people grew better as they grew older. Assuming that tendencies toward good and evil were innate, parents did not regard themselves as responsible for the outcomes of their offspring. People felt sorry for parents with "bad" children and regarded them as unlucky or as having to bear such crosses because it was God's will.

For many centuries this concept was part of certain religious dogmas and so was given the additional authority of the church. More recently, it had the apparent endorsement of science. Darwin's concept of evolution, for example, seemed to give credence to the basic animal quality of human nature. Freudian psychology also seemed to support this view in its concept of the *id*, defined as primeval impulses representing a person's roots in the uncivilized animal world. The concept of persons as basically evil is very old. Even today the principles of this essentially pessimistic view of human beings are accepted by people in all walks of life, including some members of the helping professions.

The Person at War with Self

The concept of the person at war with her or his self is even more common than original sin. Those who hold this view see the person as a battleground on which both good and evil forces are constantly striving for supremacy. It is supported by the observations we make about the behavior of people around us. People do indeed behave well and badly. Conflict, competition, and struggle seem to be going on everywhere. Reflecting on our own behavior, we can recall our struggles against temptation, our grief or shame over harmful actions, and our feelings of self-approval from fighting against an evil impulse. The personality-in-conflict view seems to explain a great many of our experiences.

The concept of the person divided can also be found deeply imbedded in tradition not only in Western culture but in most others. It exists in the folklore, myths, fables, and traditions of primitive tribes and of highly civilized cultures. In the Western world it has long been a classic concept of Judeo-Christian philosophy. In psychology the concept of conflict is illustrated by need systems like succorance–nurturance, dependence–abasement, and aggression–deference. It is also advanced by psychoanalysts who describe maladjustment as the outcome of a person's struggles between the primitive impulses of the id and the civilized functions of the superego.

Some Implications of Older Concepts

Human nature as seen from these older points of view poses difficult problems for the helping professions. The original sin and the person-in-conflict views require working with an organism that can never be trusted. If human nature is inherently evil, one is always confronted with the possibility of a reversion to bestiality the moment a person is permitted to operate freely. Helpers proceeding from this frame of reference constantly struggle against great odds, and their task is doomed to eventual defeat. The person in need of help must be regarded with suspicion. The helper must always be on guard for signs of reversion to type and must be ready to head off such tendencies as they appear. With this view and its characteristic lack of trust, helper and helpee are cast in the roles of antagonists.

The methods required to deal with such perverse tendencies must be powerful ones. Saving people in spite of themselves calls for vigorous measures. People growing up in such traditions often come to believe that there is something innately good about work and that discipline for its own sake is a wonderful thing. They operate on the philosophy "if it's hard, it's good for them." Helpers with this orientation believe that they are battling for the very salvation of the individual and the maintenance of civilization. This is a task that can brook no nonsense.

Such a philosophy calls for methods of helping people that rely on various forms of control and direction, for example, rewarding the taking of right paths and punishing the taking of wrong ones. This results in a way of dealing with people that is sometimes called the fencing-in approach, in which people are guided toward chosen goals through the imposition or removal of barriers, much like rats in a maze. Controls may be physical (walls, traffic lights, electric shocks) or verbal (prohibitions, threats).

Unfortunately, most of the public schools are run on the basis of control and direction, punishment and reward, and the futility of this kind of approach was made only too clear in a recent study of teaching.[1] An analysis of time-on-task revealed that the group of teachers studied spent about ten percent of their time teaching. The rest of their time—almost all of it—was spent in managing their classes!

A PERCEPTUAL VIEW OF MOTIVE

Humanistically oriented psychologists have arrived at a different view of the basic nature of human beings. They agree that people do indeed sometimes behave well and sometimes badly. These psychologists point out, however, that because people *behave* so, it cannot be assumed that they *are* so. Who has not hurt or embarrassed a friend while intending to be especially nice? Perceptual psychologists have developed a conception that provides a different understanding of motivation and establishes a different set of guidelines for the helping professions.

From biology we learn that a basic characteristic of protoplasm is its "irritability," that is, its capacity to respond. Awareness is thus a quality of life itself. The ability of organisms to respond, furthermore, is not haphazard; it is response with direction. Haphazard or fortuitous response would quickly result in elimination of the organism in the course of evolution. The response of an organism is not accidental; it is goal-directed toward fulfillment. Even the lowly amoeba moves toward food and away from danger, at least as far as it is capable of doing so. Mushrooms turn away from light, whereas sunflowers grow toward it. Wounded flesh heals. Animals mate and care for their young. Each life in its own peculiar way continuously seeks fulfillment.

Human beings, like all other organisms, are continuously in search of fulfillment. The dynamic, striving character of people has its origins in the nature of protoplasm itself. People begin their lives with a built-in motivation toward self-fulfillment and thereafter make of it what they can within the limits of their capacities.

The expression of our basic striving translated into behavior may seem good or evil to an outside observer. But movement toward fulfillment is neither good nor bad. That is a value judgment about behavior made by people observing it from the frame of reference of a particular culture. We cannot say that an organism is basically good or evil. However, because striving for fulfillment seems to be a constructive force in human existence, there is some justification for considering this basic drive to be more positive than negative.

The Growth Principle

The basic striving of organisms for fulfillment has been called the *growth principle*, because the effect is to move them continuously toward health and growth for as long as possible. This is true whether we are talking of a single cell like a paramecium or of the great organization of cells that make up a complex mammal like a human being. Growth is characteristic of the very essence of life and finds expression in all of life's ramifications.

The growth principle is so important to the physiological well-being of people that the practice of medicine is predicated on it. The physician knows that it is not she who cures her patient; rather, it is the patient who cures himself. When the body is invaded by germs many forces swing into action to defend the organism by destroying or immobilizing the offending invaders. The physician's task is to minister to this process. She assists the body in its normal striving toward a healthy condition. To this end, she may try to impede or destroy the invading germs with medication or resort to surgery to remove or repair a disabled organ. By prescribing rest, nourishing food, and proper inoculations, the physician may further assist the body's attempts to return to a state of health by building up its resources. But no matter what the physician does to help the process along, in the final analysis the body gets well by itself.

The growth principle operates in behavioral terms as well as in physiological terms. The entire organism strives toward growth. Not only do people seek to be physically adequate, but more importantly, they also strive for personal fulfillment. To achieve psychological satisfaction they will even risk their physical beings. To feel important or worthwhile they may even court death. Examples in everyday life are the professional football player, the racing driver, the test pilot, and the astronaut. Throughout history, heroes have gone to certain death for their fellows. In doing so they sacrifice their physical selves to enhance other selves that are more important to them: their self-concepts.

NEED FOR SELF-ACTUALIZATION

We have seen in Chapter Three how the self-concept transcends the physical body. The fulfillment of self that human beings seek is actualization of the *concept of self*, not simply its container. Consequently, people may strive for self-enhancement not only in the present but for the future as well. Many people spend large portions of their lives and fortunes seeking to perpetuate a favorable image of self in the minds of others. In certain cultures even suicide may be seen as a form of self-enhancement. To achieve as adequate and effective a self as possible, a man may kill himself today rather than suffer the humiliation he knows is coming tomorrow. For the Japanese, a person of noble rank who commits hara-kiri is guaranteed prestigious immortality.

The growth principle at work has also been called by biologists "homeostasis," "the wisdom of the body," and "the drive to health." Among psychologists, it has been described by Maslow[2] as a need for self-actualization, by Allport[3] as a process of becoming, by Lecky[4] as self-consistency, by Festinger[5] as dissonance reduction, by Frankl[6] as a search for meaning, and by Rogers[7] as a search for self-fulfillment. In their earliest work Combs and

Snygg[8] described it as a need for the maintenance and enhancement of the self; in a later work it was described as a need for personal adequacy.[9] Whatever it is called, the principle refers to the striving of human beings constantly searching for personal adequacy or fulfillment.

Maslow's Hierarchy of Needs

People do not seek enhancement in the same ways or through the same goals. They have learned many different ways of seeking fulfillment and operate on varied levels of enhancement. Abraham Maslow[10] called these goals *needs* and arranged them in a kind of hierarchy from basic physiological ones to high-level self-actualization as follows:

1. Physiological needs (i.e., food, water, oxygen)
2. Safety needs—security, stability, freedom from fear (e.g., needs for structure, limits)
3. Belongingness and love needs—affectionate relationships with people and the feeling that one belongs in some social context
4. Esteem needs—achievement, adequacy, mastery (e.g., needs for reputation, recognition, importance)
5. Self-actualization needs—self-fulfillment, to actualize one's potential, "to become more and more what one idiosyncratically is, to become everything that one is capable of becoming"

Maslow suggests that such hierarchies of need represent a demand system in which the more basic needs must be satisfied before higher ones can be achieved. However, a need at any level does not have to be completely satisfied before one can go on to the next.

The more basic a need, the more urgent its fulfillment and the more dominant it will be. For example, a person who is being deprived of a physiological need (air, water, etc.) will not have time to focus on anything except attempting to satisfy that need. All thought and effort will be directed toward its satisfaction. If the need is at least temporarily or partially filled, and deprivation is not at a life-threatening level, the person can and will seek fulfillment at a higher level.

One can and often does voluntarily circumvent a lower-order need in search of fulfillment of a higher-level need. Examples are the starving artist and the fasting monk. Control of deprivation is in their hands, not in those of other individuals or of fate, and they know they can end the deprivation at will.

People go up and down the need hierarchy, depending on what is *the* dominant need at any given moment: Are they hungry or in need of love? Do they need to create? But usually one is operating on a dominant theme or need level, the satisfaction of which occupies the individual's life. This is quite evident in the United States. Most Americans do not find it particularly difficult to satisfy their physiological and safety needs. Yet one need only examine the advertising media to discover what levels they *are* hung up on. It is virtually impossible for a person to go even for a moment when he or she is not either seeking satisfaction on the levels of belongingness and love or esteem, or interacting with someone else who is. Most advertisements in the United States—on billboards, TV, and radio and in magazines and newspapers—claim that whatever they are selling will bring us love or status. And if we are honest with ourselves, we must admit that much of our behavior is indeed directed toward the fulfillment of such needs.

The hierarchy also tells us something important about communication. It tells us that if we have any hope of communicating with others, as individuals or professionals, we had better first ascertain on what level or levels of need satisfaction those with whom we are trying to communicate are operating. Otherwise, communication will fail.

Problems on a personal and even international scale can develop if we do not understand this fact. If a group of human beings are severely deprived of a physiological or safety need, and we try to communicate with them on some other level, our efforts will be futile. Teachers who try to teach hungry children that are also afraid are wasting their time. If we, as a nation, approach other nations spouting platitudes of neighborly love, democracy, or even human rights, and those people are starving or afraid, our words will fall on deaf ears. If deprivation exists at one level of the hierarchy, we must end that deprivation before going on to a loftier level of need satisfaction or communication. One should never lose sight of the fact, however, that it is always self-fulfillment or enhancement that humans are seeking. The levels of the hierarchy simply tell us the best way to deal with that search at any given time in an individual's life.

A Trustworthy, Predictable Organism

An understanding of the hierarchy also makes the behavior of human beings predictable and the organism trustworthy, providing we know the peculiar expression of need in a given person.[11] From the person's own point of view, far from being at war with himself, he is an organized totality with direction and purpose. "But," one may argue, "that does not seem to fit my personal experience. I remember when I had to make this or that difficult choice and it wasn't easy. Isn't this an indication that I was at war with myself?" Not at all.

When we examine our own behavior we must remember that we are looking at it after the fact. That is, we observe it like any other outsider. From this position there may appear to be simultaneously existing desires, but this seems so only because the matter is being observed externally. At the moment of behaving the individual does what seems *at that instant* most likely to lead to fulfillment and actualization. To be sure, it may be perceived quite differently before or after the act. The illusion of conflict occurs because one is looking at two different events separated in time. You may test this against your own experience. Recall some recent instance in which you may have "misbehaved." Looking back from your present position, it may seem as though the act was stupid, undesirable, or even morally wrong. Even before the act occurred, if you had contemplated its consequences, the action may have seemed unsatisfying or immoral. At the moment it happened, however, it seemed like a good thing to do. The act appeared desirable and need-fulfilling, perhaps even necessary, to accomplish your purpose at that instant.

Although there may be occasional confusion about ways of achieving fulfillment, there is no conflict of motives. Fulfillment is the motive no matter how it is accomplished. This basic drive for fulfillment is also characteristic of the societies that people create to achieve their purposes. All kinds of groups—schools, clubs, communities, nations—are formed to provide fulfillment for their members. They thrive so long as they achieve it and are destroyed or disintegrate when they can no longer provide it.

Is Human Nature Selfish?

Perhaps it is distressing to some readers that the basic nature of human beings as we have described it here is a striving for self-fulfillment. They may ask, "Is human nature really so fundamentally selfish?" The answer is yes and no. There is no doubt that the basic drive for self-fulfillment is a concern for self. We have also seen how the self-concept is the individual's basic frame of reference. In this sense, human beings appear to be selfish. The picture, however, is not nearly so egocentric as it seems.

As discussed in Chapter Three the self-concept is capable of expansion. If a child who is born with a basic drive for self-fulfillment has good experiences with the people about her, then little by little she comes to expand her self to include those significant others. She comes to feel "one" with parents, siblings, playmates, and friends. As she grows older, the circle of those she includes within her self may expand to include wider and wider groups of people. In time, she may come to identify with "my country" and "my school." In the case of saintly persons, the feeling of identification may eventually extend to all humanity. In that state the problem of selfishness has disappeared; when the self is identified with all humankind, then what one does for self, one does for everyone, and what one does for everyone, one does for self. Selfishness is determined by the boundaries of the self. A restricted self is a selfish one; an expanded self is a saintly one. Basic nature is selfish only in the extent to which the self has failed to grow by identification with others.

MALADJUSTMENT—A PROBLEM OF DEPRIVATION

The striving of human beings for self-actualization goes on as long as it is possible to do so. The need is insatiable. As soon as a person has achieved one goal, there is always another just beyond so that no one is ever completely fulfilled and the drive for self-actualization continues as long as one lives. For some people, unhappily, the force of this drive may be more or less permanently blunted or its direction diverted to unfortunate channels because of some form of deprivation.

The achievement of a satisfactory degree of fulfillment constitutes psychological health. People who are successful in attaining a measure of self-actualization are likely to be happy and contented with themselves and effective in their relationships with the world. People who are unsuccessful or frustrated in their attempts to achieve fulfillment become sick and maladjusted. Just as the body's failure to achieve proper growth and fulfillment results in physiological disease, so too failure of the individual to achieve satisfactory fulfillment of self brings psychological ill health.

Maladjusted people are unfulfilled, and the seriousness of their condition is almost directly a function of the degree of deprivation they have suffered or think they have suffered. Most of us can tolerate mild degrees of failure to achieve fulfillment. When failures become chronic or strike people in important aspects of self-structure, people soon become unhappy. If deprivations are serious or persist for long periods, people become increasingly neurotic. Depending on the degree of frustration, people become discouraged, dispirited, angry, or hostile. Almost certainly, deprived people will frustrate other people. If deprivation is too great or too long continued, people finally may feel defeated and without hope. When this happens they become burdens or dangerous to the rest of us. Such unfortunates are the people who fill the mental hospitals and penitentiaries.

People are not "naturally" sick. We now understand that sickness and maladjustment are products of human deprivation, failure, and frustration. In earlier times we regarded criminality as willful immorality. Treatments devised for this condition were appropriate to that belief and were often unbelievably harsh and brutal. Today we have a more enlightened view and regard such persons as psychologically sick rather than as inherently evil. Slowly we are learning to extend this understanding to the problems of the less dramatically ill, the poor, and the victims of prejudice. At one time we could regard the problem of the sick and the deprived as inevitable expressions of the will of God. We no longer regard them as inevitable, and if they continue to exist, they do so not as the will of God but as the lack of will of human beings.

Seen in this light, maladjustment is not a willful seeking of destructive or negative behavior. The observed behavior of people suffering from deprivation and low self-esteem must be understood as efforts to protect the self or achieve some measure of personal fulfillment. Maslow described the behaviors of the maladjusted as "the screams of the tortured at the crushing of their psychological bones."[12]

Failure to understand the defensive character of such behavior often results in the complaint "They like it that way." This statement is usually made in a tone of shock, frustration, disappointment, or condemnation, depending on whether the speaker is surprised, thwarted, blaming, or reject-ing. It is often used to explain the failure of social reforms when, for example, we provide new housing for ghetto areas and the residents destroy the property. We apply it also to our friends and neighbors whose be-havior we do not comprehend. The assumption is that what people do is what they want to do. If that is so, it follows that they deserve what happens to them.

"They like it that way" is not only a judgment about other people but also a beautiful excuse for inaction. If "they like it that way," we ought not interfere. What happens to other people can thus be ignored without feeling guilty for not having helped. For some, belief in this myth is more than an excuse for inaction. It provides an outlet for hostility and a satisfying feeling of superiority over the stupidity of other people. There are even people for whom the myth may be a source of enjoyment when watching others "get what's coming to them."

If the view of human nature that we have been discussing is accurate, vastly different attitudes toward human frailty and error are called for. Many of us are quick to blame our fellows for their foibles and misbehaviors. We get angry at parents for what they do to children. We scorn parents for the stupidities that made them ill and blame teachers for their inabilities to cope with the children they send to the counselor. We overlook the fact that the behaver always acts in ways that seem reasonable, even necessary, under the circumstances. We forget that others have problems and that their behavior is a consequence of those conditions. If the basic character of human beings is striving for fulfillment, if every person is forever engaged in a search for self-actualization, if each human being is searching to be the best she or he can, who, then, can we blame for what?

FREEDOM AND THE RIGHTS OF OTHERS

To this point we have spoken of the individual's need to achieve per-sonal fulfillment. But what of fulfilling society's needs? The answer to that question is that if a person is truly free to seek self-fulfillment and is achiev-ing it to a reasonably satisfactory degree, the person will behave in ways that satisfy the needs of society as well. Why should this be so?

First, it is necessary to remind ourselves that we live deeply embedded in a social structure. We have created a world so cooperative and inter-dependent that few of us could last but a few hours without the aid and assistance of other people. The self-concept is learned from the behavior of others toward us, and most of our satisfactions are results of human relationships in one form or another. Human maladjustment is a product of the breakdown of this vital condition. Dialogue between the person and society is necessary for effective living. This means that successful fulfill-ment can be achieved only through some form of successful interaction with others.

We have already seen that selfishness disappears as people become ful-filled. As the self expands, an increasing number of other people are brought into its organization and treated as extensions of self. In the degree to which fulfillment occurs, then, people become increasingly responsible. In fact, the dynamics we are describing are an essential precondition for truly responsi-ble behavior. Irresponsible behavior is a consequence of the breakdown of dialogue, a feeling of alienation, or lack of commitment to others. Because the self is learned from the feedback of others, its enhancement depends on successful interaction. *Providing they are free to do so,* it follows that people can, will, *must* move in directions that are good not only for themselves but for others as well.

This relationship between the person and society was described by Ruth Benedict as *high-synergy culture* and defined as one "in which the individual by the same act and at the same time serves his own advantage and that of the group."[13] Fred and Anne Richards have further described a high-synergy so-ciety as

> the healthy or helping society in which the individual process of self-actual-ization and the cultural process of socialization, rather than mutually antag-onistic, are complementary or reciprocal. The fulfillment of one's potential for growth and well-being and the realization of society's provides the max-imum climate for the full development of the potentiality of the greatest number of its members. . . . The individual, by participating in the social order, participates in and affirms his own personal growth.[14]

People who are confronted with this idea for the first time will no doubt find that it strains their credulity To them, it may even seem to be hopelessly naive. However, if the basic motive of the organism is a drive toward health, and if it is free to move, it *must* progress in healthy directions. The essential condition in this statement lies in the phrase "if it is free to move." The drive toward fulfillment is innate, but the conditions for freedom are not; they exist in the perceptions of the individual and in the world she or he must cope with. If creation of those conditions is in fact feasible, the democratic concept that "when people are free they can find their own best ways" becomes a clearly defensible principle. What is more, if people are interacting openly and meaningfully with others, the ways they find for achieving self-fulfill-ment will contribute to the fulfillment of all.

The growth principle can be counted on to provide the motive power for the helping professions. The problem for helpers is to create the conditions for freedom in which the principle can operate. Just as the physician attempts to free the physical organism to move toward recovery and growth, the task of counselors, teachers, parents, psychologists, social workers, and all others engaged in the helping professions is to minister to human beings in such fashion that this basic drive may be set free. If we are successful in creating these conditions, the person's own basic drive for actualiza-tion and fulfillment can be counted on to move him or her in positive directions.

SOME IMPLICATIONS FOR THE HELPING PROFESSIONS

People Are on Our Side

If it is true that human beings are relentlessly driven toward health and adequacy, it follows that the helping professions always have a powerful ally—the person himself. The discovery that the human organism is trustworthy means that the people whom helpers seek to assist are not enemies who are perversely, stubbornly, or maliciously resisting the efforts of professional workers. Rather, they are deeply and fundamentally motivated by the need to be the best they can as they see it. Therefore, those who are engaged in the helping professions are not dealing with unpredictable, fortuitous matters. They can formulate ways of working with their clients, students, or patients with real hope that these may result in certain and predictable outcomes. Helper and helpee seek the same goal—fulfillment of the client. This makes the relationship a kind of partnership. Such a partnership, to be sure, might occasionally be uneasy or filled with difficulties. A partnership, however, no matter how uneasy, is far more likely to produce positive results than it is to produce open battle between enemies.

People Are Always Motivated

Most people regard the problem of motivation as a matter of management or manipulation to get others to do the things they would like them to. Motivation is accomplished by rewards or punishments designed to get other people to do "what is good for them" or to keep them from behaving in some fashion considered harmful or against the best interests of the motivator. In light of the growth principle we have been discussing, a different view of motivation is called for.

If people are always seeking self-fulfillment, then they are forever motivated. They are never unmotivated until they die. To be sure, they may not be motivated to do what some outsider believes they ought or should. The little boy in school who pokes the person in front of him during the arithmetic lesson is not very motivated to do arithmetic at that moment, but he is surely not unmotivated! In light of our discussion of the growth principle, motivation is not a problem of external manipulations; it has to do with what goes on inside people. It is always there, a characteristic of the life force itself.

Looked at externally, motivating people is a problem of getting them to do the right things. From the internal point of view, the task of the helper becomes one of helping the person to discover new ways of becoming more effective as a human being. To do this, teachers, for example, seek to help each person fulfill the needs he already has and then help him discover additional needs he never knew he had. As Frymier and Thompson describe it:

Motivation to learn in school is something which students *have* or *are* rather than that which teachers *do* to help them learn. It is a function of one's personality structure, his goals and values, his conception of self and others, and his attitude toward change. These aspects of human behavior are learned and they are subject to modification. Nevertheless, teachers concerned about their youngster's motivations have to do much more than use a carrot on a stick or a paddle on the behind if they hope for significant changes in any way.[15]

Understanding human motives in the terms we have described will have salutary effects on helpers' relationships with clients, patients, or students. Rapport is likely to be much better, because helpers will more likely be seen as compassionate, concerned, and sympathetic. Operating under the assumption that human nature is fundamentally perverse is apt to make helpers suspicious of helpees. When behavior is not understood in relation to the individual's fundamental need for fulfillment, it is likely to seem puzzling, stupid, and depraved to the outside observer. Such an attitude will not endear the helper to those he or she seeks to help.

In the view of motivation based on the concepts of a person-centered approach, the goal of the helping professions becomes one of ministering to a trustworthy, striving organism rather than controlling a perverse, unpredictable one. It calls for methods of helping designed to encourage and facilitate growth and provides assurance that if helpers are successful in creating the conditions for freedom, then people will move toward whatever degree of fulfillment is possible for them. This understanding of human nature is also basic to democracy. The basic tenets of democracy are not just "nice ideas" but also have roots in the fundamental character of life itself. Helpers need not be split personalities. The beliefs they hold for working with their students, clients, or patients can be consistent with those they employ for guiding their own behavior and that of the societies in which they operate.

The purpose of helping relationships is the stimulation and encouragement of growth. This growth is internal and calls for encouragement and stimulation rather than threat and coercion. To grow a healthy plant we use the best possible seed we can find and plant it in the best possible soil available. We provide it with optimum conditions of light, moisture, and temperature and with the nutrients it needs to grow. After that, we get out of its way and let it grow. In similar fashion, applied to people, helpers actively involve themselves in searching, perceiving themselves as facilitators in a cooperative process of exploration and discovery. The work of helpers is congruent with the fundamental striving of people toward health. They seek to "get with it" by entering an encounter with clients or students that is designed to help explore and discover more effective relationships between self and the world.

Expertise rests not so much in knowing answers as in providing processes by which they may be discovered. This removes a tremendous weight from the shoulders of helpers. They do not have to play God or know in advance exactly how clients or students will emerge from the experience. Helpers can devote full attention to the creation of conditions for freedom and rest assured that the end results will be positive if they are successful in doing so.

Notes and References

1. ASCD *Update* 24 (1982):6.
2. A. H. Maslow, *Motivation and Personality*, 2d ed. (New York: Harper & Row, 1970).
3. G. W. Allport, *Becoming* (New Haven, Conn.: Yale University Press, 1955).
4. P. Lecky, *Self-Consistency: A Theory of Personality* (New York: Island Press, 1945).
5. L. Festinger, *A Theory of Cognitive Dissonance* (Palo Alto, Calif.: Stanford University Press, 1957).
6. V. E. Frankl, *Man's Search for Meaning: An Introduction to Logotherapy* (New York: Washington Square Press, 1963).
7. C. R. Rogers, *On Becoming a Person: A Therapist's View of Psychotherapy* (Boston: Houghton Mifflin, 1961).
8. D. Snygg and A. W. Combs, *Individual Behavior* (New York: Harper & Bros., 1949).
9. A. W. Combs and D. Snygg, *Individual Behavior: A Perceptual Approach to Behavior* (New York: Harper & Bros., 1959).
10. A. H. Maslow, *Motivation and Personality*, 2d ed. (New York: Harper & Row, 1970).
11. This does not mean that every person is trustworthy in a moral sense. The authors too have been robbed, lied to, and deceived in their lifetimes. The point here is that there is nothing *innately* untrustworthy about people. The human organism can be counted on to behave in predictable fashion. If it appears untrustworthy, this judgment lies in the "eye of the beholder," who may not have enough data to make accurate predictions. Had the authors known enough about their deceivers, they could have predicted the times they were robbed and lied to.
12. From unpublished comment at the First **Annual** Conference on Personality Theory and Counseling Practice, University of Florida, Gainesville, 1961.
13. As quoted by A. H. Maslow in "Synergy in the Society and in the Individual," *Journal of Individual Psychology*, 1964:153–164.
14. F. Richards and A. C. Richards, *Homonouous: The New Man* (Boulder, Colo.: Shields, 1973), p. 22.
15. J. R. Frymier and J. H. Thompson, "Motivation: The Learner's Mainspring," *Educational Leadership* 22 (1965):567–570.

FIVE

PERSONAL MEANING AND THE HELPING RELATIONSHIP

How people behave at any moment is a function of how things seem to them. Helping people achieve more satisfying ways of living and being is, therefore, a matter of facilitating change in what people think about themselves and the world. To do this well, effective helpers need to understand the nature of personal meaning and how the perceptual field is modified and enriched.

FACTS, MEANINGS, AND REALITY

No matter how strongly it may be bombarded from without, a person's perceptual field of feelings, attitudes, ideas, and convictions remains forever the sovereign possession of the person himself. Meanings are the facts of life. In behavioral terms, a fact for any person is what that person *believes is so.* If Tom Green believes that his boss is unfair, he behaves as though he were. Whether other people think Tom's boss is unfair has little or nothing to do with the matter. Tom can behave only in terms of what seems to him to be the fact of the matter. So far as Tom's behavior is concerned, the "real" facts as they appear to an outsider are irrelevant and immaterial. Indeed, if we try to convince Tom that he is wrong, we run the risk of having him conclude that we don't understand him either!

The simplest, most obvious facts about the world around us are true only for members of a common culture. So long as we stay in the same culture, a given fact may never be seriously questioned. When we step outside our own culture we quickly discover that many facts we consider to be reality have no validity in the new setting. Even something so commonplace as a "table" may be called a different name in another culture or may not even be regarded as a table. Instead, it may be seen as a platform for dancing, a seat for the village chief, a bed to lie on, a shelter from the rains, or a useless object to be used for firewood.

The personal quality of meanings and the importance they have in the private worlds of individuals are of tremendous significance to workers in the helping professions. The moment we understand other people in terms of personal meaning, a great deal that was formerly puzzling or inexplicable becomes meaningful and reasonable. A student in one of the authors' psychology classes raised this question: "I just got a paper from home. I read where a man was arrested for shoplifting. He had a whole sack of things he had taken. When they searched him, he had a hundred pounds on him! How do you account for his stealing?" Obviously, the student was puzzled. The instructor too was puzzled. Here was a statement of fact. There is nothing puzzling about a man being caught with a hundred pounds of shoplifted loot. Why should this student be so puzzled about that? Then, suddenly, the teacher remembered that the student was from Jamaica, a former British colony. In the eyes of the student, "pounds" did not refer to weight but to money! At once the problem was clear. Why, indeed, should a man shoplift when he has several hundred dollars in his pocket? The puzzle was clear enough when the instructor was able to perceive the problem through the eyes of his student.

Because of the individual character of meaning, people often fail to understand one another. This is particularly true of people who are raised in different cultures, but it is also true of people with different experiences who are raised in the same culture. Witness the difficulties in communication for men and women, adults and teenagers, and people of different occupations, religion, and locality. Without an understanding of the unique meanings existing for the individual, the problems of helping are almost insurmountable.

SOME DYNAMICS OF MEANING

Stability of Meaning

Development of meaning is a creative act occurring as a consequence of people interacting with the world they live in. People invest events with meaning. The perceptual field is a gestalt, an organization, in which some meanings develop an importance or centrality around which other meanings are organized. The most important of these fundamental meanings is the self-concept. Other organizations, called *anchorages*, provide additional orientation and direction by providing a kind of reference point to which other meanings can be referred. Some anchorages are aspects of the physical world like the horizon, which orients us with respect to distance and location. Others are the relative positions of earth and sky, the discovery that far objects are smaller than near ones and that close things are generally brighter than far ones. For most of us these seem so natural that we take them for granted. But we were not born with them. We learned them and, having discovered their stability, came to rely on them.

Anchorages also exist in respect to personal, social, and political relations. Children, for example, may regard one or more parents as infallible referents for what is or is not so. For many a young child "my daddy told me!" is the clincher—the quintessence of truth in an argument. Later, "my teacher told me" may become the ultimate weapon at the dinner table.

Adults develop similar highly stable feelings about husbands and wives, religious beliefs, and even philosophies or governments.

Anchorages have great value in providing expectancies or handy frames of reference against which new experience can be quickly tested and judged. They can also cause great distress when eliminated from experience. In experiences on sensory deprivation, for example, psychologists sometimes suspend subjects in water at body temperature with ears plugged and eyes blindfolded. Cut off from the usual anchors to reality, most subjects under these conditions have difficulty concentrating and often experience wild delusions. Similar anxiety and distress, usually on a less intense scale, may be experienced by almost anyone when his or her anchors to reality are destroyed. The first reaction to the loss of a husband or wife may be to deny the fact. Little children may cling to the idea of Santa Claus long after they have begun to suspect that he does not exist, and they may become extremely upset at the efforts of others to deny his existence.

Values, generalized attitudes toward events or people, are organizations of meanings much like anchorages. Like all other meanings, they are learned from experience, but because of their generalized character, they tend to add to the stability of the person's perceptual field. They also provide a frame of reference for experience—a kind of shorthand determination of the meaning of events for the behaver. This often makes a person's behavior so predictable that other people, observing its stability, develop an expectancy and sometimes say, "Well, of course! What do you expect of Jane? You know how she is!" So important is the stabilizing effect of values on behavior that in time it can be truly said of an individual that he becomes his beliefs.

Selective Effect of Existing Meaning

We have seen how perceptions are affected by need and by the self-concept. We now add a third factor: the effect of the existing field of meanings on new experience. Meanings, once discovered, tend to be relied on and are seldom questioned unless the person is forced to do so because new experience does not fit her expectations. In part this is because some perceptions cannot be made until others have preceded them. The best examples of this are to be seen in learning school subjects with a highly sequential character, for instance, mathematics. Here, concepts are built in step-by-step fashion. Before one can grasp complex concepts, one must first perceive simpler ones. In this fashion the existing field of meaning exerts a degree of control on what further meanings can be readily acquired. Piaget spent a large part of his career studying concept formation in children and was able to delineate the step-by-step progressions by which the children he studied moved from simple to more and more complex concepts.[1] Although the children often moved through these phases at varying speeds, the sequences of development were highly stable.

The individual's need for adequacy also exerts a selective effect on perception. To achieve fulfillment, the organism requires a stable perceptual field. New experience that fits the existing organization is quickly and easily incorporated. It corroborates and reinforces what is already differentiated. When, however, new experience does not fit existing meanings, the behaver is confronted with a problem of disparate perceptions (called cognitive dissonance[2] by some psychologists) and some adjustment must be made. Generally speaking, this may occur in one of three ways:

1. New experience may be denied or ignored while the person clings to old meanings. Facts that do not fit existing patterns may simply be bypassed. Letters about overdue payments may remain unread. Warning signs may not be seen. Unacceptable evidence is treated as though it did not exist.

2. A second way of handling meanings that do not fit is to distort them so they will. In this way the experience is given a meaning that does not require reorganization of the field. This can often be observed in the common practice of rationalization wherein a good reason for behavior is substituted for the real one. "I bought it because my old car was beginning to use oil." "I really need to eat to keep my strength up." "She probably had a date already." "The speed limit on this stretch of road is absolutely ridiculous."

3. A third way of dealing with divergent meanings is to confront the new experience and make whatever changes are appropriate in existing meanings. This could result in either acceptance or rejection of the new concept. Such actions, however, are taken on the basis of willingness to confront the matter at hand and subject the existing field of meanings to the new data. This way of dealing with new experience is probably the healthiest in the long run.

These ways of dealing with new meanings are seldom found in isolation. More often than not, when confronted with a new problem, the person will use all three ways. Depending on what seems to satisfy need most effectively, some meanings will be ignored, some distorted, and some changes will be made in the individual's personal field of meaning.

The Circular Effect of Meaning

Discovering meaning from the world on the one hand and imposing it on the other produces a circular effect. Having acquired a particular field of meanings, people behave in ways that tend to call forth from others reactions that corroborate existing meanings. For example, the child who is afraid of the water may be so terrified in early attempts to swim that she behaves out of panic and splashes water in her face, which frightens her more and proves what she believed at the start. Similarly, what teachers or counselors believe about children or clients is likely to cause the children or clients to behave in ways that confirm existing beliefs. The "incorrigible" boy is likely to be watched more carefully and restricted, thus producing a feeling that he is "being picked on"—a feeling almost certain to result in aggressive behavior and further defiance of authority.

In a very real sense each person is the architect of his own personality. Every experience a person has that produces a change in meanings must have its effects on behavior and therefore changes the person himself. Each choice we make in life both opens up new possibilities and closes others. When a person decides to become a priest, it is unlikely that he will become an engineer. At the same time such a decision opens up new areas of meaning that are unlikely to exist in similar degrees for the person who decides to become an engineer. As Paul Tillich points out, "Man is his choices."[3] People are also increasingly unique, for they acquire fields of meaning from their own individual experiences. Thus, the longer people live, the more unlike one another and the more individual they become.

LEARNING AS DISCOVERY OF MEANING

Learning—A Human Problem

Effective learning always involves two aspects: the acquisition of new information or experience and the individual's personal discovery of the meaning of the experience. The provision of information can be controlled by an outsider with or without the cooperation of the learner. It can even be done, when necessary, by mechanical means that do not require a person. The discovery of meaning, however, can occur only with the involvement of people.

To assume that the acquisition of facts alone will make a difference in human behavior is naive. All we need do is examine ourselves to be quickly aware of how false this assumption may be. Most of us know what we ought to eat, but we don't eat those foods. We know how we ought to drive, but we don't drive that way. We know we ought not to be prejudiced, but we are. Few of us misbehave because we do not know any better. Most of us have more information than we can ever use. School dropouts are not dropouts because they did not receive the same information as everyone else did; they received it but, unhappily, never discovered what it meant.

A great deal of what passes for learning is no more than the production of temporary awareness. Consequently, students do not behave in the terms they set down on the test, nor do clients or patients do what they know they should. The capacity to report back acquired information is but the first faint glimmer of meaning. Unfortunately, it can seldom be relied on to produce a change in behavior the moment the necessity for reproducing it is past. Real learning—learning that produces a change in behavior—calls for a deeper, more extensive discovery of meaning. It calls especially for the discovery of the relationship of events to the self, because truly effective learning is a deeply personal matter.

Learning and the Self

Whether or not any meaning is sufficiently important to exert an effect on behavior is a function of its relationship to the person's self. Combs and Snygg have stated this basic principle of learning: "Any information will affect a person's behavior only in the degree to which a person has discovered its personal meaning for him or her."[4]

Let us use an example to see how this works.

At breakfast you read in the paper the statistics on pulmonic stenosis. Thirty-five cases have been reported in your state during the past year. Will this affect your behavior? Probably not. For most readers, this bit of information is probably little more than a foreign language. Later in the day you hear pulmonic stenosis mentioned. Because you have nothing better to do and a dictionary is handy, you look up the ailment and learn that it is a disorder of the heart having to do with a narrowing or closing up of the pulmonary artery. You continue to read and discover that some children are born with this disorder. The information now has more meaning, and you may feel vaguely uncomfortable. Now, let us suppose you are a teacher and you hear that a child in a school across town is afflicted with the disorder. The matter is closer now to your personal concerns because it has more effect on your behavior. Perhaps you pay more attention, listen more intently, think about the matter.

Suppose we give this topic even more personal meaning. Let us say that you are a teacher who has received a letter from the mother of a child in your class. She writes that her child has the disorder and will need to be operated on soon. She asks that you consider the child's problem in assigning her school tasks. This item of information now has a much more personal bearing and produces a number of effects on your behavior. Perhaps you write a note to the mother. You certainly discuss the matter with other teachers and are especially nice to the child. No longer is this mere "information"; it is now something that is happening to one of *your* children. Moreover, because the information has more personal meaning, your behavior is more sharply focused and more precisely oriented.

Let us go one step further and assume that you have just been told by a doctor that your son or daughter has the disorder. Now, indeed your behavior is deeply affected.

To conceive of this matter visibly, we might think of a person's field of experience, as shown in Figure 5.1. Let us assume that all information can be spread out on a continuum ranging from that closely related to self at point A to that having no relationship to self at point E. The closer events are perceived to the self, the greater the effect such perceptions will have in producing behavior. The farther they exist toward the periphery of the perceptual field, the less influence they will exert. Plotting our discussion about the concept of pulmonic stenosis from the preceding paragraphs, we might illustrate the relationships to self on the line A–E and represent them as shown

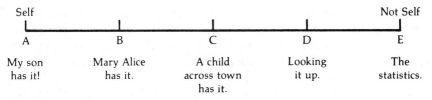

Figure 5.1   Diagram for learning and the self.

in Figure 5.1. Helping people learn is a matter of helping them discover closer, more meaningful relationships of information to self.

A Source of Learning Failures

Students who do not see the personal meanings of events are likely to be unaffected by learning experiences. For a long time a great deal of educational theory has been operating from an inadequate concept of learning, generally based on some form of repetition. Seeing the problem of learning in this way leads logically to a preoccupation with manipulation of events outside the learner. The distressing thing about this is not that it is wrong but that it is partly right. People do indeed need new information or experience. Preoccupation with this phase of learning, however, can have disastrous results by encouraging the belief that the problems of learning will be solved if we continue doing what we have been more precisely, more frequently, and more intensely. We are led to polish and repolish our techniques of providing information in the fond belief that if a little is good, a lot must be better.

Failure to deal with the second aspect of the learning equation explains why so much of what is learned in school is forgotten. Most of us at one time knew what the capital of North Dakota is, how many miles it is to the moon, when the Battle of Waterloo was fought, and a million other facts. But where are these facts now? A great deal of educational activity often seems expressly designed to discourage the search for personal meaning and to concentrate almost exclusively on the ingestion of information. Preoccupation with the information half of the learning equation is also responsible for many of the problems of dehumanization, depersonalization, and alienation we have created for young people.

Knowing and Behaving

There is a vast difference between knowing and behaving. Knowing comes from getting new information. Change in behavior comes from the discovery of meaning. Some of our most important learnings have nothing to do with new information but everything to do with the deeper and richer discovery of the meanings we already have. The majority of North Americans know there is a strong possibility that smoking will shorten their lives significantly. They have had access to innumerable "facts" about the matter. Yet the behavior of many clearly demonstrates that they do not believe the facts. Smoking continues to be, for them, more self-enhancing than the possibility of developing lung cancer. They manage to hold the facts at arm's length and keep from perceiving the relevance to self.

Most people in the helping professions know how to give information well. Exposure to new information can often be greatly speeded up. Changing meaning is a slower, more difficult task that cannot be done by an outsider. It must be done by the learner himself. People need information, of course. The danger comes when we lose our perspective and expect that "telling" or giving advice will result in permanent changes. The things we have learned but have not yet seen in relationship to self are quickly discarded when school is out or the pastor is not around. Good examples of reversion to what is personally significant can be found in the training of people for the helping professions. Teaching beginners a new concept or technique is fairly easy. A counselor, for example, learns several "proper" approaches to working with clients. She knows them, can pass a test about them, can even talk about them convincingly. Then she goes to work with a client and may behave as though she had never heard of the approaches. Confronted with real problems, she does not have time to think about what to do. Instead, she does what comes naturally to her, the things most closely related to self and past experience.

EFFECTS OF THREAT AND CHALLENGE ON PERCEPTION AND LEARNING

Effect of Threat on Perception

Of special concern to the professional helper is the *effect* of challenge and threat on people, because one of the helper's most important tasks is to make the helping relationship one (challenging) and not the other (threatening). Let's first examine the effects of threat on an individual.

Tunnel Vision

Psychologists are aware of two effects of the experience of threat. One effect is *tunnel vision*. When a person feels threatened the perceptual field narrows and focuses on the object of threat. Almost everyone has experienced this phenomenon under frightening circumstances. What can be perceived is narrowed to the point where it is difficult to see anything but the threatening object—like looking through a tunnel. One of us recalls asking his daughter at the dinner table what she had learned in school that day. "Oh, nothing," she replied. "But was our teacher mad!" Under the threat of an angry teacher, little or nothing else made much impression.

If the threat is great, attention becomes sharply focused on the threatening event, to the exclusion of all else. The child in school, for example, who feels threatened by his mother's having to be hospitalized is obviously in no condition to perceive the nuances of a Shakespearean line, the importance of the raw products of Arizona, or the implications of constitutional law. Sometimes the narrowing effect of threat may even result in apparently stupid actions in an emergency. Once, during a party given by one of the authors at his home, a grass mat in front of the fireplace caught fire. Seeing this, the author picked up the burning rug, ran across the crowded room to the front door, and threw the rug outside, into the snow. When everything had quieted down, someone asked, "Why didn't you just kick the mat into the fireplace?" Why not, indeed? At the moment of the emergency the only thing he could think of was to get the burning rug out of the house, and the simple solution of kicking it into the fireplace never occurred to him. His perceptions were focused on getting the fire out, not in!

The tunnel vision effect is equally operative when the feeling of threat is only mild. Combs and Taylor conducted an experiment in which subjects were asked to translate short sentences into a simple code.[5] Some of the sentences were mildly threatening or unflattering. The investigators found that, even under conditions of mild degrees of threat, performance in translating was significantly disturbed; nearly every subject made more errors and took longer to complete the code.

This restricting effect of threat on perception is antithetical to effective learning and helping whether it takes place in the classroom, during a group activity, or in the counseling office. We do not want our clientele's perceptions narrowed. What we seek is the broadest, richest experience possible.

Defense of Self

A second effect of threat on perception makes it an even more important consideration in helping relationships. When a person feels threatened she is forced to defend the perceptions she already has. Although this effect of threat on perception is well known, it is truly amazing how little attention it has received as a principle that affects learning. One need only look about to see examples of the principle in operation. People who are arguing do not seem to hear what others are saying. Children dig in their heels and refuse to cooperate. Grown men and women become unreasonably stubborn. People resist clear demonstrations of how wrong they are. Almost everyone is aware that when an individual feels threatened, the first reaction is to defend the self in any way possible. What is more, the greater the degree of threat to which a person is exposed, the more tenaciously he or she holds to the perceptions, ideas, or practices he or she already has.

The fundamental need of the organism to maintain and enhance the self will not ignore threats to self. The self must be protected. This defensive stance under threat, however, is the reverse of what is needed for effective learning and helping. Helpers want their clients to change their self-perceptions, not defend them! Events that force people into strongly defensive positions are contrary to what we are trying to accomplish in the helping professions.

The effects of threat on perception are especially important for members of the helping professions who are expected to help persons in trouble. The degree of threat experienced by a person is directly related to feelings of personal adequacy. People with highly positive feelings about self are less likely to feel threatened by any given event than are those with inadequate self-concepts. People with low self-esteem are likely to be highly sensitive to threat. Those who are most in need of the helping professions are thus also the most sensitive to the experience of threat.

Challenge

Some people do not react to threat in the ways we have been describing. Instead, they seem to be challenged to do better work. What is the difference between threat and challenge?

People feel threatened when confronted with situations that they think they are unable to cope with. People feel challenged by problems that interest them and that they think they can handle reasonably well. The behavior of people who feel threatened is likely to be tenuous, unsure, inaccurate, and inadequate. Such people may even attempt to escape the situation. Under the same circumstances, others who think they are able to deal with the problem may not feel threatened at all. The situation may be perceived as a challenge with important opportunities for self-enhancement. It may even be greeted with joy as a new test of adequacy.

Again, we need to remind ourselves that the distinction lies not in the eyes of the outsider but in the eyes of the beholder. The teacher who encourages the shy child to "share and tell" may believe that she is offering a challenge. From the child's point of view the experience may seem like a terrifying possibility of humiliation. The differences between threat and challenge are so important and the effects of these diverse experiences are so great that every person in the helping professions needs to be keenly aware of them. A large part of the helper's efforts are devoted to finding effective ways for challenging the people he or she is trying to help, without threatening them.

RELATION OF MEANING TO MEMORY, EMOTION, AND FEELING

Memory

The importance of personal meaning extends far beyond its significance for human learning. It is also important for memory, feeling, and emotion. When a person looks back at some past event, what he remembers is not what really happened but the meaning it had then or has now. He remembers what seemed to be happening at the time or, even more inaccurately, what now seems *must* have happened! The memory of an event is a belief about it, not an accurate record. Any teacher who has ever given an examination is familiar with the maddening and sometimes hilarious meanings that students retain from the most carefully planned lesson. Students do not recall what was said; they recall what they comprehended. The crucial character of meaning in remembering may also be observed in counseling. During the counseling hour clients may spend long periods exploring memories of early life, and in the course of these explorations may often change their minds. They exclaim, "You know, I don't believe it ever really happened like that at all!"

Additional errors in remembering may be produced by the selective effect of need, self-concept, or the existing field of meanings. Memories may be distorted in ways more advantageous to the reporter. Who has not been guilty of reporting what happened in the best possible light? And who has not embroidered a story in a way that made the storyteller appear blameless, more righteous, brave, or smart? Memories may also be distorted in ways to make them fit the existing field. This occurs when people remember what *must* have happened. Magicians make good use of this characteristic by purposely establishing in the observer a reasonable "set," so that what is seen later is interpreted in terms of what it seems to the observer must have occurred.

In courts of law the notorious inaccuracies of human memory make the "credibility of witnesses" an ever-present problem for defendants, lawyers, judges, and juries. Many courtroom rules of procedure, puzzling to the lay person, were established as devices to assure the most accurate reports possible of exactly what happened in a given case. Even under oath the story told by the most well-intentioned witness may be in error for any of the reasons we have reviewed.

Emotion

For the psychologist, emotion is a state of acceleration. It is the response of the organism that makes it ready to act. Ordinarily, emotion is low when one is sleeping, with one's "motor barely turning over." On awakening, more energy is required, and body processes accelerate to adjust to greater demands. Emotion reaches its greatest heights in emergency situations in which the self is in danger, as in anger or fear, or when it is engaged in important enhancing experiences, such as ecstasy or triumph. At such times the organism is capable of tremendous bursts of energy for short periods.

Emotion is an artifact of the meanings existing for the individual at any moment. Generally speaking, the closer the event is perceived to self, the more intense the behavior and the emotion experienced by the behaver. In the pulmonic stenosis illustration used earlier, we observed that effects on a person's behavior increased with the closeness of meaning to self. The experience of emotion is also affected by the degree of personal meaning. As

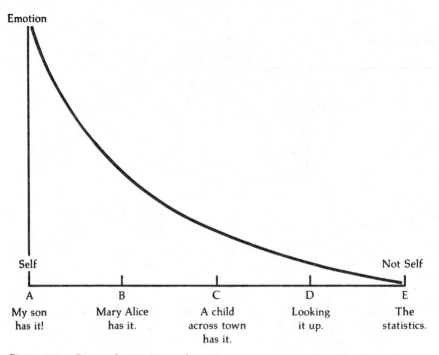

Figure 5.2   Personal meaning and emotion.

shown in Figure 5.2, the degree of emotion experienced is a consequence of the relationship of the event to self.

Gordon Bower further clarifies the relationship between meaning, memory, and emotion with a construct he calls *state-dependent* memory.[6] He has demonstrated that one's ability to recall events accurately, or at all, depends on recapturing the emotional state one was in at the time of a given experience. Bower provides the example of a Vietnamese veteran who was found walking in the jungle by a U.S. army patrol. He had no idea what happened to him during the week before the time he was discovered, and it was several years before he could do so. Under the care of a psychiatrist, who was treating him for depression, the soldier was hypnotized and encouraged to recall the events before and after his blackout period. Recall went smoothly until the subject reached the point just before he lost his memory. At this juncture he became agitated and the story unfolded. Approximating the emotional state he was in when his ability to recall began to fail him, the memories came flowing out. He had found the remains of his Vietnamese girlfriend when he blacked out; she had been killed by enemy mortar fire. He then obtained a jeep and for the next seven days, in a fit of passion and anger, went about the jungle killing Vietcong, setting booby traps, and capturing weapons.

Bower cites other research illustrating that when and how we see an event depends on the mood we are in. He has demonstrated, for example, that whether we see the future as gloomy or bright, or think of another person, a TV show, or even the performance of our car as good or bad depends on the mood we are in when we make such evaluations. Even self-judgments depend on one's emotional state at the time those judgments are made. Bower found that when subjects were happy they judged themselves as confident, competent, and warmly sociable. The same subjects, however, judged themselves as inept, unsociable, and awkward when they were depressed!

SOME IMPLICATIONS FOR HELPERS

The Fetish of Objectivity

Workers in counseling and education often refer to the "affective domain" as though emotional aspects of human experiences were somehow separate from cognitive ones. Critics of education, for example, have asked, "Do you want to educate for knowledge or adjustment?" The attempt to separate these matters in such an either/or fashion damages our understanding of human dynamics. Truly intelligent behavior cannot be segregated so neatly. Both the knowledge to cope with life and the personal discovery of meaning are needed to make it viable. Feeling and emotion are indicators of personal relevance. As students or clients talk about events, they reveal the degree of importance they attach to those events by the levels of feeling and emotion they express. The relationship is so close, in fact, that by attending to levels of feeling observers can gather significant clues to the personal involvement of students or clients in helping relationships. One can, for example, gauge the involvement of members in a group experience by listening to levels of talk. Early in a group experience, with little or no commitment yet established, people talk to one another at fingertip lengths. Their talk is mostly descriptive, usually pertaining to events outside themselves: "There was this man . . . ," "Did you read where . . . ?" "My cousin once . . . ." As commitment begins, one is likely to hear occasional references to self: "I read that . . . ," "Can you tell me if . . . ?" "I went to see . . . ." Such comments are still likely to be highly descriptive. With greater commitment, tentative involvements of self begin to show themselves: "I don't know about that . . . ," "I am not sure about this, but . . . ," "It seems to me . . . ." Much closer to self are comments like "Well, I thought . . . ," "I don't really care for . . . ," "I enjoy . . . ." At the deepest levels of commitment one may even hear what some psychologists call "gut" talk: "I hate . . . ," "That makes me so mad," "I love . . . ."

The attempt to treat knowing and feeling, or cognition and emotion, as though they were unrelated matters obeying different laws can lead only to failure. We do not experience cognition and emotion as separate entities. Things that have no personal meaning arouse no emotions. In light of these facts, the fetish that some people make over the necessity for objectivity becomes ridiculous. Complete objectivity is an illusion. Whatever is experienced is experienced in a person and that fact inescapably influences what is perceived. One can "be objective" only about events with little or no personal relevance. What is not relevant to self is in turn unlikely to affect one's behavior. If learning is not affective, it is probably not happening. The practice of education, counseling, social work, or pastoral care that rules out feeling makes itself ineffective.

Society is properly impressed by the large contributions made by science through the application of objective methods. Because of these successes, many people have attempted to translate such methods directly to problems of dealing with people. Unfortunately, the answers to human problems arrived at through complete objectivity frequently apply only to people who are operating under laboratory conditions. They do not hold up for the person in the street, the child in the classroom, or the client in the counselor's office. For the helping professions, the attempt to deal with people in purely objective terms may result only in making the helper ineffectual. Some research on the helping professions has found that objectivity on the part of teachers, counselors, and priests actually correlated with ineffectiveness!

Discovering Meaning Takes Time

It takes time to discover meaning. This fact is easily forgotten in the desire to help someone. The teacher who has studied a subject for twenty or thirty years and now believes that the subject can be taught in a few weeks or months has embarked on a frustrating course. The maximum speed for the discovery of meaning depends on a number of factors having to do with the nature of the individual, the subject under investigation, the student's previous experience, present circumstances, and so forth. Attempting to push discovery of meaning too fast may actually destroy the possibilities of the person's discovery of meaning. When people are pushed beyond the point where they believe that they can cope effectively with events, resistance sets in and destroys the possibilities for effective learning. Generally speaking, the more important the meaning to be grasped, the slower the discovery of its significance is likely to be.

A major requirement for helping is patience. Many a helper has made herself ineffective in her zeal to move too fast in carrying out the helping function. People who are being helped are also anxious, understandably, to get on with finding the solutions to their particular problems. They are often likely, therefore, to put great pressure on the helper to speed things up. Because the helper too is anxious to help the client, he or she can easily succumb to temptation and attempt to direct and control the process of learning with firmness and dispatch. This usually slows the process of meaning discovery—if it does not defeat it altogether. Although it is incumbent on helpers to aid in the quickest way possible, it is also necessary that they have clear conceptions of the goals, purposes, and dynamics of the processes they are engaged in. There are limits to how much learning can be accelerated. A vast difference exists between merely possessing information and being so aware of its meanings that one is able to behave in terms of it. Attempts to bypass the discovery process may provide only an illusion of aid, which quickly breaks down when subjected to the test of application.

More often than not, the best clues to maximum speed are provided by the people being helped. As seen in earlier chapters, the individual's need for adequacy provides the motivation to move with dispatch when the way seems open to do so. Experts in the helping professions discovered this fact long ago and have learned to work with, rather than against, it by following the lead of their subjects. They have learned that aiding the discovery of meaning most efficiently is not so much a question of manipulating people as it is a matter of guiding them toward discovering alternatives.

Discovery of meaning comes about through a process of increasing differentiation of experience. Usually this occurs as a consequence of a series of slow steps in which one differentiation is followed by another and another until the new event is learned or its personal meaning discovered. This is true even in those instances in which insight seems to come about in a sudden flash of recognition—what the French call the "aha moment." Even in such instances, however, what appears to be a sudden flash of meaning usually turns out on closer examination to be but the final differentiation in a series of previous, almost imperceptible stages leading to the final denouement. This is somewhat like finding the key piece in a jigsaw puzzle that makes all the surrounding parts comprehensible. Without the discoveries preceding it, finding the key piece would have been of little or no consequence. Its extraordinary value depends on the hard work that went before. So it is with personal meaning; the fruit comes only when the ground has been plowed, the seed has been planted, and conditions favorable for growth have been established.

Helping: A Problem in Learning

Learning, we have seen, always has two aspects: the acquisition of knowledge or experience and the discovery of its meaning. Professional helpers provide their subjects with information and experience in the helpers' particular area of concern. The teacher provides the student with information about a subject. The social worker introduces a client to a new group setting and therefore provides new experiences of other people. Similarly, the counselor interprets a psychological test for a client, the nurse shows a new mother how to bathe a baby, and the priest or rabbi interprets the Bible for his flock.

Helping does not stop with the provision of information. Almost anyone can provide other people with new information or experience. You don't need a professional just to give information. In fact, with our shiny new hardware we can often do this better without any human intervention. Problems of humanization and personal discovery must be solved in the final analysis by human commitment and involvement, in the interaction of people with people. This is what the helping professions are all about.

Notes and References

1. J. Piaget, *Judgement and Reasoning in the Child*, trans. M. Warden (Paterson, N.J.: Littlefield, Adams, 1959).
2. L. Festinger, "Cognitive Dissonance," *Scientific American* 207 (1964):93–107.
3. P. Tillich, *The Courage to Be* (New Haven, Conn.: Yale University Press, 1959).
4. A. W. Combs and D. Snygg, *Individual Behavior: A Perceptual Approach to Behavior* (New York: Harper & Bros., 1959).
5. A. W. Combs and C. Taylor, "The Effect of Perception of Mild Degrees of Threat on Performance," *Journal of Abnormal and Social Psychology* 47 (1952):420–424.
6. G. Bower, "Mood and Memory," *American Psychologist* 36 (1981):129–148.

SIX

APPROACHING PROBLEMS IN HELPING

Although the problems that clients, patients, or parishioners bring to helpers are of many kinds, they generally fall into one of two categories. First, there are those problems that, while not necessarily easy to deal with, are easily defined and for which rather straightforward clear alternatives are available for solutions. These problems would be encountered, for example, in educational and vocational counseling, in certain teaching–learning situations, and in medical settings.

At other times the helpee will confront the helper with much more difficult situations—conditions in which neither the nature of the problem, the procedures for attacking it, nor the solutions for it are clear. These are usually personal conflicts, such as emotional, interpersonal, or marital problems. The two categories of problems require entirely different approaches by the professional helper.

STRUCTURED PROBLEM SOLVING

Clear-cut problems call for what may be termed a "structured" approach. When confronted with such problems, a helper takes on the role of the authority or expert in her field. She views the problem objectively and applies her technical knowledge and skills to the client's difficulties. The procedure goes something like this:

1. *The problem is defined*   Let's say the problem is that Janie can't read.
2. *Objectives are defined in the clearest possible terms*   In this case the goal may be to get Janie to read a certain number of words per minute or at a particular grade level.
3. *The machinery needed to reach the objective is specified*   Popular techniques to help illiterate individuals read are available, and the one deemed most suitable for this particular child is selected.
4. *An intervention program is instituted*
5. *Progress is checked periodically*   If the objectives are being achieved, the program continues. If they are not being achieved, alternate intervention strategies are examined and treatment of the client is changed until the objectives are met.

The structured approach is most appropriate when desired outcomes are known in advance, when goals can be clearly defined, and when problems have clear beginnings and ends. Objectives can usually be expressed in terms of specific acts or behaviors and can be subjected to precise methods of measurement or assessment.

OPEN PROBLEM SOLVING

Many of the problems that helpers encounter are so ambiguous and complex that it is not only undesirable but also impossible to take such a systematic approach. In many instances neither the helper nor the helpee will have the slightest idea, in the beginning, what the problem is, let alone have a solution for it. At such times an open approach to problem solving is the most useful.

Problems requiring an open approach are not easy to define. Outcomes will often be unknown in advance or may exist as holistic objectives capable of statement in general terms only. In counseling, for example, the goals of the client and counselor may be to help the client become more aware of self or to improve a marital relationship. What that will mean or how that will come about neither counselor nor client can perceive at the start of the process. The open approach is *discovery* oriented. In fact, sometimes the explorations that are involved in the process are more important than the outcomes, and often goals may change during the course of interaction. An open system is especially useful to helpers who have to deal with internal, subjective matters like feelings, attitudes, beliefs, values, fears, loves, and aspirations.

The decision as to which approach to take to a problem—structured or open—is an important one and should be made carefully. The implications of what the helper does, what he or she becomes, and the objectives to be achieved are radically different, depending on which approach is selected.

The Authority

If the helper selects the structured approach to problem solving, he immediately accepts a tremendous responsibility. He becomes *the* authority and administrator of the situation, answerable for the ends that are achieved. This pattern of helping is similar to the medical model with which most of us are familiar. A person goes to the doctor and states the problem. The doctor then diagnoses the situation, determines the goals to be achieved, and writes a prescription for the patient, who is expected to carry out the doctor's orders. Responsibility for control and direction is almost exclusively that of the helper–manager, with the student, client, or patient in a passive or subservient role. To do this well, the helper must be an expert diagnostician, who knows at any moment what is going on and where events must be channeled next. In the medical profession this leads to the principle of "total responsibility" for the patient. The model is also familiar in the structure of modern industry, in the military, and in many other institutions. Such an "expert" role places a heavy burden on the helper.

The open approach has a different focus of responsibility. Because operations are problem centered, products are not known in advance. Responsibility for outcomes, therefore, cannot be centered in a leader or manager; it is shared by all who confront the problem. This jointly shared responsibility removes a great burden from the helper. The helper does not *have* to be right. Mistakes need not be seen as disastrous calamities or as evidence of personal failure. They can be taken in stride as normal, even acceptable, aspects of process. The emphasis here is on participation of all, with shared power and decision making. The role of the helper is not director but facilitator. Skill is expressed in the advancement of processes, in creating conditions that are conducive to solving problems. The appropriate role is helper, aid, minister, assistant, consultant. Such an emphasis calls for skill in facilitating interaction.

The Objective

A second implication of deciding which approach to choose in an attempt to solve a problem has to do with what becomes the objective of the helping relationship. If the helper selects the structured approach, then the goal of the relationship becomes the solution of the problem. If he or she decides on the open approach, then the objective becomes the establishment of an atmosphere that is conducive to problem solving. As stated earlier, these two objectives are quite different and call for different kinds of responsibilities and behaviors.

Consideration of these two approaches is not a question of right or wrong, good or bad, but one of appropriateness. Certainly there are times when a helper should take on the responsibility implied by the structured mode. After all, she has studied her profession for anywhere from four to twelve years and should have learned something that is immediately useful for helpees. When she does take on such responsibility, however, she should realize the significance of what she is doing and be aware of her limitations. Human problems are much too complex for any individual ever to conclude that she has developed the expertise needed to solve everyone's problems. Humbleness and humility should be the key to the helper's behavior when dealing with the lives of others.

THE PSYCHOLOGY OF PROBLEM SOLVING

Besides the two approaches to problem solving that we have been discussing, there are many theoretical explanations for assisting the professional helper in understanding behavior.[1] Most of these explanations come from the discipline of psychology. Some are based on the structured approach, some rely solely on the open, and others use a combination. Of the three most common primary psychological positions, two are based on the structured approach and one on the open.

Psychoanalysis

Out of the structured mode have come two great movements. The first is that generated by Sigmund Freud, which resulted in the most influential force to appear in psychology up to that time—psychoanalysis. No other psychologist's thought has had as great an impact on our culture as Freud's. He has had an effect on literature, theater, child-rearing practices, all the helping professions, and just about every other aspect of our social structure. Although the influence of psychoanalysis has decreased over the years, words like ego, conscious and unconscious, and defense mechanisms still permeate our basic vocabulary.

As a scientific statement, psychoanalysis generated controversy and was challenged from the moment it was introduced. This movement is no longer the dominant position in helping, but it behooves us to accept its tremendous contributions and to recognize its true significance. What Freud essentially did with the introduction of psychoanalysis was to give birth to applied psychology and inject a new vitality into the helping professions.

Although the validity of a good many of the concepts constituting basic psychoanalysis have been challenged, at least four of its principles are basic to almost all psychological theory.

1. *Effects of internal stimuli*   The first major contribution of the psychoanalytic movement was the attention it called to internal stimuli affecting behavior. Freud and his students pointed out that people do not behave only in terms of external stimuli. Some of our most important behaviors, they said, are a consequence of stimuli arising from within. These include such factors as human values, wants, desires, and appetites and needs for food, water, warmth, affection, and sexual satisfaction.

2. *Unconscious stimuli*   A second great contribution of the psychoanalytic movement was the attention it called to the importance of "unconscious" stimuli in the determination of behavior. Freud pointed out that not all the events to which the individual reacts can be clearly perceived either by outside observers or by the individual himself or herself. Many of the stimuli that affect behavior exist at such low levels of awareness that the person may not be able to report them to others when asked to do so.

3. *Defense mechanisms*   A third contribution was the attention Freud focused on the importance of protecting the ego, or—as more generally used now—the self. He pointed out that one of the most important concerns of the individual is the protection of self and that we each go about doing this in rather systematic, if unconscious, ways. He referred to these as

ego defense mechanisms, most of which are common household words today, such as rationalization, fantasy, and compensation.

4. *Effects of early stimuli*   Finally, although not the first to suggest it, Freud was the first person to make the world realize the true significance and importance of the influence of early experience on an individual's life. He believed that what happened to a person in, roughly, the first five years of life was far more influential than anything else that would ever happen to him or her. One's basic personality, behavior patterns, and attitudes toward life are formed at this time. Furthermore, Freud believed that after being established during this period, these characteristics were difficult to change.

This last contribution may be Freud's greatest, for it is the most universally accepted. Even though there is some question as to just what happens, what span constitutes the "critical" period, and how firmly characteristics are established, subsequent research continues to bear out the importance of the early years.

Behaviorism

The second great movement in psychology is behaviorism, also known as stimulus–response psychology, the S–R approach, or objective psychology. Behaviorism is not a theory in the sense of other psychologies, although a theory can certainly be generated from it if one wishes. If one were trying to capture the real history and nature of the movement, one would be more accurate to speak of behaviorists and not of behaviorism. What truly sets behaviorists—particularly modern behaviorists—apart from others is that they were and are primarily concerned with applying the scientific method to the solution of psychological problems. Rather than spending a lot of time theorizing about what is or what might or could be, behaviorists are likely to say,"Let's do this and see what happens." Put another way, they are interested in setting up a controlled situation, manipulating the variables in that situation, and trying to identify the functional relationships that occur.

Generated from this kind of manipulation and control are terms with which we are all familiar: positive and negative reinforcement, schedules of reinforcement, reward and punishment, contingencies of reinforcement, and the like. All these, however, describe empirical events; they are not theoretical constructs. The great contribution of the behaviorists, then, is not theory but method. From this approach have been generated many techniques and principles that are very useful to the helping professions.

Third-Force Psychology

Psychoanalysis and behaviorism are structured approaches to helping. The third great movement is primarily an open approach. It is often referred to as third-force psychology because it came in that order in the development of psychological thought. The approach is expressed in a number of varieties of what are collectively referred to as humanistic psychology. These latest psychologies are expressly designed to understand the internal life of human beings and the qualities of human interactions. Because feelings, values, beliefs, and purposes lie inside people and are not available for direct observation by outsiders, psychologists dealing with these matters have chosen to operate from the internal frame of reference, also called the phenomenological, or perceptual, frame of reference.

Psychologists in the humanist movement call themselves by a bewildering variety of names. This often occurs when scholars from widely different backgrounds and experience begin to explore a new subject and create their own vocabularies and concepts. Psychologists working in the humanist movement sometimes call themselves transactionalists, personalists, phenomenologists, self-psychologists, humanists, existentialists, or perceptualists. By whatever name, they are trying to understand behavior as the person himself or herself experiences it. The authors of this book are primarily associated with that branch of the humanist movement called *perceptual psychology*.

The humanist movement in psychology is much newer than the other psychologies. It came into vigorous being in the 1950s, largely in response to the great human problems of modern society. It is primarily the product of applied psychologists—people who are engaged in one way or another with the practice of psychology. Most of its contributors have come from the ranks of social work, teaching, counseling, clinical or child psychology, and psychiatry. The influence of these kinds of workers on humanistic psychology has been so great that it has sometimes been called the "practitioner's" psychology. It has special relevance for the work of those who are engaged in the helping professions, and the majority of the material in this text is based on this position.

THE BEHAVIORIST–HUMANIST ARGUMENT

Like structured and open approaches, psychologies are neither right nor wrong. They are simply alternative ways of explaining behavior, offering different techniques to helpers, and must be judged in terms of their appropriateness for the problem at hand. Unfortunately, many people in the helping professions do not understand this. Consequently, a tremendous amount of unnecessary controversy and conflict have been generated in the professions. Too often it is the differences between positions that are stressed rather than the possible rapprochements that can be made. This has been particularly true with regard to behaviorism and humanism. One symposium on phenomenology and behaviorism, for example, was described as aggressive, hostile, and emotional with little likelihood of a reconciliation between the two schools of thought.[2] Such arguments can be highly confusing to students of helping processes, and a comment about this debate may be helpful.

Developments during the first half of this century made the human-ist–behaviorist debate understandable as well as inevitable. Behaviorism was originally concerned, almost entirely, with the development of a *science* of living organisms. It was essentially amoral and asocial, having as its purpose the discovery of theories, principles, laws, and processes that would make the study of behavior a true science. Its thrust was not much concerned with the human condition, solutions to human problems, or the relief of pain and suffering. Leading behaviorists saw the goal of psychology as the attainment of a high level of quantification of behavior theory and the development of a science of organisms, with the emphasis on science.

Humanists, on the other hand, although concerned with the develop-ment of a science, also had the social workers' burning desire to make things better, to apply research and theory in a way that would produce happier, more productive people and relieve suffering. Sometimes their enthusiasm to foster the cause of humanity and alleviate pain and suffering caused human-ists to develop ideas and engage in practices that had little, if any, scientific basis. This kind of willingness to go "beyond the data" was unacceptable to behaviorists, who regarded such behavior as a violation of the basic require-ment for a true science.

Humanists, dynamic psychologists, and other professional helpers, how-ever, believed that they must act. Although they were professionals and had a high regard for science, their primary concern was to help develop more adequate people and minister to the desperate, disabled, and deprived. They simply could not wait for totally verifiable principles to develop a pure sci-ence that could *then* be applied to the problems of the suffering. Something had to be done!

Thus, battle lines were drawn and the humanist–behaviorist debate began. Humanists were labeled "soft-headed" and were accused of having "bleeding hearts" and generating untestable concepts. Behaviorists, on the other hand, were labeled "hard-headed" because of their amoral attitude and refusal to deal with anything but empirical data. To this day we speak of hard and soft psychologies with these distinctions in mind. Humanists, to be sure, hypothesize about internal conditions that cannot be directly observed and are hard to verify. But behaviorists often generalize from subhuman to human behavior, and behavioristic positions are as hard to verify with human populations as are humanistic ones because of the many legal, social, and moral restrictions placed on the manipulation of human behavior. In any event, developments in the second half of this century have made vitupera-tive argument over humanist–behaviorist positions futile.

One such development is a major change in the attitudes of behaviorists themselves. Following the lead of such pioneers as Joseph Wolpe and B. F. Skinner, many behaviorists have begun to move behaviorism from the labo-ratory to therapeutic and educational settings, even to preventive and reme-dial suggestions for society. Increasingly, they have become concerned with the human condition and how to improve it, developing in the process a number of techniques for making people more successful and healthier.

Another factor inflaming the humanist–behaviorist debate centers around the term "humanist." Describing one's self as a humanist seems to imply that others are *nonhumanists*, a category few people find acceptable. As a matter of fact, people who call themselves humanists are so diverse that often as much disagreement exists among them as between humanists and behaviorists. For example, some humanists use sensitivity groups extensively, whereas others will have no part of them. Some consider nude encounters to be therapeutic, whereas others consider such events to be forms of self-indulgence. Understanding this diversity has gone far to discourage dichotomous labeling.

A third event that detracts from the validity of the humanist–behaviorist debate is the increasing amount and sophistication of humanistic research. Recent humanists are not satisfied with the exclusive philosophical approaches of earlier workers. Just as behaviorists are moving toward application, humanistic psychologists are devoting more time and attention to sophisticated research.

Finally, behaviorists and humanists alike increasingly see the futility of hostile exchanges and are coming to the conclusion that their positions are not mutually exclusive. Behaviorists, for example, are becoming concerned with the importance of internal conditions, and humanists now appreciate the usefulness of behavioristic techniques for the pursuit of humanistic goals. The authors believe that there are complementary aspects to these positions and that seeking them is far more fruitful than open warfare.

A FINAL NOTE ON MOVEMENTS

Are the battles over? Probably not. But these authors hope they are waning and truly believe that they are. The future of helping lies in "putting it all together," not in fighting. The great movements and great contributions of one individual probably *are* over. In the future it is more likely that helping will build and grow from the contributions of many different individuals supplying smaller pieces to the great puzzle. It has been a long time since a powerful theory or great experiment with the impact of those in the past has been introduced into psychology. The next great leap to take place in the helping professions seems, to these authors, to be an integration of all that has gone in the past with that which is to come. The time for fighting is over. What we need most is an Einstein who will take all we have, give it new meaning, and develop for us a new functionality. Perhaps you will be that person.

There are those who might disagree with some of what we have just said. A number of professional helpers believe that a fourth force is on the horizon. It is seen as coming from the integration of the psychology of the East (Buddhism, Shintoism, etc.) with the psychology of the West (the new transpersonal psychologies and the holistic health movement). It is too early to tell what effect these enterprises will have on helping. They may simply be fads, old ideas in new clothes, or they may just integrate into the great new frame of reference that we need.

Notes and References

1. The typical text on personality theory will examine twelve to fifteen different approaches. Some texts available are:

    DiCapario, N. S. *Personality Theories: Guides to Living.* Philadelphia: W. B. Saunders Co., 1974.

    Pervin, L. A. *Personality: Theory Assessment and Research.* New York: John Wiley & Sons, 1980.

    Rychlak, J. F. *Personality and Psychotherapy.* Boston: Houghton Mifflin, 1981.

2. W. D. Hitt, "Two Models of Man," *American Psychologist* 24 (1969):651–658.

SEVEN

THE ATMOSPHERE FOR HELPING

One of the most important aspects of a successful helping relationship is the atmosphere in which it occurs. In fact, this may be the most important part of a helping relationship because it is the first thing to which a client is exposed; it sets the scene for all that follows. If a proper atmosphere is not established, the relationship is probably doomed.

THE SPECIAL NATURE OF THE HELPING ATMOSPHERE

Helping relationships are special. Most ordinary life experiences are dialogues in which all parties seek personal enhancement. In the helping relationship one party resolves to set aside personal needs temporarily to help another. For many people who seek help the helping relationship is a new experience and often begins with students or clients spending considerable time exploring the atmosphere of the helping–learning encounter. The techniques that helpers use to help clients or students discover what the encounter is like and how to use it most effectively is sometimes called "structuring the relationship."

Establishing atmospheres to aid clients or students work out new and more satisfying relationships often requires temporarily protecting people or sheltering them from the accustomed pressures of the world they live in. Social expectancies may be short-circuited and the usual consequences of a person's acts may be temporarily set aside. A child can express hatred of a teacher without being told he "mustn't feel that way" or that he is "naughty." The anger of a worker toward a foreman can be safely expressed without fear of reprisal. The helping relationship thus provides a haven in which the helpee is, for a limited time, excused for errors. Hindrances to communication may also be systematically eliminated or reduced so that free expression becomes possible in a manner rarely experienced in daily life. As quickly as possible, the helper seeks to establish conditions in which a person feels (a) it is safe to try, (b) assured that he or she can deal with events, (c) encouraged to make the attempt, and (d) more fulfilled for having done so. The relationship that the helper creates must be seen by the client as promising fulfillment on the one hand and as safe enough to risk encounter on the other.

THE HELPER'S IMPACT ON
THE ATMOSPHERE FOR HELPING

The helper is not a passive object in helping relationships. There can be no relationship with a nonentity. The helper has to *be* somebody. Her actions give direction to the helping process. The choices she makes in responding to a student or client communicate messages about the relationship. The teacher who ignores a child's behavior is not inert. He is teaching the child something about herself and her place in the class. From being ignored, she may learn patience, the "right" way to behave, that her teacher doesn't like her, or a hundred other lessons. The message communicated by a teacher's behavior is real to the child and helps establish the nature of the dialogue whether the teacher wishes it so or not.

Whatever a helper does or does not do inevitably affects the relationships he or she establishes. Some of the effects are direct, straightforward outcomes and are exactly what the helper intended. Others are concomitant effects occurring in more or less subtle ways and are the consequences of the student–client's personal interpretation of what is going on. Such side effects cannot be ignored. They must be perceived clearly and taken into account. Because side effects can never be eliminated, they should be understood and can be used to advantage if the helper is keenly enough aware of their existence.

To develop awareness of potential side effects the helper may find it useful to ask himself or herself three basic questions.

1. *Are the objectives in this relationship the important ones?*   Not all objectives are equally important. It is easy to be seduced by quick, easy, or dramatic results that provide illusions of growth without making a significant impact on the helpee. An example of this may be seen in the teacher's acceptance of easily measured achievements in basic skills as evidence of learning while overlooking important educational objectives like creativity, responsibility, concern for other people, problem-solving ability, and intelligent behavior.

2. *What is the effect of the helper's choices on the helpee?*   Whatever the helper's purposes, their expression in practice inevitably affects the way the helper is perceived by those she or he is seeking to assist. Even when the helper's purposes are simple and clear in her or his own eyes, they may be perceived quite differently by students or clients. For example, while working with a deeply rejected client, one of the authors was annoyed by someone repeatedly knocking on his office door despite the "Do Not Disturb" sign hanging there. When the knocking continued, he excused

himself, went to the door, and angrily asked the person who was knocking to observe and honor the sign. Returning to his chair he found his client halfway to the door. "What's the trouble?" he asked. "I guess you are too busy to see me today," said the client. "Not at all, not at all," said the author. He then had to spend the next five minutes reassuring his client that this was her time and hers alone. Helpers cannot escape creating expectancies in the eyes of those they seek to help. They can, however, be aware of their impact and thus be in a better position to correct inhibiting impressions and reinforce more positive ones.

3. *What is the effect of the helper's purposes on the helpee?*   Nowhere is sensitivity more important than in providing continuous clues for helpers about the dynamics of the relationships they are engaged in. Checking the outcomes of helping from the point of view of students or clients is not simply a device for measuring final outcomes. It is a process that is used continuously by effective helpers in every phase of the relationship.

The Helper as Model

People in the helping professions expect to exert their influence as significant others in the lives of those with whom they work. The more significant they become, the greater the degree to which they will be regarded as models by their students or clients. This will occur whether the helpers want to be placed in that position or not.

Helpers cannot escape being models. Because their actions indicate who they are and what they believe more clearly than speech, what they say will often not be heard. The helper who advocates that the helpee do something that the helper himself is unwilling to do will not be very convincing. This is not to suggest that helpers must be paragons of virtue—only that one of the best ways to convince other people that a certain behavior is worthwhile is to see it manifest in the helper's own behavior.

Helper Authenticity

A good deal of discussion goes on among those in the helping professions concerning the proper role of the counselor, teacher, administrator, social worker, or nurse. Examining the functions of the professional helper in that light, however, is not likely to be helpful. The word "role" ordinarily refers to some form of acting; we speak of "playing a role." This focuses attention on the wrong question. It is possible, of course, for a teacher, counselor, or social worker to act a part in a relationship with a client or student. But such a relationship can seldom be maintained for long, for one behaves according to one's perceptions—and the moment one's guard is down, fundamental beliefs become apparent to others in spite of oneself.

A person with a position is likely to reveal a stronger posture than is a person without one. It may be easier for a student or client to relate to a negative conviction—if it is clear and unambiguous—than to a vacillating stance. This is one of the reasons for rejecting eclecticism as a workable philosophy for helpers. Choosing methods or techniques from widely divergent sources may be highly effective, providing the methods and techniques are tied together by an internally consistent theoretical or philosophical position. An eclectic approach in which a helper is trying things simply "because they might work" will likely be a disaster.

Helpers with consistent systems of beliefs can disclose themselves and maintain their clients' confidence; helpers without such systems dare not disclose themselves lest their clients discover the disordered state of the helpers' thinking. Authentic helpers are more visible, and the impressions they convey are likely to be those of confidence, assurance, and strength. Without authenticity, helpers are likely to create impressions of doubt, hesitation, and dishonesty and a sneaking suspicion in the minds of clients that they are frauds. With authenticity, many things become easy; without it, helpers create unnecessary barriers for themselves and those they seek to help. Helpers who are willing to be open and honest have a tremendous advantage. Because they can forget themselves they can give themselves more freely to the task at hand. Interactions tend to be straightforward, uncomplicated, and hence more appropriate.

Making Self Visible

The kind of communication required for most helping relationships calls for openness in the helper, a willingness to level with students or clients. Carl Rogers includes the quality of genuineness in the counselor as one of the basic requirements for successful counseling, along with congruence, empathy, and unconditional positive regard.[1] Aspy,[2] Carkhuff,[3] Truax, and others have tested these hypotheses with counselors and teachers, and they find that these are indeed qualities of effective helpers. Sidney Jourard, in a series of research, demonstrated the importance of self-disclosure for helping relationships in several professional groups.[4] Further confirmation is found in studies reporting good helpers to be "self-revealing" and poor ones, "self-concealing."[5]

The quality of sharing self is important for effective helping relationships. To interact effectively with a helper, the helpee needs to know what to expect in order to select his own behavior safely. This requires feedback that has the feel of solidity. Psychologists sometimes refer to such interaction as "making one's self visible." Without this quality, the atmosphere for helping becomes confused and frustrating.

This can be observed in the "controlled panic" that is experienced by some beginning teachers. First efforts at capturing the attention of an unusually lively or difficult class meet with little success. The teacher then searches for "methods to handle them." If these methods are authentic, the class may quiet down. If they are not, the class senses this and begins to explore the teacher's limits. This launches a spiral of trying and testing, which rises higher and higher as the teacher desperately tries to control the class by using methods in which he really has no confidence or skill; the students, made more and more uncertain by lack of consistent structure, search ever more wildly to discover the limits. If long continued, this state of confusion may end with the students in control and the teacher reduced to a state of utter helplessness. Many beginning teachers suffer through this nightmare brought on by a "gimmick approach," and some become so demoralized that they leave the profession.

The helper must select methods that fit her so she can use them smoothly and naturally. Preoccupation with techniques is certain to make them seem contrived. When learning to dance, one watches one's feet and falls all over them. When one learns to relax and follow the music, dancing improves and becomes a pleasurable experience for both dancer and partner. So it is with methods. Authenticity frees the helper to devote full attention to the problems at hand. Her behavior can be smoothly congruent, en rapport with students, clients, and the world.

HELPING BEGINS WITH ACCEPTANCE

Acceptance is a major requirement for creating an atmosphere for change. Growth cannot proceed from where people are not; it can begin only from where people are. Accordingly, the atmosphere for helping must start from a base that accepts the person as is. Acceptance, as we are using the term here, does not mean approval or disapproval. Acceptance has to do with confrontation, one's willingness to face the world the way it is. Students, clients, or patients are accepted just as they are in the helping relationship.

The experience of being accepted reduces the feeling of threat and so makes possible more open approaches to examining self and the world. The counselor, for example, accepts unjudgmentally a client's expression of hatred for a brother and thus makes it possible for the client to look at personal feelings. The teacher may accept a student's error without judgment as simply a matter of fact. This makes it possible for student and teacher to find a better solution. The pastor too accepts a parishioner's sin as understandable and so makes it possible to talk about and find more effective ways of behaving. In the following report a nurse describes the value of acceptance for one of her patients.

While making the rounds of my floor, I saw a woman patient start to cry. Her face just crumpled in spite of what seemed to be great efforts to maintain composure. I went into her room and stood by the bed; her eyes were closed with tears running from under the lids. She seemed to sense my presence for she took my hand and held on to it with a very tight grip. I waited, for I didn't wish to pry, yet felt that this was not a casual thing which was occurring. For several minutes I stood there while she cried silently. After a time, she told me why she was crying. She had had surgery three days previously; her physician had just told her that she had inoperable carcinoma. She had been given the hope that a relatively new antimetabolite might offer relief, longer life, and she hoped, a cure. Her choice was to accept the risks inherent in the treatment or to refuse. She was also trying to decide what to tell her husband and son. There was nothing I could offer her except myself as a person to listen; her decision had to be hers. I stood and listened while she cried and talked.

The knowledge I had about the course of her illness, the new treatment, the support she would need from her family, physician, other people, none of this was what she needed. The need at this moment was for a fellow human to listen to her. I felt that I was such a person, one who could listen. Her world had turned inside out and upside down. She was the very attractive wife of a successful businessman, the mother of a handsome son, an interesting, vital, well-educated woman who was having to accept the fact that she was facing invalidism, prolonged illness, and death. She said that she was not a woman who cried easily, yet she seemed to accept a nurse as a person with whom she could cry; by some very great effort she regained her composure before her son and husband came to visit her.

For many people the experience of being accepted is in itself a most important release from the negative effects of threat.

Because the way things seem to us has such a feeling of reality, it is easy to reject the reality of others and demonstrate a lack of acceptance in relationships. Helpers have been known, for example, to reject the surly, unmannerly delinquent on first contact. He has grown up in a world that largely rejects him and he comes in with a chip on his shoulder. In his world, toughness and defiance are the means to prestige and status, so he slouches in his chair and snarls his replies to questions. Such behavior can be infuriating to the helper who does not understand his business, and it seems "only natural" to lash out and demand that the subject "Behave yourself! Be polite! Sit up and pay attention!" From the point of view of the delinquent, such behaviors are undesirable; being polite in the world he lives in could ruin him. Even from the helper's point of view such demands do not make much sense. One hopes for courteous and respectful behavior from the subject *when he gets better*. To demand such behavior now is like a doctor saying to a patient: "Go away and get better. Then come back and I'll help you!"

To begin the helping process with a denial of the facts of the situation is hardly likely to create an atmosphere for facilitating change and growth. Nevertheless, with the best of intentions many helpers fail to be effective by closing the doors to consideration of events at the beginning of a conference. A child who expresses a shocking or naughty attitude may be told, "Why, Jimmy, you mustn't feel that way!" Thus his feelings, the very things he must explore to get over his difficulty, are barred from examination. Before one can examine feelings one must be allowed to have them. The experience of being accepted provides the atmosphere in which exploration of self and the world can take place.

CHALLENGE AND THREAT IN
THE ATMOSPHERE FOR CHANGE

To a large extent, creating the proper atmosphere for learning involves dealing with challenge and threat. As we have observed in Chapter Five, people feel challenged when confronted with problems that interest them and seem to lie within their capacities. People feel threatened when confronted with problems they do not feel able to deal with. Producing the kind of atmosphere usually needed for the helping process requires the creation of challenge and the avoidance of threat.

Behavior can, of course, be changed by threat. People do learn from such experiences. As we have seen, however, the effect of threat is to narrow perceptions to the threatening object. What is learned, therefore, is likely to be both highly specific and negative—one learns what *not* to do. Thus a spanking may teach a child not to cross a street, and a fine may teach a grown-up not to speed (at least not when a police officer is in sight). When the goal is simple and clearly defined, threat can result in learning. For thousands of years this technique has been used by those in authority to control others. Because a device sometimes works, however, is no good reason to adopt it as a general principle for continuing action. Helpers' tools must be used with precision and must be applied to the problems for which they are uniquely appropriate. This is especially true in the use of threat, for its side effects extend far beyond what is directly observable. Operating without awareness of these side effects may destroy with one hand what is so carefully built with the other.

Most clients achieve health from the attainment of positive goals rather than negative ones, from seeking or obtaining rather than avoiding. The specificity of goals required for the use of threat is seldom appropriate for the helping professions. The learning of subject matter, the solving of personal problems, or the achievement of maximum self-actualization can rarely be defined in precise terms. Goals like these require openness to experience and freedom to depart from specifics. The purpose of the helping professions is to expand, to open up, to encourage exploration and discovery. These ends can seldom be achieved by experiences of threat. One does not get a mouse to come out of a mouse hole by poking it with a broomstick. One must entice it out by making things more desirable outside the hole than in. Just so, a person's self must be encouraged toward expression; it cannot be heedlessly placed in jeopardy. The self can be committed only when there is some likelihood that "coming out of the hole" will result in a measure of fulfillment and the self will not be damaged in the process.

Even when the specific and negative aspects of threat can be overcome, its use in the helping professions would still be limited for another reason: the destructive effect of the use of threat on the helping relationship itself. Most of us do not take kindly to people who threaten us. Threatening people are regarded with suspicion, and what they have to say is generally heard with reservations if indeed it is heard at all. Most people respond to threat with resistance, suppression, negativism, or rationalization—responses that are unlikely to enhance the relationship between helper and helpee. Helping relationships depend on establishing rapport between helper and client. Whatever destroys this capacity for dialogue interferes with the process.

Two effects of the experience of threat—narrowing of perception and defense of self—are directly contrary to the primary goals of helping: to produce some change in personal meaning. For this reason workers in the helping professions generally seek to create nonthreatening atmospheres for helping–learning processes and advocate such conditions as warmth, understanding, acceptance, congruence, support, and freedom.

One may think this matter so universally accepted that it need not be mentioned. Thomas McDaniel, for example, points out that none of the three major models being applied to the conduct of human affairs—the behavioral, human relations, and preventive models—advocates threat.[6] Universal acceptance, however, does not seem to be enough, for far too many professional helpers continue to use this technique despite the fact that almost everyone agrees it is not good for human beings.

REMOVING BARRIERS TO INVOLVEMENT

The creation of a freeing atmosphere is partly a matter of the client's finding promise of satisfaction. It is also a matter of eliminating as nearly as possible the blocks that lie in the path of the client's innate move toward health. This is accomplished by awareness of the nature of such barriers and a systematic attempt to find ways of removing them. The following anecdote illustrates how this was first learned by one of the authors.

In his distant past one of the authors was employed as school psychologist in a large high school in a northern city. He was also faculty adviser for the Hi-Y, a service club for boys. The school had a regulation that any money a service club obtained from students during the year had to be returned to the students in some form before the end of the year. One year the club ended up with a surplus in the treasury. What to do with it? The club held a meeting to decide.

Somebody suggested giving a party for the school. Another said, "Well, it ought to be for everybody." The adviser said, "Let's see if we can figure out a way to get everybody into the act." Someone else suggested, "Well, we could have a dance. But if we do have a dance, the people who can't dance won't come." Then another person said, "Well, maybe we could have a dance that everybody will come to." That was a novel idea, and the question immediately arose as to what kind of dance it could be. Somebody came up with the idea, "Let's have a square dance, and we'll teach them when they get there." Because this was a large city high school and nobody knew how to square dance, as far as anyone knew this met the criterion.

Then somebody said, "Even if we have a square dance, some people won't come because they don't have the right clothes." The reply: "Well, this is a country dance; we won't let anyone in who looks too sharp." And that was adopted as policy. Somebody else pointed out, "Well, they won't come if they aren't able to get a date," and somebody else countered, "We could make it stag. We could let the boys in one door and the girls in the other on opposite sides of the gym, and nobody would know who had a date."

Then somebody suggested, "Some people won't come because they won't have enough money and after the dance was over they would want to buy something to eat for the girl they were with." So it was decided, "Let's feed them at the dance." A committee was set up to enlist the aid of mothers in baking cakes and another was set up to make a deal with a soft-drink distributor. After all this, someone said, "We've still got a problem: Some people won't come because they can't afford it." After much figuring on the cost of the band and an estimate of how many people would come, the price of the dance was finally set low enough for everyone.

Many people doubted that such a program would succeed and said, "It will never work!" When the night of the dance finally came, the largest crowd turned out that had ever been in the gymnasium. In fact, so many came that nobody could dance!

A similar technique can be applied to any helping relationship by systematically searching for the barriers to commitment and eliminating them. Such barriers may be attitudinal, physical, or inherent in the structure of the relationship and may be contained in rules, regulations, or administrative machinery. They may even be found in the helper himself. The authors have successfully applied the method to the practice of counseling, psychotherapy, teacher education, group process, and consulting relationships of many varieties. Not all barriers are easily removed, of course, and some may have to be lived with. The device has value, however, for focusing on the critical barriers to the helping process and helping create more effective atmospheres. A search for barriers in any of the helping institutions will almost certainly reveal an extraordinary number of hindering concepts or practices. Some of these are expressions of myths, generally held ideas about people or events that are not true.[7] Others are practices established to solve problems that have changed or that no longer exist. Still others seem to continue for no clear reasons. A discussion of a few common barriers that often impede the helping atmosphere follows.

The Dependence Barrier

The goal of helping is the production of free and intelligent people who are able to operate by themselves as free and autonomous agents. Whatever increases dependence and interferes with independent self-direction, therefore, obstructs the helping encounter. Dependence, instead of strengthening the self, requires surrender. Too great a dependence on the helper gets in the way of the free atmosphere desired for effective helping.

People who need help are often willing—even anxious—to let someone else solve their dilemmas, and helpers with the best of intentions can easily be seduced into developing dependent relationships. Our own perceptions feel so right, and our perceptions of situations often seem so uncomplicated, that we come to believe that surely they must be similarly appropriate for others. It seems quicker to tell others the obvious answers, and we may feel we are being cruel and heartless to permit them to flounder about in search of solutions. So not with malice but rather with generosity and goodwill the helper may tell those he would like to help the answers to their problems. In so doing he may create dependence and destroy self-direction in the people he seeks to help. Those who are skilled in the helping professions have generally learned to avoid "telling" and "advising," not only because their advice may be wrong but also because the advising itself may create dependence and interfere with self-propulsion.

Restricting Effects of Evaluative Processes

Many barriers to exploration masquerade as aids to learning. Devices established ostensibly to motivate people turn out, instead, to get in the way of learning. Perhaps the worst offender is overemphasis on evaluation. Educators, for example, begin with the assumption that people need to know where they stand. Surely, no one could take much issue with that! They also believe that people need to be motivated to do their very best. Accordingly, a grading system is introduced to perform two excellent functions: to let people know where they stand and to provide a system of rewards and punishments to spur them on. The theory sounds unassailable, but all too often it fails in practice. In the first place, it frequently evaluates people who neither want nor need it—at least not in the terms provided. For some, grades become the goal of learning; worse still, students sometimes give up their own goals for the meaningless symbols of grades. For others, grades appear irrelevant, a waste of time, to be met with a minimum of involvement. Thus the grading system, which sets out to bring about involvement in exploration, often ends by diverting, restricting, narrowing, or even shutting off the very events it was designed to encourage.[8]

Evaluation is more a convenience for the helper than a procedure of value to the helpee. This is especially true of evaluative techniques that compare the helpee's performance with the performance of others. Generally speaking, information evaluations, which help the student or client assess where he is and what he needs to do next, are likely to be far superior to formalized, standardized assessment devices. The procedures finally used must be adopted with full understanding of the probable meanings they convey to the helpee. It is no accident that psychotherapists generally avoid making evaluations and judgments in counseling practice. This is because they have discovered from long experience that evaluating tends to destroy rapport, creates resistance, and generally interferes with the free atmosphere so essential for encouraging discovery of personal meaning.

Fear of Making Mistakes

One of the most certain destroyers of the atmosphere for exploration and discovery is the fear of making mistakes. This fear is often held by both helpers and those they seek to assist. Many helpers, acting out of kindness, try to keep their students, clients, or patients from making mistakes. With the best of intentions, they point out the horrible pitfalls along the way or seek to protect their clients from them. Sometimes helpers may even punish helpees to make certain they do not fall into error. Unfortunately, a rejection of mistake making can often destroy the very things that both helper and helpee are seeking. The atmosphere for helping must encourage looking. A fear of mistakes has the opposite effect; it discourages searching and exploration, no matter what the intentions of the helper. People who are afraid to make mistakes are afraid to try. And when people are afraid to try, their sources of creativity and innovation dry up.

By protecting helpees from error, helpers can often cut them off from important learning experiences. For example, a consultant arrived at a school shortly after the election of a new student-body president. He found the administrators and teachers in a high state of indignation because the students had elected a youngster who had campaigned vigorously for office on a platform he obviously could not deliver. He had promised his constituents such things as no detention halls, every Friday afternoon off, free dances every week, and a dozen other equally unlikely benefits. The faculty was so incensed by the young man's election that they were seriously considering invalidating the election. They asked the consultant whether or not he agreed that this action should be taken. He disagreed and pointed out to the faculty that, with the best of intentions, they were about to rob the students of a valuable lesson in practical democracy. How else can one learn the value of a vote? What better way to learn the importance of a careful choice of leadership than having to live for a while with a bad one you elected yourself? Counselors and social workers call this "confrontation with reality." They recognize its value. Instead of overly protecting their clients from making mistakes, they seek instead to help their clients explore and discover the meanings to be gained from such experiences.

LIMITS IN HELPING RELATIONSHIPS

Every life situation has limits. This holds for helping relationships as well. People need limits; few of us could live without them. Knowing the boundaries of a situation provides a feeling of security and so has the effect of creating freedom. The traffic light on the corner limits freedom in one sense, but its existence enables people to go where they desire in safety. The amount of freedom we have is often determined by our willingness to give up some degree of autonomy in one area for the greater good of increased freedom in another.

We are surrounded by limits of many kinds and become so used to them that the first thing most people do on entering a new situation is to begin testing the limits. Students do this on the first day of class when they ask the teacher: "How many books shall I read?" "Do you want the papers in on Tuesday?" "How long do I have to get ready for my presentation?" They also ask one another: "Do you think she means it?" "What kind of guy is he?" People cannot deal constructively with events until they establish boundaries.

The establishment of clear limits is particularly important for children, because a large part of their growth is accomplished by pushing against limits. In this way they find out what they can and cannot do. Substitute teachers know how avidly children pursue the search to discover what this new person is like, what he will stand for and what he will not, whether he means what he says, knows whereof he speaks, and the like.

Freedom and License

Lay people often mistakenly believe that "experts" in human behavior advocate that helping relationships should be free of limits. Many parents and educators labor under this misconception, probably because of confusion over the term "permissive" and the advice of child care specialists to involve children in self-directed activity. The helper's concern to create freeing atmospheres has often been translated by parents and citizens as "letting people do as they please." In part, such concern arises from age-old beliefs in the untrustworthy nature of the human organism and the personal experience of most people with authoritarian ways of dealing with others, which is so characteristic of much of our culture.

Freedom, for the professional helper, is not license to "do whatever one pleases." To the helper, freedom means creating conditions that are designed to free clientele to confront significant problems effectively and efficiently. That is no laissez-faire abrogation of responsibility. It is a purposeful, meaningful design for helping, supported by fundamental theory and successful practice. Likewise, "permissive" for the professional helper does not mean "no control," as lay people often fear; it means permitting clients or students to explore what is personally relevant, to play a major role in their own growth. As far as we are aware, no professional person has ever advocated rearing children or conducting helping relationships without limits. No human being could exist very long without them. The important question is not *whether* limits but *what* limits, and the answer must be decided in terms of their effects on the people they are applied to.

Effective helping relationships need limits, and the sooner the limits are understood, the sooner both helper and helpee can proceed toward more creative and fruitful endeavors. Sometimes this may be accomplished by stating limits outright at the beginning of a relationship. Most helpers, however, have learned by sad experience that this seldom works. In the opening sessions of a helping relationship, statements about limits will frequently not be heard. People are often confused and a little suspicious and therefore often fail to hear what is said. Furthermore, they may be trying to see if what the helper says matches what she does and consequently may miss many of the words being spoken.

Generally speaking, the establishment of limits is best governed by the behavior of the helper. Most people learn, beginning in early childhood, the superiority of action over words for understanding what others are really about, so they learn most effectively about the structure of helping relationships primarily from their own experience of them. Even so, they may need to reexplore limits now and then, if only to assure themselves that the limits have not changed. When young children are involved, it may be necessary to provide continuous reminders of what the limits are as long as the relationship exists.

Stability of Limits

It is important that the limits of helping relationships be stable. If the limits keep shifting, people do not know how to respond. They become upset and begin to mistrust the helper. One of the authors overheard three little boys discussing their next year's teacher at the end of the term. One of them asked another, "Who you got next year?" "I got Miss Johnson," was the reply. "Oh, I feel sorry for you. She's terrible!" Then the first boy went on in great detail about how bad Miss Johnson was. The third child finally ended the conversation, saying, "Yeah, she's bad. So okay! You'll get used to her!" This is true. People can adjust to almost anything if it stands still. It's the ambiguity and the contradictions that drive people wild and keep them constantly reexamining the limits.

The helper is often admonished to be consistent. This is often interpreted as a demand to behave in the same fashion. He should, indeed, be consistent, but the consistency required is of his belief system, not his behavior. Behavior, as we have seen, is only the external expression of personal meanings or beliefs. A given belief may produce many kinds of behavior, or different beliefs may result in similar behavior, depending on the people and the circumstances involved. The limits established by the clinician for the sick child and for the healthy one, for example, will necessarily be quite different, although the basic intent of the clinician may be the same with both children.

Helpers who seek consistency by concentrating on behavior will succeed only in becoming rigid and inflexible. Truly consistent helpers are those who have acquired internally consistent understanding about themselves, other people, the goals and purposes of helping, and the techniques or methods appropriate for the particular tasks they confront. The development of such congruent frames of reference takes time, experience, and continuous exploration of the helper's personal meanings.

Notes and References

1. C. R. Rogers, "The Characteristics of a Helping Relationship," *Personnel and Guidance Journal* 37 (1958):6–16.
2. D. N. Aspy, "The Effect of Teacher-Offered Conditions of Empathy, Positive Regard, and Congruence upon Student Achievement," *Florida Journal of Educational Research* 11 (1969):39–49.
3. R. R. Carkhuff and C. B. Truax, "Toward Explaining Success and Failure in Interpersonal Learning Experiences," *Personnel and Guidance Journal* 44 (1966):723–728; R. R. Carkhuff and C. B. Truax, *Toward Counseling and Psychotherapy: Training and Practice* (Chicago, Ill.: Aldine, 1967).
4. S. Jourard, "Healthy Personality and Self-Disclosure," in H. G. Brown et al., eds., *Behavioral Implications for Curriculum and Teaching: Interdisciplinary Readings* (Dubuque, Iowa: William C. Brown, 1969).
5. A. W. Combs et al., *Florida Studies in the Helping Professions*, Social Science Monograph No. 37 (Gainesville, Fla.: University of Florida Press, 1969).
6. T. R. McDaniel, "Exploring Alternatives to Punishment: The Keys to Effective Discipline," *Phi Delta Kappan* 61 (1980):455–58.
7. For a more extensive discussion of myths as they apply to education, see A. W. Combs, *Myths in Education: Beliefs that Hinder Progress and Their Alternatives* (Boston: Allyn and Bacon, 1979).
8. An analysis of grades and grading practices may be found in H. Kirschenbaum et al., *Wad Ja Get? The Grading Game in American Education* (New York: Hart Pub. Co., 1971) and in S. B. Simon and J. A. Bellanca, *Degrading the Grading Myths: A Primer of Alternatives and Marks* (Washington, D.C.: Association for Supervision and Curriculum Development, 1976).

EIGHT

SELF-FULFILLMENT: THE PRIMARY PURPOSE OF HELPING

Human beings strive for personal fulfillment every moment of their lives: to be healthy and happy, to function at their fullest potential, and to be productive and contributing members of society. The purpose of helpers is to aid in this search for personal fulfillment in their own unique way. Maximum attainment of personal fulfillment requires both rich and extensive fields of perception and the achievement of personal growth characteristic of self-actualization. In order to help students or clients toward self-fulfillment, helpers need to understand the nature of self-actualization, what highly self-actualizing people are like, and the dynamics involved in growth toward personal fulfillment.

WHAT IS SELF-ACTUALIZATION?

Scholars recently have devoted attention to the study of self-actualization, what people could become if they were maximally free to use their potentialities to the utmost. These scholars ask, "What would such people be like?" and "What can we do to help people achieve these exalted ends?" Some have described self-actualizing people objectively, in terms of typical behaviors or personality traits. Maslow,[1] for example, has described a long list of characteristics, including more efficient perceptions of reality and more comfortable relationships with it; acceptance of self, others, and nature; spontaneity; problem centering; the quality of detachment; autonomy; independence of culture and environment; freshness of appreciation; the "mystic" experience; feelings of oneness with others; democratic character structure; clear discrimination between means and ends; an unhostile sense of humor; creativeness; and resistance to enculturation. Carl Rogers[2] has added some traits to Maslow's list: openness to experience, living in a more existential fashion, being and becoming a process, and an increasing trust in the organism.

Listing the traits of self-actualizing people is helpful and informative but still essentially descriptive. Knowing that self-actualizing people are creative, trust their organisms, or have freshness of appreciation or an unhostile sense of humor still leaves us with the problem of how to facilitate growth and development of these traits. Trait descriptions, however accurate, do not in themselves provide us with guidelines to effective action. We need to understand self-actualizing people in dynamic terms that tell us how such traits come into being. To this end some writers have chosen to examine self-actualization in subjective terms. Earl Kelley,[3] for example, has described the fully functioning personality in the following terms: thinks well of himself; thinks well of others; sees his stake in others; sees himself as a part of a world in movement, in process of becoming; sees the value of mistakes; develops and holds human values; knows no other way to live except in keeping with his values. Approaching the matter in perceptual terms, Combs, Richards, and Richards[4] have described three factors especially characteristic of self-actualizing people. These factors are a positive view of self, openness to experience, and identification with others.

POSITIVE VIEW OF SELF

Scientists who have written about the nature of self-actualization generally agree that one of its characteristics is a high degree of self-esteem. Highly self-actualized people see themselves in essentially positive ways. With a positive view of self one can dare, be open to experience, confront the world openly and with certainty. Negative views of self may lock a person in a vicious circle in which efforts to deal with life are always too little, too late, or inappropriate.

Bolstering Effect of a Positive View of Self

The self is involved in every interaction with the world. Whatever its nature the self-concept goes along. Even a poor, ragged, unhappy self must be dragged by its owner into every activity. A positive self has vital effects on a person's efficiency and on a person's freedom to confront new matters. Having a positive view of self is like owning a stout ship. With a sturdy vessel underfoot one may go sailing far from shore. When one has doubts about one's ship and concern about its seaworthiness, one must play it safe and stay close to harbor. A positive self is like that. It provides a firm foundation from which to deal with the problems of life with security and confidence.

Self-actualizing people see themselves as liked, wanted, acceptable, able, dignified, and worthy. These deep feelings of personal security make it much easier for them to confront the emergencies of life. They believe that they are people of dignity and worth, and they *behave* as though they are. Rogers has pointed out that one of the characteristics of healthy personalities is trust in the organism.[5] With greater feelings of certainty about themselves, people can trust their impulses more. They experience their selves as trustworthy and dependable.

Whatever demeans the self, on the other hand, undermines confidence and produces fear and withdrawal. People with long histories of failure cannot handle emergency situations. This assurance-producing character of a positive view of self can be observed in the behavior of children with positive and negative views of self as they confront the problem of what to do about poor schoolwork. When examiners[6] asked children with positive views of self and histories of success in school, "What can you do about it if you had a bad grade in spelling?" (arithmetic, social studies, or whatever), the children suggested all kinds of possibilities: "Study harder," "Ask my teacher," "Ask my mother to help me," "Practice," "Try to find out what I'm doing wrong," and so on. When the same question was asked of children with negative self-concepts and histories of failure, the reply was, almost without exception, "Nothing!" These children regarded the matter as hopeless, the problem insoluble. It is a pity to encounter individuals with such low self-esteem, especially at such an early age.

The Fallacy of the Value of Failure

Many believe that failure is good for people, that it is a valuable stimulant for growth. This idea seems to have arisen from the observation that people are often strengthened by confrontation with problems. This, of course, is true. Many people also believe that failure is a strengthening thing. They adopt the attitude "if it's hard, it's good for me," and honestly believe that the experience of failure builds character, courage, and stimulation to succeed. This belief is a fallacy. From what we know about healthy people, such an assumption is not only false but can also be downright destructive.

Earlier in this book we described psychological illness as a problem of deprivation, a failure of the organism to achieve fulfillment. Psychological failure is like physiological disease. We do not say about diseases, "Let us give these diseases to our children as soon as possible!" Rather, we say, "Let us keep this child from getting diseases just as long as we possibly can." Or, alternatively, we may say, "Let us give her the disease in such an attenuated form that we know she will be successful with it." This is what we do with an inoculation or a vaccination, because we know that the body is strengthened by *successful* experience with the disease. The same principle holds true psychologically. A diet of failure is destructive to human personality. A person learns that he is adequate and able from success experience. The best guarantee we have that a person will be able to deal with exigencies in the future is that he has been successful in the past. Even the self-made man who beats his chest and proclaims to the world that he came up the hard way overlooks the fact that he became a self-made man by being successful. He became what he is today precisely because he successfully avoided failure!

Positive effects from feelings of success and negative effects from experiences of failure are beautifully illustrated in this report from a nursing supervisor.

Louise was in her second year as a sophomore in our College of Nursing program when she was assigned to my instruction. She was the motherless daughter of a small-town general practitioner. Her older brother was a medical student and progressing well.

Her intellectual test scores placed her as "barely able" to achieve in college. The previous year she had failed the first semester of the sophomore year. She decided to repeat that semester the following year. She attained a "D" grade. Her evaluation gave little hope for her success. The instructor in effect was saying, "I tried, but I couldn't find enough evidence on which to base a grade of 'F'."

Louise was very plain, the only student who insisted upon wearing her mousy brown hair in a net. She had "I can't succeed" written all over her face. She trembled when asked to recite formally or when asked a question informally.

I felt, as her clinical instructor, that the patients would suffer if Louise's assignments were too difficult. I felt she would make mistakes, possibly drastic ones, and I did not want that burden. Looking back, I never thought I was providing success for Louise by giving her patient assignments she could handle. I never thought of Louise in that way at all. I was concerned with myself and the patients for whom my students were caring.

The other instructors were interested in Louise's progress. As the weeks passed, I proudly related how well she could perform with her simple assignments (four to six months behind) and that her trembling had stopped. She could smile and relate to others more freely.

I was told by my superiors, however, that I was handling the situation terribly. (This was damaging to my self-concept, I realize.) The only way to approach extremely weak students like Louise, they said, was to give them the roughest assignment possible for that level students, supervise them heavily, collect the data to fail them, show them where they have failed, write it up and put an "F" on the evaluation.

They convinced me! I did a bang-up job and you know what? Louise behaved true to her perceptions. She blundered miserably, made hair-raising mistakes, and failed.

I did such a good job. I was praised highly. Louise did not return this past September. And I feel like a failure knowing that I am a part of Louise's nightmare of failure.

It is dismaying to observe how our society believes in the value of failure. When modern educators suggest eliminating failure from the classroom, they are often met with storms of protest from parents and community, who fear that this would destroy the very basis of the public schools. There is no word in the vocabulary of the English language that distinguishes between the act of failing and judging it "non-negatively" and noncritically. The word "failure" is derogatory, implying a sense of "no goodness"; that one is vanquished, defeated, and inadequate. A person learns very early that if an act does not reach its expected or desired outcome, then he or she is a failure. A society that does not distinguish between "non-accomplishment" and "failure" runs a serious risk of demoralizing and discouraging vast numbers of its populace.

By rejecting the value of failure we do not mean that people must be protected from difficult kinds of experience. People like to work hard when tasks provide a feeling of self-accomplishment and goals are perceived as possible. People enjoy being challenged. It is the experience of long-continued failure that produces destructive outcomes and feelings of inadequacy. Failure is debilitating and weakening. There is enough failure in the natural order of things without anyone, especially professional helpers, planning and plotting to make sure that another human being gets enough of it.

OPENNESS TO EXPERIENCE

A second characteristic required for maximum self-actualization is openness to experience. This has to do with a person's ability to perceive the world. It is the capacity to confront what is, to enter into transaction with it, and develop new meanings as a consequence. Highly self-actualizing, fully functioning personalities seem able to deal with the world with a minimum of distortion. They see themselves more accurately and realistically.

Psychologists call openness to experience "acceptance," by which they mean the ability to confront what is—whether it be in self or in the outside world. The word "acceptance" used in this way does not mean "giving in to" or "being resigned to." Persons can accept the fact that someone dislikes them, for example, without necessarily agreeing that they are, therefore, totally inadequate. Persons in the helping professions are often called on to accept the fact of a client's misbehavior without rejecting the client.

The first requirement for being able to deal with the world or with one's self must be the capacity to perceive it, to enter into a dialogue with it. Whether this is possible will depend in large measure on a person's feelings of self-esteem. Highly self-actualizing people find acceptance easy. Deeply deprived and maladjusted people often find it difficult or impossible to achieve. This relationship of openness to positive views of self was measured in a simple experiment carried out by one of the authors.[7] All the sixth-grade children in a school were given standard tests of adjustment. On a list of things "Boys and Girls Sometimes Do" they were asked to indicate those items that were true of themselves. All the items on the list were behaviors that were probably true of every child but that were somewhat unflattering to admit. Some samples: "Sometimes I have lied to my mother," "Sometimes I forget to brush my teeth on purpose," and "Sometimes I have been unkind to animals." When the results of the study were analyzed, it was discovered (as predicted) that the children who were better adjusted admitted that more of the unflattering things were true of them than did the children who were maladjusted. One little boy, who had the highest adjustment score in the group, agreed that nineteen of the twenty unflattering items were true of him.

Highly self-actualizing people have such a degree of trust in themselves that they are much more able to look at any data without the necessity for defending themselves or distorting events in ways they would like them to be. Lack of acceptance, on the other hand, is a major characteristic of neurosis and shows itself in myriad forms—in the inability of a young child to accept her baby brother, in the failure of prejudiced people to accept members of minority groups, in the resistance of males to accept the principles of "women's lib," and many more. People with extreme inabilities to accept reality end up in mental hospitals and are described as being "out of touch with reality."

Openness and a Positive View of Self

The walls people build to keep others out also keep themselves in. Protections set up to avoid injury can also destroy openness to new experiences. People who reject themselves are likely to reject others as well and so contribute to closing themselves off from the very experiences that might eventually result in personal fulfillment.

The interdependency of self-acceptance, acceptance of others, and openness to experience were beautifully illustrated by two severely handicapped young women known to one of the authors. They both sought entrance into a graduate training program in clinical psychology and came to the author's office on successive days. Because the office was on the third floor, each had to be carried up for an interview. The first woman was hard and bitter. She had an attractive face, but her dour, angry, defiant stance spoiled what good possibilities she had, and her attitude at once repelled her audience. In the course of conversation the author said, "I wonder if you have given any thought to the degree to which your handicap . . . " That's as far as he got. She snapped, "I don't have a handicap!" Unable to accept herself, she was also unable to deal effectively with herself or with others. The second candidate had the same condition, but what a difference! She was not as physically attractive but had a much more open, friendly personality—a person one felt immediately drawn to. The author said the same thing to this woman as he had said to the first young woman, but this time he was allowed to complete his sentence: "I wonder if you have given any thought to the degree to which your handicap might make it difficult for you to work in this field?" This is what she replied:

> I have thought a lot about that. You know, in addition to polio I had TB some years ago. At that time I lay on my back for two years in a hospital and had lots of time to think. It seems to me that experience could be helpful. You know, I kind of feel that somebody who has gone through this much will be better able to understand other people who have suffered.

People who are open to experience enjoy exploring. They are freewheelers who are able to move off in new directions, which is what creativity means. They are neither thrown by their experience nor defensive against it, and the more reticent among us must be prepared for the fact that these freewheelers are open to *all kinds* of experiences. For example, some helpers—and surely a number of parents whether helpers or not—will find disturbing a recent study of young girls attending birth control centers.[8] A group of 486 of these girls, ranging in age from thirteen to twenty, were evaluated on several factors, including their perceived level of self-esteem and their attitudes about sex. A clear distinction was found between those girls with high and low self-esteem and their attitudes toward sex. Girls with high self-esteem were more accepting of premarital intercourse, as long as it was the result of a loving relationship, were more willing to take the sexual initiative, and felt less guilt about intimate relationships. Girls with low self-esteem endorsed abstinence as the best course to follow.

The authors are not taking sides on the issue of premarital sex, but the study does make two points: (1) that the pursuit of fulfillment may take any direction and (2) that the professional helper will have to deal with a helpee on whatever level of need enhancement the helpee is operating on. This is true, even if the nature of that quest may conflict with the helper's own personal values.

Lest we leave someone in a panic, let us assure you that all is not lost. James E. Elias, who studies such matters, tells us that the sexual revolution is a myth anyway.[9] He points out that our society operates on three levels— the media, attitudinal, and behavioral. Each of these levels reflects a different picture of what is really going on in a society.

The *media level,* which often has little to do with reality, currently projects the image of the United States as a sensuous and sexually oriented society in which anything goes. The *attitudinal level,* which represents the feelings and attitudes of society and is closer to the truth, is mostly characterized at present by a willingness on the part of individuals to be more accepting of the behavior of others. The *behavioral level* is the prime indicator of what is really happening, and Dr. Elias believes that, particularly with the younger folks, not much has changed over the past few decades.

The authors have corroborated this point of view through personal experience. When they sit and chat with young students or clients, they find the moral values and beliefs of these young people not much different from those of young people twenty or so years ago. True, they are much more tolerant of the behaviors of others, but when it comes to deciding what is right and wrong for them, they are a pretty conservative lot.

Sexual preferences of any sort probably occur no more frequently than in the past but are occurring more openly than ever before, particularly those that some consider atypical. The true status of the sexual revolution lies somewhere between the sublime character of TV commercials and the ridiculousness of letters to the editor of *Penthouse* magazine.

Openness becomes a particular problem with regard to sex, because people in our society have so much difficulty dealing with this aspect of human behavior. In fact, the topic is so sensitive that openness can become a double-edged sword in the helping professions, for it is often a subject that is as difficult for the helper to deal with as it is for the helpee. This is unfortunate, because the kind of openness we are speaking of is not something that can be turned on and off. It is an attitude that permeates one's life, allowing one to be accepting of all aspects of self and others.

FREEDOM AND IDENTIFICATION

A third major quality of self-actualizing people is identification, the feeling of oneness with others. Humans are social beings. The degree to which they are able to attain fulfillment depends on how successful they are in working out effective relationships with other people who make up the society or culture in which they live. We are so dependent on other people that some measure of successful interaction with them is essential to life itself. Experiments with monkeys deprived of opportunities to interact with other monkeys demonstrate that such isolation causes them to grow into distorted, maladjusted personalities.[10] Raised out of touch with one another, they frequently cannot even be induced to mate. Apparently, without the experience that helps them discover who and what they are, they do not know that they are monkeys. Similarly, people become human through human interaction. Feelings of identification contribute to that process and so to the humanization of persons. People are the most important aspects of our world, the sources of most of our satisfactions and frustrations. In fact, other people are the only really important ingredients of life. Material possessions, whether they be money, cars, or clothes, gain meaning and importance only when they are shared with other human beings. The nature of our relationships with others determines our freedom and personal fulfillment.

Identification with Ideas

Identification is equally significant with respect to ideas. We have already observed the intimate relationship between the self-concept and learning. Whether any information is likely to result in changed behavior will depend on the closeness with which that information is perceived to the self. Ideas incorporated into the self-structure can be counted on to determine future behavior. There is simply no learning of consequence without involvement of the person in the process. Ideas by themselves are mere illusions. It is only in people that they come alive and only through the personal discovery of their relationship to self that they affect behavior.

Real learning and the richness it bestows on life come about only with self-involvement. People who will not or cannot enter into dialogue with ideas are cut off from experience. This principle was vividly brought home to one of the authors while visiting a museum with an artist friend. The author was working hard at trying to understand one of the modern paintings but was getting nowhere. Then his friend said to him, "Stop working at it. You are looking at it from afar, groping for it with your fingertips. Let it come to you. Try to be with it. Let yourself get involved. Let it flow into you." Looking at the painting in this way, the author almost at once experienced a whole new relationship with it. He discovered a new beauty, meaning, and sensual delight as he let himself "be with it." Instead of *looking at* the painting, he learned to enter into a *dialogue with it* and thereby opened a whole new world of experience for exploration. The self at war with experience is shutting itself off from meaning, reducing psychological freedom. The self capable of entering interaction with ideas or concepts is opening and expanding its world, simultaneously broadening its base of operations and increasing its chances for the achievement of self-fulfillment.

Nowhere is this relationship between the self and ideas so important as in education. A major purpose of schools is to bring students into effective relationships with the accumulated experience of other human beings. The success of schools in accomplishing this task depends on their degree of success in inducing students to invest themselves in learning. We have all had the experience of being or not being "with it" in school. In those classes in which, for some reason, we refused to invest ourselves in the learning process we learned little or nothing. On the other hand, in those classes in which we worked hard and interacted with our classmates we learned a great deal. It made no difference whether our interest came from within or was the result of an inspiring teacher or exciting subject matter. Once involved, we *were* with it and we learned. Also, what was learned was far more likely to be retained and acted on. People do not sabotage their own projects.

Identification and Self-Actualization

Deep feelings of identification with others is a major characteristic of highly self-actualizing people. Possessing such feelings in turn produces interactions with their fellows that corroborate and strengthen existing beliefs. Broad feelings of identification, for example, make it possible to place more trust in others. Relationships with others can be entered into much more openly and freely. When one is certain of being welcome, one walks more boldly and dares to do or say what others less certain could not risk. Interactions with others can thus be entered with an *expectancy* of success. Because they feel they belong, broadly identified people establish relationships with others as though they were members of the family rather than strangers. Fulfillment comes much easier to those who are capable of such involvement. The feedback they experience from these interactions is also more supporting and enhancing than that of less self-actualizing people.

Those who identify strongly with others are likely to experience deep compassion for people. Others quickly discover this fact and respond in kind. They also discover that deeply identified people are highly responsible and trustworthy, for what such people do for others, they do for themselves and vice versa. Consequently, others respond to them warmly and openly. Because broadly identified people are less threatening, others can afford to relax their defenses and enter into more responsive relationships with them. This was true so frequently in the lives of some of the self-actualizing people that Maslow studied as to sometimes become an embarrassment.[11] Because they were warm, open, compassionate, and understanding, they tended to attract people with problems and thus found themselves at times surrounded by unhappy people in need of help!

Deep feelings of identification are also likely to contribute to more intelligent behavior. With positive feelings toward others, people can approach relationships with the expectancy of success. With a feeling of oneness they have little to fear and so can commit themselves wholeheartedly to interactions. People without such feelings operate under great handicaps. They must deal with others defensively as strangers or as enemies rather than as possible friends. Accordingly, they tend to approach interactions with hesitation. Expecting resistance, they are likely to get it and thus defeat themselves almost before they begin.

Identification and Psychological Health

Many of the great social and personal problems of our time have been brought about by the terrible dehumanizing forces we have set loose in our midst. The net effect of many of our technological innovations has been to depersonalize the individual and make satisfying human interrelationships increasingly difficult to achieve. We have created a society in which millions of people believe that they are of little account. A large part of the activities of those in the helping professions is directed toward helping people discover and enter into new and more satisfying relationships between themselves and other people.

The problems of alienation and loneliness exist at every level of our social structure. They are especially poignant with respect to the young. It is probably no accident that one of the best cures for juvenile delinquency seems to be marriage. Of all the things associated with delinquents who improve, getting married seems to be more effective and more certain than any other one thing that we know about. When one has somebody who cares, somebody to live for, somebody to share things with, one is provided a measure of relief from the boredom and feelings of alienation that lie at the basis of much delinquent behavior. Many young people grow up with deep feelings of alienation from the society they live in. Many are desperately lonely and find themselves at loose ends without satisfying commitments. We cannot afford this waste. On humanitarian grounds the loss in human potential involved in such rejection is tremendous. The loss in human happiness is even greater. If it is not enough to be concerned about the matter because we love and respect our young people, there is another very practical reason we had better be interested: These are the citizens and voters of tomorrow!

SELF-ACTUALIZATION AND TOTAL HEALTH

Having a positive attitude toward life is not just a matter of being happier or more productive. One's health—*and even life itself*—can depend on it. Researchers Suzanne Kobasa and Salvatore Maddi have been conducting studies that demonstrate the relationship between self-actualization and physical health.

As a result of their work, Kobasa and Maddi have developed a concept they call *hardiness* to describe people with attitudes and perceptions exactly like those we have been referring to as self-actualizing. These individuals are described as having three primary characteristics. First, they are *committed,* being much more involved in their work and social lives than is typical. Second, they are *challenged* by life rather than threatened by it. And third, they believe that they are in *control* of events.

The essential purpose of the bulk of Kobasa and Maddi's research was to examine the relationship between hardiness and disease. The results of the studies showed that people who rate high on commitment, challenge, and control are healthier than those whose rating is not high. On a health rating scale, the hardiness group had a total illness rating, after two years, of 510. A group of individuals rating low on hardiness had an illness rating, on the same scale, of 1,080. One of the striking things about their study is that all the subjects were in high-stress occupations. Thus it was not the subjects' jobs that were causing the increased illnesses, but the subjects' *attitudes* toward their jobs.

Challenge appeared to be the greatest buffer between sickness and health in the hardy group, closely followed by commitment. The effect of losing a job, for example, is very different on a person, depending on whether she or he perceives it as a *catastrophe* or as an *opportunity* for new adventure and commitment.

Martin Seligman has been studying this question of health and attitude from a completely different point of view.[13] Yet the conclusions are the same. He has identified a process that he calls *learned helplessness.* When people experience failure over long periods they come to believe that they have no control over their lives, that they are pawns to be moved about by others and the whim of fate. When such an intense feeling of helplessness is reached, not only physical disease but also *the loss of life itself* can occur.

One of the most dramatic examples cited by Seligman of what can happen when one feels completely out of control of one's life is a study of fifty-five women who were about to enter a nursing home. One of the things the women were asked at the time was how much choice did they feel they had in what they were about to do. Thirty-eight said they had at least some and seventeen said they had none. At the end of ten weeks, after entering the home, only one of the thirty-eight who said they had some choice in the matter had died, whereas only one of those who felt they had no choice remained alive!

Current literature abounds with examples of the relationship between one's attitude toward life and the effect that life's experiences have on one. Hans Selye,[14] a leading expert on stress, agrees that it is not what happens to a person that results in diseases, but rather the way he or she looks at or evaluates what happens to him or her. This is the major premise of his book *Stress Without Distress*.[15]

SELF-FULFILLMENT AND SOME IMPLICATIONS FOR THE PRACTICE OF HELPING[16]

Contributing to a Positive Self

What can a helper do to contribute to the development of a positive view of self on the part of her helpees? At least a partial how-to guide for helping lies in the answers a helper finds to questions such as:

- How can a person feel liked unless someone likes him?
- How can a person feel acceptable unless somebody accepts her?
- How can a person feel able unless sometime he has some success?
- How can a person feel she is a person of dignity and integrity unless somebody treats her so?
- How shall a person feel that she matters unless someone cares?

Helpers must themselves be positive forces in the lives of their students or clients. In fact, at any given moment the helper may be the only affirming force in a helpee's life. This is a powerful place to be, and if that power is wielded with care, concern, and wisdom and with the welfare of the helpee in mind, it can contribute tremendously toward the development of a positive self. Helpers contribute to a positive view of self, not by what they do for or to their clients, but through what their behavior conveys of their feelings and beliefs about their clients. The criteria for self-actualization, therefore, also provide definitions for the nature of the perceptual organization that must characterize helpers themselves.

Aiding Identification and the Discovery of Meaning

It is a mistaken notion that learning is a solitary matter best achieved in isolation. The most important aspect of our world is people, and it is with and through people that our most important learnings are achieved. This is true even for the learning of highly abstract intellectual concepts. It is much truer with respect to learning the things we need to know about getting along with one another and achieving maximum fulfillment.

The feeling of oneness has important implications for the behavior of helpers in the helping process. Identification is learned from successful encounters with other people. When a helper is able to give of himself he does much more than provide a warm atmosphere. He himself is a demonstration of commitment, a living invitation to students or clients to join the human race. Empathy is an invitation, a holding out of the hand, an indication that someone cares.

To serve as significant others in the lives of those they seek to aid, helpers must commit themselves to the process. They must care. Research indicates that a feeling of oneness with others is associated with effective helpers, whereas feelings of alienation are attitudes of ineffective helpers. People do not identify very long with those who reject or are indifferent to them. Being loved is immensely reassuring, and the loving and caring attitude of helpers, in itself, provides an important ingredient for aiding the discovery of meaning.

The importance of love as a major factor in successful human relationships has been universally recognized by artists, poets, novelists, philosophers, psychologists, anthropologists, and the clergy. Yet the place of love in the helping professions is often ignored in favor of "being objective." Love is approached, if at all, with apologies, fear, or shame. Even to talk about "liking" is sometimes regarded as not really relevant to the helping process. This was beautifully expressed in a letter written by a fifth-grade boy after his teacher permitted the class to hold a free discussion that got around to the question of love. The next day the little boy wrote:

> Dear Miss Jones:
> It sure surprised me when we talked about love in our class yesterday. I learned a lot of things. I learned how people feel about each other. It sure surprised me when we talked about love. I never knew you could talk about things in school that you didn't get grades for!

What a pity that such an important factor in human life is often not regarded as part of the curriculum!

If helpers do not care, they run a grave risk of defeating themselves as professional workers or, worse yet, of interfering with the growth of those they seek to help. This does not mean that helpers have to love everyone. Some people are not very lovable and no one can turn feelings on and off at will. The authors have seen teachers and counselors who were ready to quit the profession because they felt guilty for not liking a particular child or client. Helpers are required to deliver the very best professional relationship they are capable of. That in itself is a kind of caring. But if a helper has such strong negative feelings toward a helpee that he or she can't do a good job, then something should be done. Quitting, however, is not the answer. The helper is only human, and disliking others, if it is a crime, is one all helpers will be guilty of at some time or other. In such cases, accepting the situation and making arrangements for the helpee to work with someone else is an honest, healthy, and simple solution.

Facilitating Openness

Encouraging openness is a two-way street. That is, both the helper and the helpee must be open to experience and be *aware*. A hundred-pound nurse, for example, who tells her two-hundred-fifty-pound patient that it is easy to lose weight "if you only stay on your diet" is a case in point. It is easy for the nurse who has eaten pretty much what she pleased for most of her life. For her patient on a 1200-calorie diet, it is quite another matter.

The helping encounter must actively encourage searching. This condition is achieved in part by an attitude of fearless looking, that "it is good to look and fun to try." It may be provided in the form of success experience or the discovery of challenging problems. It may be acquired by "osmosis" from the attitudes and behavior of the helper. Whatever contributes to the feeling that anything can be looked at, is likely to be helpful. On the contrary, whatever prevents such an attitude gets in the way of effective learning.

We have succeeded, almost everywhere in our institutions and child-rearing practices, in erecting an incredible number of barriers to involvement—attitudes that say to people: "Watch out!" "Don't look at that." "That is forbidden" (or inappropriate or nasty or unacceptable). Teachers do this when they say to children, "I'm not interested in what you feel about that. What does the book say?" We do it with children in our families when we teach them the "right," "nice," "proper" things to do, think, and feel. We do it with one another when we change the subject because "we would rather not think about that." Even as a society, we become highly skilled in not seeing what lies before our eyes—for example, the sick, the slums, unfair treatment of minorities, prisoners, or the fact that other countries and other cultures do not see things as we do. A major task of the helper, no matter what branch of the profession, must be to overcome the negative effects of such built-in resistance to looking.

As with the question of how to contribute to a client's development of a positive view of self, the helper can find answers with regard to how she may facilitate openness by asking herself such things as:

- Do the methods I am using assist my students or clients to accept themselves and the world?
- Is the atmosphere I am creating truly encouraging my clients to be more open to their experiences?
- Am I demonstrating by my own behavior a willingness to look at any and all events?
- Am I teaching my students or clients acceptance of themselves?
- Am I providing experience of successful confrontation with themselves and the world?

A LITTLE REALITY ORIENTATION

Writers discussing self-actualization have often been criticized as being dreamers or as being out of touch with reality. "Nonsense," some say. "No one is like that!" These authors agree, with two qualifications. The self-actualized model is an ideal toward which everyone, helper or not, can strive. The closer one comes to achieving this ideal, the happier and healthier one will be. Robert Browning said, "Ah, but a man's reach should exceed his grasp, or what's a heaven for." Whether for one's self or for others, it's no mean thing to reach for the stars.

Self-actualization is a process, not a state. This is the only point on which the authors disagree with Maslow. Maslow believed that self-actualization was a state that some, although an extremely small number, reached. These authors believe that people are only, more or less, engaging in self-actualizing behavior at any given moment, with some individuals behaving that way more frequently than others. But anyone can become involved in the self-actualizing experience. The primary criterion is not what one is doing, but the attitude one has toward what one is doing. To these authors, a person can be engaging in self-actualizing behavior if (1) he or she is experiencing personal satisfaction and (2) is contributing to the welfare of society as a whole. Thus writers of great books and songs, painters of great pictures, and world leaders can be in the process of self-actualization. So too, however, can garbage collectors, real estate agents, and even used car dealers. The authors have encountered no one who is a self-actualized person—only individuals who are more or less often engaging in self-actualizing behavior. Self-actualization is a process of becoming, not an exalted status one possesses.

We have scarcely scratched the surface of the full implications current concepts about human fulfillment and actualization may have for human existence. The little we do know, however, provides important guidelines for the efforts of helpers in working with students or clients. We need to explore these concepts much further while at the same time inventing new ways of putting them into action. We cannot turn back. Now that we know that it is possible, we must get about the business of producing more fully functioning people in every way we can. Now that we know the limitless possibilities of human capacity, we need to exploit our understandings to the limit. Not to do so is to fail ourselves, our students, our clients, our patients, and society itself.

Notes and References

1. A. H. Maslow, *Motivation and Personality*, 2d ed. (New York: Harper & Row, 1970).
2. C. R. Rogers, *Person to Person: The Problem of Being Human* (New York: Pocket Books, 1967).
3. E. C. Kelley, *In Defense of Youth* (Englewood Cliffs, N.J.: Prentice-Hall, 1962).
4. A. W. Combs, A. C. Richards, and F. Richards, *Perceptual Psychology: A Humanistic Approach to the Study of Persons* (New York: Harper & Row, 1976).
5. C. R. Rogers, *On Becoming a Person: A Therapist's View of Psychotherapy* (Boston: Houghton Mifflin, 1961).
6. E. Stotland, "Effects of Public and Private Failure on Self-Evaluation," *Journal of Abnormal and Social Psychology* 56 (1958):223–229.

7. C. Taylor and A. W. Combs, "Self-Acceptance and Adjustment," *Journal of Consulting Psychology* 16 (1952):89–91.

8. E. S. Herold and M. S. Goodwin, "Self-Esteem and Sexual Permissiveness," *Journal of Clinical Psychology* 35 (1979):908–912.

9. J. Elias, "Adolescents and Sex," in H. E. Fitzgerald and T. H. Carr, eds., *Human Development 82/83* (Guilford, Conn.: Dushkin, 1982), pp. 212–214.

10. H. Harlow and M. K. Harlow, "Social Deprivation in Infant Monkeys," *Scientific American* 207 (1962):136–146.

11. Maslow, *Motivation.*

12. Maya Pines, "Psychological Hardiness," in N. Jackson, ed., *Personal Growth and Behavior 82/83* (Guilford, Conn.: Dushkin, 1982), pp. 213–218.

13. D. Colligan, "That Helpless Feeling: The Dangers of Stress," in Jackson, *Personal Growth*, pp. 111–114.

14. Hans Selye, *The Stress of Life* (New York: McGraw-Hill Book Co., 1976).

15. Hans Selye, *Stress Without Distress* (New York: J. B. Lippincott Co., 1974).

16. For discussions of the implications of the factors that have been discussed in this chapter as they relate specifically to counseling and teaching, see A. W. Combs, "Self-Actualization and the Teaching Function of Counselors," in G. S. Belkin, ed., *Counseling: Directions in Theory and Practice* (Dubuque, Iowa: Kendall/Hunt, 1976), pp. 43–53, and A. W. Combs, *A Personal Approach to Teaching* (Boston: Allyn and Bacon, 1982).

NINE

THE RANGE OF HUMAN POTENTIAL

What helpers believe about the nature of human capacity inevitably affects the methods they use, the respect they have for their clients, and even the amount of effort they are likely to expend in trying to be helpful. Effective helpers believe that their clients are able to cope with life, whereas ineffective helpers doubt the capacities of the people they work with. What do we know about the range of human potential?

CAPACITY AND THE PHYSICAL MODEL

When we think about what is possible for people, it is natural to think in terms of experience with our physical bodies. We are obviously limited by the nature of our physiology. There are limits to how far and how fast we can run, and these usually become narrower as we grow older. We need only get sick to observe how illness may impair effectiveness. Clearly, we cannot make our bodies do what our physiology will not permit. Our physical capacities depend on our hereditary characteristics and on the condition we have managed to keep ourselves in to the present. With the physical model constantly before us, it is easy to assume that the capacity for behavior or misbehavior is similarly limited. This concept of human capacities was commonly held for generations. Until recently it was also held by most psychologists. Today we must take quite a different view.

One of the most exciting discoveries of this generation is the idea that human capacity is far greater than anything ever thought possible. The fascinating thing about human beings is not their limitations but their immense capabilities. For years we have believed that people are born with strictly limited potential and that there is little or nothing anyone can do about it.

It is true that physical condition controls our physical prowess. But most of the behaviors required for getting along effectively in the world have little to do with the state of our physiology. Behaviors like thinking, loving, hating, wanting, creating, hoping, searching, and understanding or misunderstanding one another are matters of perception. They have little to do with the nature of the physical organism in which they occur.

The body is the house in which we live. It provides the vehicle for much behavior, but it does not explain behavior. We must have eyes to see. Thereafter, what is seen, what has been seen, and what will be seen is no longer a question of the structure of the eyes alone. A study of physiology will not provide us with the full understandings we need about people. The capacity for behavior or misbehavior transcends the organism in which it occurs. The body is not the controller of behavior but the vehicle in which it occurs, and capacity lies not in the structure but in the use to which it is put.

Human Beings Are Overbuilt

The outstanding thing about the human organism is not its limitations but its potentials. It is characteristically overbuilt! When an engineer builds a bridge, she designs it with a built-in "safety factor"—a degree of sturdiness many times stronger than she expects the structure will need to withstand. People are like that too. Most of us, in the course of our daily lives, use but a small portion of what is possible for the physical organism. Some years ago one of the authors left his disabled car on the side of the road and began walking along the edge of the highway, looking for help. In the distance he saw a car approaching at great speed, weaving back and forth across the road. A moment later he realized with horror that the car was coming straight for him. In a flash he jumped the ditch beside the road and fled into the adjoining field. Brushing himself off and verbally venting his wrath on "that crazy driver," he walked back to the ditch. It looked pretty wide when he reached it, but he thought that having jumped it one way it should be no problem on the return trip. So, taking a mighty leap, he jumped—and landed in the middle of the ditch in water up to his waist! With the danger gone he was back to his normal expenditures of energy.

Such feats are really a matter of need and concentration. There is a fictitious belief, for example, that psychotics have superhuman strength. This is because, in states of desperation, they have performed acts that appear to be beyond most people's capacity. One of the authors once witnessed such an act while working in a sanatorium. A small, frail female patient in her early twenties was asked to take a bath. No one knew why, but taking a bath was one of the things this woman most hated to do. When asked, she always became extremely angry. The room in which she had to bathe was at the end of the corridor in which her room was located. One day the sanatorium attendants entered her room and told her it was time to bathe. She immediately bolted from her room, ran the length of the corridor, and disappeared into the bathing room. The attendants, knowing she had nowhere to go, began to walk slowly down the hall, but before they could reach the end the young girl reappeared, flinging an entire washbasin toward them! She had ripped it from the wall!

This young woman did not suddenly acquire superhuman strength. She had just reached her breaking point, accumulated enough need for revenge, and concentrated her entire being toward finding some way to pay back her tormentors.

In less physically related behavior the scope of human potential is even more impressive. People can learn to read a page at a glance and to perform prodigious feats of memory and perception. Human creativity goes on and on. Scientists continue to discover, painters paint, and poets write. There seems literally no limit to the possibilities for thinking, feeling, loving, hoping, and seeking and the behaviors they produce. People are always rising to new occasions. It is commonplace to find that an individual's behavior lives up to the promotion to which the person has been raised. From everything we can observe, it seems clear that few of us ever remotely approach the potentialities for effective behavior that lie within us. Indeed, it had to be so throughout human history. The human organism could only have survived the course of evolution if it had within it the capacity to rise to emergencies.

INTELLIGENCE AS FUNCTIONAL CAPACITY

Intelligence is the capacity of an individual to behave effectively and efficiently. This capacity may be looked at in two ways: ultimate capacity and functional capacity. *Ultimate capacity* is the maximum potential permitted by the physiological makeup with which a person is born; it is what the individual could deliver if every condition of her or his life was maximally operative. *Functional capacity* is the behavior a person can normally deliver when necessary. This concept refers to the person's current capacity for effective and efficient behavior. It is also what we mean in this book when we speak of intelligence.

Ultimate Physical Capacity

Every animal is ultimately limited by its physical structure. People too can do only that which inherited structure will permit. Physiologically, these limits are comparatively narrow; psychologically, they are far greater. We need, therefore, to distinguish between physiological and behavioral ultimate capacities. In Figure 9.1 we have done this. We have represented the potentials for physical activities by a dot–dash line rising in a fairly smooth curve at one end of the continuum and leveling off at a height fairly well above the baseline. The levels at which people are able to engage in their day-to-day activities lie somewhere between this line and the base of the chart. Although people may occasionally, under extraordinary circumstances, come close to the ultimate level, usually their physical activities are much lower.

Ultimate Behavioral Capacity

The curve for behavioral potential is a different shape. Of course, a comparatively small number of pitiful souls are born with such inadequate physiology or nervous systems as to be severely handicapped behaviorally as

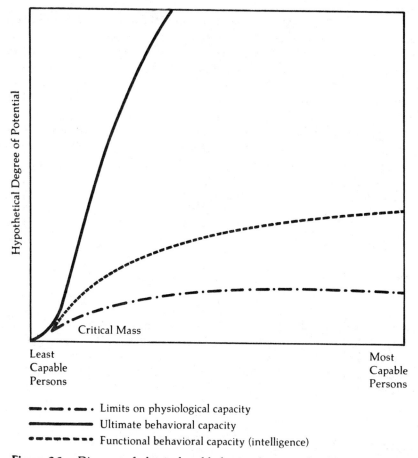

Figure 9.1   Diagram of physical and behavioral potentials of human beings.

well. Some of these, such as the "crib cases" in institutions for the mentally retarded, are destined to live out their lives as little more than human vegetables. Others, like those less severely limited by brain damage or by in utero or postnatal failures of organ development, manage to cope more or less successfully with life but are destined to limited success because of their physical problems. They are represented on the diagram at the extreme left of the ultimate behavior curve. For most of us, fortunately, the picture is quite different.

Earlier we described human behavior as the product of the person's perceptual field. Given the machinery for perceiving, even with limitations, behavioral possibilities are almost astronomical. Once a person possesses eyes and ears in reasonably workable condition, the possibilities of what she may see and hear are no longer restricted by physiological endowment. The situation is similar to the critical mass required for an atomic explosion. Up to a point the atomic pile reacts in smooth, predictable fashion, until the critical mass is reached; then a whole new set of conditions comes into being. Something like this happens with our ultimate capacity for behavior. Given the critical mass to make perceiving possible, what the organism makes of it after that is no longer a function of physical conditions. Ultimate capacity to behave is represented in Figure 9.1 by the unbroken line, which begins to rise smoothly to the critical mass, then zooms off the chart to heights unknown. Perception transcends the physical structure in which it occurs.

Intelligence: The Capacity for Effective, Efficient Behavior

Intelligence is the person's functional capacity—the ability to behave effectively and efficiently when necessary. This functional capacity is represented in Figure 9.1 by a dotted line that begins at a low level for the severely handicapped at the left-hand side of the diagram and rises to the heights achieved by the most brilliant people on the right-hand side. Owing to the limitless possibilities for human perception, none of us ever achieves more than a small part of what is possible. Because none of us ever approaches the limits of perception, ultimate behavioral possibilities are an academic question of no practical significance.

Historically, psychologists used the term "intelligence" to refer to ultimate capacity. Used in this way, intelligence was regarded as fixed and immutable, derived primarily from one's heredity and only minimally influenced by change from outside forces. Recently, many psychologists define intelligence in terms of functional capacity. This is a much more useful concept for the helping professions. A person's current capacity for effective and efficient behavior is what most people mean by "intelligent behavior." The production of intelligent behavior is a major goal of education and of the helping professions.

Defined as the capacity for effective and efficient behavior, intelligence is not a hereditary problem, nor is it a static, unchangeable potential. Rather, it represents a comparatively low level of achievement with vast possibilities for improvement. It is interesting that this was the position taken by Alfred Binet, originator of the first intelligence tests. He declared:

> Some recent philosophers appear to have given their support to the deplorable verdict that intelligence of an individual is a fixed quantity—we must protest and act against this brutal pessimism—a child's mind is like a field in which an expert farmer has advised a change in the method of cultivation with the result that in place of desert land we now have a harvest. It is in this particular sense, the one which is significant, that we say that the intelligence of children may be increased. One increases that which constitutes the intelligence of a school child, namely, the capacity to learn, to improve with instruction.[1]

Unfortunately, Binet's warning was largely overlooked for a good many years after his death, and it is only recently that intelligence is once again being regarded as a broader human function capable of change. We will not stop here to review all the research leading to the conclusion that capacity for behavior can be created. The evidence is so extensive and varied as to call for a book in its own right, and J. McV. Hunt has answered the call superbly in a volume called *Intelligence and Experience*.[2] We heartily recommend this book to readers who are interested in pursuing the evidence for intelligence change in greater detail.

The idea that human capacity is not so fixed and immutable as we thought in generations past is a concept of tremendous significance for the helping professions. Later in this chapter we will explore its implications further.

WHAT INTELLIGENCE TESTS MEASURE

For many years intelligence tests have been used for the determination of human potentialities and have often been regarded by the public and some users of tests as infallible indications of a person's possibilities. Most of the early intelligence tests were manufactured by those who regarded intelligence as a capacity of the organism, obtained primarily from heredity. People might fall short of their possibilities; they could never rise above them. The early test makers tried to measure that ultimate potential.

Because ultimate capacity is not open to direct measurement, those who made up intelligence tests had to find another way of estimating it. They did this by assuming that all people taking the test had had an equal opportunity to learn the material it contained. If everyone had an equal opportunity to learn the material, they reasoned, then those who did better must have already possessed greater innate capacity. Over the years we have come to understand that that basic assumption is rarely tenable. If behavior is truly a function of the private world of perceptions for each individual, there can never be common experience for any two persons, even in the same externally observed situation. Even in a family of identical twins, apparently treated identically, twin A's experience is largely created by twin B and twin B's is supplied by twin A!

A great deal of mischief has been done over the years through the misuse of intelligence tests. This is especially true when the tests have been used to label people or establish expectancy levels. We have already seen how important the self-concept is in determining a person's behavior. Labeling people, therefore, as "dull," "moron," "below average," "average," and the like, especially when such labels are backed up by the "scientific" tests of intelligence, can have devastating effects on the performance of those who come to believe them. Sometimes the results of intelligence tests assume a position of such unquestioning authority that schoolchildren are described as "overachievers," as though it were possible for a person to exceed his or her potential! It would be more accurate to describe such children as misjudged or underestimated. In a similar vein, counselors and administrators have been known to advise students and clients not to go to college or try some new experience because intelligence test results show "they would never make it." Such use of tests as infallible indicators of potential is unwarranted.

Intelligence tests measure the degree to which a person's cultural milieu fits the sampling of items selected by the test's constructors. If a person's life experience does not include the type of behavior demanded by the test, he probably will not do well. Yet the same person may behave "brilliantly" in a situation with which he is familiar. This is why so many minority group members and champions of lower socioeconomic groups argue so fervently against IQ tests. They state, and rightly so, that the experiences of these people are so different from the normalization samples of the test that their true ability is judged falsely. Typical middle-class children often do well on standardized tests, but how intelligently would they behave or how long would they last on the inner-city streets of New York, Chicago, or Los Angeles? The ability to survive and live effectively in the world is, after all, what intelligence is all about, and different worlds call for different kinds of knowledge and skills.

INTELLIGENCE AS MEDIATED EXPERIENCE

Reuven Feuerstein, a psychologist who is beginning to have a major influence on the way children are taught, believes that we have been terribly misled by the established ways we currently measure intelligence.[3] Feuerstein took up the task after World War II of psychologically evaluating children who were victims of the Holocaust. All these young people were quite limited in experience in the traditional sense. Many of them had been in concentration camps and had lost their parents.

Included in the tools Feuerstein used to evaluate these displaced youth were traditional intelligence tests. But he soon realized that these tests were useless for trying to ascertain the potential of this particular group. For one thing, a totally unacceptable proportion of the children were being identified as being retarded. This, Feuerstein could not accept, for intelligence was not the criteria the Nazis had used to select them for abuse, so there was no reason to believe that they were biased in the direction of being mentally handicapped. Second, he concluded that this group of children simply could not be evaluated by traditional measures of intelligence because of the basic assumption of those instruments. Measures based on the assumptions that intelligence is immutable and that the individuals being examined have had equal opportunity of experience had no relevance for a population that had spent much of their lives sleeping in doorways and fighting for survival in concentration camps.

Feuerstein decided at this point that instead of attempting to measure past learning and inferring ability, he ought to measure learning ability directly. As a result, he and his colleagues developed what they call the Learning Potential Assessment Device (LPAD), an evaluation procedure that bears little resemblance to previous measures of ability. Traditional IQ measures depend on experience and recall. The LPAD does not. Instead of an examination process, it is conducted more like a tutorial session in which the subjects are taught various skills and attention is paid to how well and how quickly an examinee learns. During the administration of traditional IQ tests the examiner offers no hints, no explanations, no feedback. The purpose of the test is to find out what a child already knows. The purpose behind the LPAD is to find out what a child can learn. Consequently, the "examiner" constantly intervenes. During the administration of an LPAD, explanations are required and given, experiences are summed up, and the examiner asks for repetition, anticipates difficulties, and warns the child about them. And it is believed that the process itself creates reflective, insightful thinking.

Turning to this new approach, Feuerstein began to get a different picture of his refugee population. Children who had previously manifested a marked ignorance of facts proved that they could acquire them. Those who showed little or no grasp of even basic concepts, such as right and left, mastered them. Children who were originally unable to reason abstractly began to do so. The dramatically different pictures painted of his youngsters by traditional measures of intelligence and by the LPAD eventually led Feuerstein to develop a construct he terms *mediated experience*.

Essentially, he sees two kinds of experience: direct and mediated. Direct experience is of a spontaneous nature, the kind of ordinary interaction we all have with our environment. Although useful, the benefit derived from such experience is circumstantial, chancy, and of limited value in the acquisition of mental skills. What's important is mediated experience.

In mediated experience a more knowledgeable individual intervenes between a learner and his or her environment. The situation is transformed, reordered, organized, and grouped, and the stimuli are framed in the direction of some specified goal or purpose by the mediator. Any experience is mediated when someone intervenes to order and clarify it.

Feuerstein believes that too few mediated experiences lead to poor thinking skills, which, in turn, reduce the individual's ability to learn from further experience. *However, this is a reversible process.* Feuerstein further believes that traditional IQ measures involve only the evaluation of direct experience and therefore give us a distorted picture of one's true capabilities and the limits of what we can do in the process of teaching and learning.

Feuerstein's view of intelligence gives us a completely different view of human potential, a view in concert with that supported in this chapter. He believes that intelligence is a soft plastic that can be shaped at will and that subnormal intelligence, as measured by any technique, can be improved. Furthermore, he believes that many people with IQs of 80, 60, or even as low as 40, with proper mediation, can be assisted to perform at normal, or even above average, levels. And he thinks he has proven this! He has developed remedial training procedures for people who initially tested as having low IQs that he calls Instrumental Enrichment programs and points out that many of his students have gone on to become teachers, school principals, professors, executives, and government officials.

Anything Left?

Have we been trying to say that traditional measures of intelligence are worthless? No, not at all. But we have been trying to dispel the notions that intelligence is immutable and that there is no help for those who score at the lower ends of the intellectual continuum. Scarr and Weinberg, after reviewing some of the literature on the subject, say that "genes do not fit behavior; rather, they establish a range of possible reactions to the range of possible experiences that the environment provides," and that "how people behave or what their I.Q.'s turn out to be depends on the quality of their environments and on the genetic endowments they have at birth."[4]

As tests of achievement, IQ measures can locate a person with respect to a given body of information. In the degree to which they have been carefully constructed, they can also give us an indication of a person's current level of functioning. That, of course, is valuable information. The use of intelligence tests as indicators of what a person can or will do in the future, however, is highly questionable. We would rather dwell on the idea of intelligence as a functional capacity as it is seen by Feuerstein, Scarr, Weinberg, and these authors.

SOME PARTICULARS OF FUNCTIONAL INTELLIGENCE

Given a reasonably adequate physiology to start with, the capacity for intelligent behavior depends on two things: the meanings a person possesses and her freedom to use them. How intelligently a person can behave at any moment depends on the richness, extent, and availability of meanings in her perceptual field. This is to say that the capacity to behave effectively and efficiently requires, in the first place, that a person possess the necessary or appropriate meanings for the situation that confronts her. The richer the field of meanings, the greater the potential for effective behavior. But mere possession of a rich and extensive perceptual field is not enough. It is also necessary that meanings be available for use when they are needed.

In earlier chapters we discussed the effect of need, self-concept, and the existing field of meanings on the determination of behavior, and so on intelligence. But other factors must be added.

Physical Condition

The acuity of sight, hearing, touch, smell, and taste certainly affect the nature of a person's experience. These senses are our "windows on the world" through which interaction occurs. The physical vehicle we ride around in also has its effect through the feedback it produces in the reactions of other people. The experiences of a beautiful young woman are different from those of her less attractive sisters. Similarly, the physical prowess that makes a young man a football hero may bring him vastly different meanings than those he might have had without his magnificent physical condition. Feedback of a less happy nature is received by adolescents with acne or by handicapped persons. Their physical conditions may impede full participation in the life around them and may distort others' reactions to them.

Whatever reduces body vigor may also impair the possibilities of experience. Because a sick or lethargic child does not get involved in school or in play with his peers, the meanings he develops may be limited. Almost everyone has had the experience of feeling "too tired to care" or so ill that all one wanted to do was sleep. So almost anything that reduces the body's readiness and capability for involvement may reduce experience. Reducers may include such things as malnutrition, focal infections, glandular disturbances, injuries, and the like. Some people with severe impediments manage to develop great breadth and depth in their field of meanings despite physiological limitations. Conceivably, some handicaps might enrich a person's field of meanings, making him or her more accomplished in some ways than more fortunate humans, such as Beethoven's playing and writing music, the accomplishments of Helen Keller, and a man with one hand and only half a foot setting a record for the longest field goal in the history of professional football.

Time

Developing a field of meanings takes time. People need to have lived long enough to have had some kinds of experiences, especially those that are dependent in sequential fashion on earlier ones. Despite the doubts of young people, there really is some advantage in experience. The mere fact of living longer means more possibilities for experience but does not guarantee them. Existing meanings may restrict further possibilities for perceiving. This often happens when older people become unable to accept new meanings.

The authors are also aware that some people can be so closed to experience that they fail to benefit from it and others, so open that they get much more out of each experience than most people do. Thus we have some twenty-year-olds who are more mature and wiser than people in their forties and fifties. We also know that it is possible for a person to live through what should have been a significant experience and not benefit from or even understand it.

But age is hardly the handicap we once thought it to be. Because people are living longer and the older population is growing rapidly, scientists of every kind have begun to direct more of their attention to this group of individuals. As a result, our ideas about them are changing tremendously.

Not long ago most people believed that getting older meant decreasing intellectual ability, almost complete loss of meaningful physical capacity, and destitute loneliness, to name only a few of the specters considered inevitable for those "passing their prime." Not so says Joann Ellison Rodgers. In an article examining the most recent data on aging, she states that researchers are challenging traditional views with tough new studies, and if "what they are now reporting continues to be confirmed, this much is for sure: there's a lot of untapped middle-aged brain power out there and a lot less for all of us to be anxious about as we grow older."[5] Rodgers reports, as an example, on the conclusions of David Arenberg of the National Institute on Aging.[6] Dr. Arenberg says that if the adage "you can't teach an old dog new tricks" wasn't dead and buried before, the research reports since 1960 "should complete the interment." The essential message, he continues, is "that normal aging does not include gross intellectual impairment, confusion, depression, hallucinations, or delusions. We will shout, as loudly as we can, that fears of becoming 'senile' in old age are based largely on myths."[7]

The status of loneliness with regard to older citizens may surprise you even more. After studying loneliness in general, Carin Rubinstein and others report that, on the average, older people are actually less lonely than younger folks.[8] Although more old people than young live alone, and although older people see their friends less often, they are more satisfied with their friendships, have higher self-esteem, and feel more independent than their more youthful counterparts. Thus the relationship between age and intelligence is not a question of how old one is; it is a matter of what has been the nature of one's experience and what condition one is in at any age.

Opportunity

People's meanings are affected by every aspect of their environment, particularly by those with whom they come in contact. Meanings for people in the North and South are by no means the same. People who live near an ocean or in the mountains, the plains, the valleys, the desert, or the woods have different kinds of experiences and different kinds of meanings as a consequence. Such interactions with the world and the people in it create private worlds of meaning and feeling and determine the intelligence with which each person may operate. The effect of opportunity on personal meaning begins at birth and continues as long as a person lives. Because of the selective effect of existing meanings on subsequent ones, the earliest development of meanings is particularly crucial for development of intelligence.

Many children in our society are raised in poverty-stricken areas, where there is little opportunity to broaden experience beyond the deadly, daily grind of keeping body and soul together. These children have no opportunity to experience even the most common events in the lives of others, like seeing a cow, using a telephone, learning to swim, riding a bicycle, writing a letter, or counting money. They are our equivalent to the kinds of children Feuerstein worked with. They grow up with restricted meanings and often are inadequately prepared to cope with the world in which they have to live. This can result in a vicious circle that continually corroborates itself. Because they are ignorant, they cannot cope with life. Because they cannot cope, they continue to be deprived and produce for their children, in turn, the same dreary existence that so warped them in the first place. With a new awakening of conscience, we are beginning to find ways of breaking into this vicious cycle. Federal, state, and privately supported programs designed to fight poverty, improve education, provide employment, and eliminate prejudice are increasingly being instituted to enrich the lives of children caught in such traps. In doing so we are also increasing the capacity of children for more intelligent and efficient behavior in the future. Without opportunity, meanings may be restricted or distorted so that effective behavior becomes nearly impossible. The principle is nicely illustrated in the report of a colleague about his experience working with children from upper-middle-class homes compared with those from slum areas. One of the problems he presented to these children went as follows: "You are all alone in an empty room of a deserted house. Up against the ceiling, out of your reach, is a balloon with a ten-dollar bill attached to it. How would you get it down?" Many of the children from upper-middle-class homes had difficulty finding a solution to the problem and gave up. Children from slum neighborhoods, on the other hand, frequently solved the problem with great dispatch. "I'd break the window," they said, "and throw the glass at the balloon!" For these children, windows were not inviolate; they were something to be broken if need be. For the upper-middle-class children, windows had a different meaning, which made them unavailable for solving the problem.

SOME IMPLICATIONS FOR
THE HELPING PROFESSIONS

Variations in the breadth and depth of meanings that people possess fluctuate widely. At one end of the scale is the severely mentally retarded patient who spends his life in the fetal position in which he was born. Further up the scale are those who are able to "get by." That in itself is no mean feat in today's world. The richness and extent of meanings needed just to navigate safely in a large city, for example, are considerable. Most people, fortunately, manage to develop meanings that take them far beyond such minimal levels, and some, like our most gifted citizens, become truly remarkable. The perceptual fields of some people become more fertile and extensive throughout their lives. For others, unhappily, the fields of meaning may become less rich with time.

The importance of the new conceptions about human capacity can hardly be overestimated. The world can never be the same for having come to understand the plasticity of intelligence. For many years athletes believed that the four-minute mile was impossible until Roger Bannister showed it could be done. Since then, what previously had been considered impossible has been repeated by dozens of others. With the shackles off our conceptions of human potential the way is open for undreamed of heights of human achievement.

A Personal Checklist

A glance back to the determiners of effective behavior that we have been discussing will make it clear that all except one (time) are open to considerable change. The rest of the specifics, however—the physical organism, opportunity, need, self-concept, goals and values, and the nature of the current field—lend themselves to manipulation. This means intelligence can be molded, and these are some variables through which it can be accomplished. They are also the factors through which helpers may contribute effectively to the growth and fulfillment of clients, students, or patients. By converting factors that determine intelligence into questions for selecting practice, helpers may discover more effective ways of operating in their respective relationships. Here are a few examples:

1. *Physical condition*   What can I do to assist my helpees toward maximum health and vigor?
2. *Opportunity*   What kind of environments can I create to provide my students, clients, or patients with rich extensive fields of meaning? What can I do to mediate experience?
3. *Need*   Can I help my clients achieve more satisfying fulfillment of the basic need for self-actualization? What can be done to help them feel more adequate and less deprived?
4. *Self-concept*   What can I do to help my clients feel more positive about themselves?
5. *Goals and values*   How can I help my clients or students explore and discover new values and goals?
6. *Effects of threat*   What can I do to free my clientele from inhibiting effects of threat on their experience?

A systematic search for answers to questions like these may provide important clues to what helpers can do to free human potential and assist their clients toward greater personal fulfillment.

Keeping Perspective

Knowing that capacity can be created does not mean it can be done quickly or easily. A child who is growing up with a restricting self-concept is as severely limited as if he were born that way. We have also seen that, once established, the self-concept tends to resist change, and the circular effect it exerts on selection of perceptions causes it to corroborate itself. Similarly, inadequate physical bodies, impoverished environments, lack of opportunities, inhibiting goals and values, or the effects of threat on perception can all produce seriously limiting effects on intelligence. What is more, these limitations may be so difficult to eliminate that people do not have the time, energy, or economic wherewithal to deal with them. There are, indeed, limits on the growth of intelligence, and functional limits can be as formidable as hereditary ones. They have the advantage, however, that in being functional there is something we can do about them.

A great deal of difference exists between approaching a job believing that it is only a holding operation with little or no likelihood of success or believing that it offers vast possibilities. For generations many teachers believed that they could do little to increase a child's capacities. The beliefs they had about the children they worked with severely limited their expectations both for the children and for themselves. All too often both parties fulfilled those expectations. A point of view about human capacities that places many of the determiners within helpers' hands, therefore, opens whole new vistas. Helpers can approach their jobs with hope and can rest assured that what they do is significant. This knowledge can provide great challenge and satisfaction. It can also be deeply threatening. It means that failures cannot be blithely charged to heredity or God's will. To this point we still do not know the ultimate levels to which intelligence can grow. Whatever those limits are, the attainment of them will be brought about through learning how to deal with the determiners of behavior listed earlier and such others as we may yet discover. We are still a long way from knowing how to create intelligence with skill and certainty, but we can do much with what we already know. A great deal more research is necessary to help us better understand those determiners and to find effective ways of putting that knowledge to work.

One place we can look for clues to that research is in the lives of gifted people. We have been accustomed to looking at such people as happy accidents of heredity. If it is true that intelligence can be created, however, these are no happy accidents. Rather, they represent our crowning achievement— the people with whom we have already been especially successful! Our problem is not to find and coddle them. We need to find out how we produced them so that we can set about producing many more of them as rapidly as we can!

Notes and References

1. A. Binet, *Les Idées Modernes sur les Enfants* (Paris: Ernest Flam Marion, 1909), pp. 54–55.
2. J. McV. Hunt, *Intelligence and Experience* (New York: Ronald Press Co., 1961), p. 346.
3. P. Chance, "The Remedial Thinker," *Psychology Today* 15 (October 1981):62–73.
4. S. Scarr and R. Weinberg, "Attitudes, Interests, and I.Q.," in T. H. Carr and H. E. Fitzgerald, eds., *Psychology 82/83* (Guilford, Conn.: Dushkin, 1982), pp. 168–174.
5. J. E. Rodgers, "Our Insatiable Brain," in Carr and Fitzgerald, *Psychology 82/83*, pp. 111–113.
6. Ibid.
7. Ibid.
8. Carin Rubinstein et al., "Loneliness," in N. Jackson, ed., *Personal Growth 82/83* (Guilford, Conn.: Dushkin, 1982), pp. 151–157.

TEN

EMPATHY: ESSENTIAL SKILL OF HELPING

Helper sensitivity is so important for the helping process that Carl Rogers named the quality of empathy first among his three "necessary and sufficient conditions" for effective helping relationships: empathy, congruence, and positive regard. The crucial character of sensitivity in the helping process has also been demonstrated in a series of research studies with helpers like counselors, teachers, and pastors.[1] Such studies show that effective helpers are characteristically sensitive to the ways their helpees are seeing themselves and the world in the moment-to-moment encounters of helping. Ineffective helpers are more concerned with how things look to themselves than with how things look to their clients or students.

In an earlier chapter we observed that the dynamics of helping can be understood only in terms of the helper's goals and the helpee's perceptions. These perceptions are the primary data for understanding the helpee's world. Such data are equally important for the helper's own behavior and provide feedback by which to judge the effects of the things the helper does or says in the process of helping. What a helper intended, after all, is irrelevant and immaterial if the client did not perceive it so. To monitor his or her own activities and provide the data for further decisions, the helper needs accurate conceptions of the ways his or her clients are thinking, feeling, and perceiving themselves and their worlds.

DEVELOPING SENSITIVITY

Everyone has some measure of sensitivity to other people. Without this, no one could exist for very long in modern interdependent society. Some people develop high degrees of empathy as a normal part of their growing up. Others have to sharpen their capacities, by accident or by design, in the course of training or experience in the professions. Either way, the development of sensitivity is essential for effective use of the helper's self.

The development of sensitivity does not require learning a new skill. Most of us are already sensitive to those who are important to us. Even little children are keenly aware of the feelings and attitudes of the adults who surround them and may be heard warning one another: "Watch out for Daddy!

He's angry!" For little children, sensitivity is a matter of survival. On the way from childhood to maturity, however, most of us discover that it is not necessary to be sensitive to everyone, only to those who have important roles with respect to us. So we continue to be sensitive to our sweethearts, our bosses, our supervisors, and those who are in positions to help us or harm us. Conversely, we may lose sensitivity for the feelings of those who are less important or subservient to us. Learning to be more sensitive is not a question of learning something new; it is a matter of learning to do explicitly and frequently what we naturally do implicitly and occasionally. This seems easy enough. All one needs to do is decide what is really important and then go ahead and do it. Unfortunately, it is not that simple.

Believing Sensitivity Is Important

Obvious things are often the most difficult to perceive. We do not lack for data about people and their behavior. We are immersed in such data every hour of our experience. We need but open our eyes to see and our ears to hear, and others will be willing and eager to impress on us their personal interpretations of people and the world. We are surrounded by people who are clamoring to be heard, often desperately seeking to be understood. But what we see and hear largely depends on what we believe is important.

One can live in the middle of events and never know they exist until they are brought into figure by a change in need. One can drive past a house a hundred times and never really see it until one needs to call on someone who lives in it. The teacher who is preoccupied with "getting the lesson across" may miss completely what her students are really comprehending. For many years one of the authors had passed through the Grand Concourse of Grand Central Station in New York City several times a day. Then, one evening at Christmastime, while standing in line for tickets, he became aware of an Englishman just in front of him. The man, apparently newly arrived in the United States, stood entranced, looking up at the ceiling and murmuring, "Incredible, simply incredible! Magnificent!" At this the author looked up too and discovered to his astonishment that indeed it was incredible. He was looking at the beautiful ceiling for the very first time! Perception is a selective process. What is perceived depends on the need of the observer. Unless it seems important to understand someone, it is practically certain he will not be understood. In order to develop sensitivity it is necessary to want to.

The way things seem to each individual has such a complete feeling of reality that one seldom questions it. Because one's own experience seems so right and so real, it is difficult to understand the world of another without making an effort. It is even more difficult when another person's reality seems contrary to one's own. Then one is faced with the distasteful possibility of being wrong. The development of sensitivity requires an understanding of this characteristic of one's perceptions and a willingness to accept the reality of another's perceptions as real *for him.* For example, one day when one of the authors was visiting a ward in a mental hospital a patient tore open his shirt and rushed up to the author. In obvious pain the patient exclaimed, "Doctor, there are fourteen devils on my chest! They are stabbing me with spears! See them?" Of course, the author did not see them, but it was clear the patient felt them. The author replied, "No, Joe, I don't, but I can see that you feel them. I am sorry about that." Had the author scoffed at the devils the patient saw and felt, he would have demonstrated how little he understood. By being willing to accept the patient's reality as real for him, the doors of communication were kept open and it was possible to maintain the rapport necessary for long hours of further discussion. It is not necessary to give up one's own reality to understand that of another. What is required is a willingness to recognize that someone else's ways of perceiving are equally real to him.

Reading Behavior Backward

Basically, developing sensitivity is a matter of learning to read behavior backward. When we see a child drink we can infer that he was thirsty. When we see a player duck the ball thrown at her we can infer that she was afraid it was going to hit her. If a person's behavior is a function of perceptions, it follows that if we observe behavior carefully, it should be possible to reconstruct the feelings, attitudes, and purposes in the perceptual field of the behaver that produced the acts we observed.

"Getting the feel" of other people in this fashion is something that everyone does automatically. The teacher, for example, observes a child who is not reading well. As he watches her, he asks: "Now what is her trouble? How is she seeing what she is doing?" He formulates inferences as he makes observations. "Does she understand the sound?" he wonders and then tests this hypothesis by further observing the child's behavior in reading various materials selected to test that hypothesis. As a result, he may decide that she does hear the sound. If so, he makes a new hypothesis: "Maybe she is not distinguishing between *a* and *o*, *t* and *th*." Then he tests this hypothesis, perhaps through the use of diagnostic tests. By such a process of observation, inference, and test he arrives at an understanding of how things are with the child, and he may then be in a position to help her perceive more adequately in the future.

Can Inference Be Scientific?

Some objective psychologists take exception to the use of inference as a technique for understanding behavior. They think it is too subjective, too open to possibilities of error and distortion introduced by the person doing the observing. Their concern is certainly a valid one. The use of self as an instrument for making observations does indeed add a possible source of distortion not present in more mechanical ways of observing and recording behavior. This does not warrant rejection of the method, however, if the sources of error can be controlled.

All sciences depend on the making and testing of hypotheses. To control the accuracy of this process, scientists have invented tests of validity to be applied to the testing of hypotheses as follows:

1. Does the hypothesis seem reasonable and accurate to the possessor?
2. Is the hypothesis consistent with all the known facts? Does it fit? Does it provide an adequate explanation of all the data?
3. Will it stand the test of mental juggling? Will it still ring true when confronted intellectually and subjected to the impact of other concepts, explanations, or suppositions?
4. Can it be used to predict? Using the hypothesis to make predictions, will these predictions be borne out in fact?
5. Is the hypothesis acceptable to other workers, especially recognized experts? Have other people independently reached the same conclusions?
6. Is the hypothesis internally consistent? Does the hypothesis stand up when various interpretations are made to confront one another?

The products of all the sciences (including the physical ones that we customarily regard as the essence of accuracy and precision), in the final analysis, depend on one or more of these tests in establishing what is "fact." These tests may be used to determine the acceptability of inferences about human behavior in the same fashion as the astronomer tests his inferences about a new galaxy or the physicist tests her inference about some new theory. The making of inferences in itself is not unscientific. Every science, including the science of people, depends on inference to extend its horizons beyond the immediate and the palpable. To reject the use of inference would seriously hamper any attempts to understand people. The problem is not to reject this valuable tool but to learn to use it properly.

Learning to Listen

For most people, real listening is a seldom used art. The purpose of much conversation is not to hear what the other person has to say but to enjoy the opportunity to express one's self. Eavesdropping on the conversation at a tea or cocktail party or the casual conversation on the street quickly reveals that no one is really listening. The speakers are amusing themselves while the audience patiently, or not so patiently, waits to get the floor to tell about their operations or trips to San Francisco.

The kind of listening required for effective helping is much more than mere attention to words. It is an active search for meaning and calls for sharply focused attention and interest. Such "listening with the third ear" involves attending to all that the client, student, or patient is expressing—not just verbally but nonverbally as well—in gestures, movements, inflections, even to what is not specifically said. Carl Rogers has called the disciplined listening of helpers "non-evaluative listening."[2] By this he means a reading of the whole person, an attempt to understand the nature of the helpee without the distortion of the helper's own judgments, preconceptions, or values.

People are always telling us how things are with them through the ways in which they behave. Psychologists have learned to use play, for example, both as a diagnostic device to explore how children are thinking and feeling and as treatment in helping them change their perceptions of themselves and the world. One need not be a mind reader to get the message about how a child feels as one watches him lambaste the "baby brother" doll or flush a drawing of his teacher down the toilet! The behavior of adults is also revealing. Most of us soon know what to expect from friends, neighbors, bosses, or enemies as we have opportunities to observe them in action.

Philip Jackson, in an interview study with teachers, reports how teachers use fleeting behavioral cues to tell how well they are doing on their jobs.[3] Here are a few excerpts from those interviews:

Interviewer*:   How can you tell when you are doing a good job?

Teacher: Oh, look at their faces.

Interviewer: Will you tell me more about that?

Teacher: Why, sure, they look alert; they look interested; they look questioning—like they're ready to question something. They look like they're anxious to learn more about it. . . . At other times, you know you haven't done a good job when they look blah or look disinterested or I-don't-care attitude, well, then I feel bad, you know, I've done a bad job.

Another teacher says:

The reaction, I think, of the children, and what they seem to have gained from it. Their interest; their expression; the way they look.

Still another says:

I can tell by the way they sound. There is a sound that you can tell and you can tell when they are really working.

Interviewer: You mean the sound of the room in general?

Teacher: The sound of the room in general. Now it doesn't always have to be a quiet sound—it can be a noisy, buzzing sound, and you're still doing a good job and everybody is working.

---

*From *Life in Classrooms* by Philip W. Jackson. Copyright © 1968 by Holt, Rinehart and Winston. Reprinted by permission of Holt, Rinehart and Winston, CBS College Publishing.

Interviewer: But can you tell?

Teacher: I can tell. You can feel it.

And still another says:

> It's the easiest thing in the world. You know you're missing
> at the first yawn. Teaching and learning, if they're not enjoy-
> able and fun, are both very difficult to accomplish. When the
> kids aren't having a good time, if they're not paying attention
> and sitting up, that's it—a theatrical sense is something you
> can't learn, but a good actor can sense his audience. He
> knows when a performance is going well or not going well,
> simply by the feeling in the air. And it's that way in the class-
> room. You can feel when the kids are resistant.

The Listening Game

One technique devised by counselors for teaching beginners to listen is
called the Listening Game, which you might like to try. In a group session all
the participants agree that no one may speak until he or she has first stated
the gist of what the previous speaker had to say, in a fashion satisfactory to
the previous speaker. It is fascinating how the application of this rule slows
down the conversation! Most people playing this game quickly discover that
listening is indeed a difficult art, and they are chagrined to discover how little
they normally hear of what is being expressed by those around them. The
discipline of paying close attention and seeing through another's eyes can
greatly improve the helper's capacity for empathy.

Attending to Meanings

Developing sensitivity is a matter of listening to *meanings* as well as observing behavior. Every behavior is in some measure expressive of perceptions, but behaviors resulting from strong feelings are almost impossible to
dissemble. The very attempts that others make to hide their feelings only
serve to reveal them more. Like the comment by Hamlet's mother, "The lady
doth protest too much methinks," our suspicions are aroused by overdone
behavior. A counseling client of one of the authors once said it this way:
"Sometimes when I am talking to you I try to keep you from really knowing.
I act like a mother bird defending her nest by pretending she has a broken
wing to lead you away from what I don't want you to see. But you know; you
always know."

Concentration of attention on the person's meaning is characteristic of
effective helpers in all branches of the helping professions. It is a widely used
technique in counseling and psychotherapy, in social work, in pastoral
counseling, and in the interactions of group leaders with members in a wide

variety of group experiences. One can hear it used by the teacher who says, "Jimmy, I can see you are very angry at Paul. I can understand that, but you must not hit him with the shovel"; or by the nurse who says to her patient, "I realize you are not sure you can do it, Mrs. Smith. I know it will not be easy for you." Some authors[4] have also tried to make this kind of listening, so valuable to counselors and therapists, available to wider audiences of teachers, parents, and those in various administrative or leadership roles in business and industry by developing specialized training programs designed to teach parents, teachers, and others the techniques of listening to personal meanings.

Listening Is Therapeutic

The importance of listening extends far beyond its value for understanding other people. The act of listening itself conveys important messages to others. The careful listener is paying others the highest form of compliment. She is saying in effect, "You are a truly significant person to me and what you are saying is important." So also the teacher listening to a student may be conveying, "I really care about you and what you think and believe." Such a message is an active, living demonstration, which may speak loudly and clearly to students, clients, or patients. In the case of unhappy or maladjusted people with deep feelings of deprivation and alienation, being really listened to is much more than communication; it is a therapeutic experience.

Growth may be facilitated by a sympathetic listener even if she does little else. In this sense every human being who ever listened patiently to the problems of another is as much a helper at that moment as those who claim impressive titles by reason of position or academic degrees. One of the authors knew a woman whose life experience clearly demonstrated the significant role of the sympathetic listener. Most people who interacted with her came away from the experience feeling much better and looking much brighter. And almost without exception they would say something like, "Oh, what a fine person she is! She's one of the most interesting people I have ever talked with. I could talk to her all day!" From these comments one would think she must have been a dynamic person. As a matter of fact, she was never directly responsible for more than five to ten percent of the conversations she engaged in. She was actually shy and retiring, albeit most sensitive and empathic.

Reading Programs

A reading program can be one valuable source for developing sensitivity. Anything that provides insight into the nature of people and their problems, hopes, and desires may contribute greatly to the development of sensitivity, either as general background for interpretation or, more directly, as participation in human experience. In this connection one naturally thinks of professional and scientific literature about the social sciences; these materials are invaluable for those working in the helping professions. Out of such reading helpers may acquire the setting or backdrop against which the understanding of a particular individual may be seen with greater clarity. A program of reading in the social sciences, however, is by no means enough for those in the helping professions. Scientific material is usually objective and descriptive. It presents human beings as they are perceived by outside observers. Much of it is also couched in statistical or normative terms that are descriptive of populations rather than individuals. People engaged in the helping professions, therefore, must usually acquire subjective understanding from other sources or from their own experiences.

A fruitful source of subjective understanding of other people is to be found in nonscientific literature. It has often been said that the best psychologists are poets and novelists, and in a very real sense this is true. Although scientists are highly skilled in providing understanding of people in normative terms, poets and novelists are far superior in helping us grasp the essential humanity of people. Drama, poetry, autobiography, and novels can expand our experience vicariously. We can enter the world of seeing, feeling, believing, hoping, trusting, caring, loving, and hating as these are experienced by others. As we give ourselves up to the spell woven by these kinds of writers, we can be for a time what we are not, never have been, or perhaps never could be. With James Agee we can experience "A Death in the Family," even if we have never had one. With Malcolm X we can feel something of what it is like to be black and to grow up in the slums of a city. Through literature we can experience the frustrations and power of being a president, the growth of intelligence with Helen Keller, or the pitiful searching of Freddie Prinze. The understanding, empathy, and capacity for a deep sympathetic identification with others, which the poet, dramatist, and novelist put down on paper, are the same qualities that people in the helping professions must actively put to work in carrying out their respective functions.

Believe it or not, on occasion even the great wasteland—TV—can be a source of insight. One of the authors regularly watches a game show, and his friends kid him about it. He just mumbles something to the effect that part of his personality hasn't reached puberty yet. The show is called "Family Feud." The producers of the show have random samples taken of people's answers to various questions. For example, "Why is divorce harder than marriage?" or "What is the most popular car in America today?" Two groups of related individuals are then matched on the show. The family whose answers most closely match those given by the people in the random survey, wins. Pretty mundane, simple-minded stuff, right? Probably, but the author believes that by paying attention to the answers given, one can gain some useful insight into current social values and concerns. One question/answer combination was particularly revealing. The question was, "What are some of the hardest things to say to another person?" The top three answers were (1) "I love you," (2) "I'm sorry," and (3) "I'm wrong." No wonder so much conflict exists in our society! Those three phrases can end hostility quicker than any others in the English language, yet people find them the most difficult to express.

At least one writer, Anne Kilguss, even finds soap operas to be a source for increasing sensitivity and an aid to solving personal problems.[5] She says that they can be therapeutic, for they give viewers an opportunity to try on new identities and work out personal conflicts. Sources for increasing empathy are wherever you find them!

Observing

A good deal of sensitivity can also be acquired by looking receptively. The choices people make are not haphazard. They have meaning. The kind of cars people drive, the sort of houses they build, the care they give their yards, the clothes they wear, and the pictures they paint all have something to say about them. What is observed when watching others also depends on the intent of the observer. What is seen is likely to be what one expects or is prepared to see. Idly watching, one may see almost nothing. If observation is to be used for increased sensitivity, it must be directed beyond surface manifestations to the nature of personal meaning behind the behavior observed.

Every science must begin its work from disciplined observation, and most training programs for the helping professions include extensive practice in observing. The approach to making observations advocated by these programs depends on the general frame of reference stressed by the trainers. Those operating from an objective orientation emphasize careful reporting of precisely what was done by the subject. Here, for example, is part of a report made by a young social worker:

> TIME: 3:30 P.M., January 4, 1983
> PLACE: Third Avenue Playground
> When I arrived, Mr. Albert pointed out Jimmy Christianson to me. He is ten years old but seems small for his age. He was dressed in blue jeans, sneakers, and an old brown zipper jacket with a big tear under the left arm. He was sitting on the bench along the first base line with four other boys waiting his turn to go to bat. Jimmy kept swinging his feet back and forth and gripping the bench with his two hands as he did so. He seemed pretty excited about the game and kept yelling, "Sock it to 'em, Eddie! Attaboy!" to the boy up at the bat. Every once in a while he would turn and say something to one of his bench mates but I could not hear what it was he said. Once, when Eddie swung and missed, Jimmy groaned and hid his face in the back of the boy next to him. Then he picked up his first baseman's glove, pounded his fist in it and yelled, "That's O.K., Eddie! Let 'em have it!"

The purpose of such detailed reporting is to teach the beginner to make careful observations and to see what is going on with a minimum of distortion. Observations made with such care and detail are usually more valuable for the discipline they demand of the learner than for improving the capacity for empathy, because they concentrate the observer's attention on behavior rather than on the internal conditions producing behavior.

More often the helper will need to make observations from a subjective frame of reference. By operating in this way helpers are less concerned about recording details and devote attention to those aspects of special significance in understanding the behavior of the subject from his or her own point of view. It involves steeping one's self in the experience and making and re-making hypotheses consistent with the behavior observed. In this fashion the helper seeks to understand the ways in which the subject sees self and the peculiar searching and strivings that motivate him. Here is a sample from the report of a beginning teacher:

> When I arrived at Miss Anthony's class on Tuesday, the children were in the middle of a project running a store. Leslie was in a group of three who were supposed to be making a big sign for the store front. They had a large sheet of paper on the floor and were drawing on it with crayons. Like his behavior on the playground yesterday, Leslie was very bossy, continually telling the other two children what to do, how to do it, and constantly criticizing them. He seems to need to be always the center of attention. It's as though, for him, imposing his will on the other children is far more important than the production they are working on. When the teacher came close at one point he ran to her and pulled her by the hand to come see their sign, but even as he did so, he managed to stand directly in front of the other two kids so they were pretty effectively blocked off from the teacher. From the look on his face you could see he was eating up every word of praise the teacher said like it was "manna from heaven." He seems to have a terrible need for attention at all times. Even the way he poises his body seems to be saying, "Please, please, please look at me! Give me! Pay attention to me!"

THE USE OF SELF IN EMPATHY

Properly used, one's own experience may be very helpful in understanding others; improperly used, it may lead one badly astray. Scientists in all fields must calibrate their instruments to assure the most accurate measurements possible. They adjust their voltmeters to zero before reading the strength of the current and carefully balance their scales before using them to weigh things. In similar fashion the human instrument can be calibrated to provide increasingly accurate inferences about what goes on in people. It is a matter of choosing a reliable instrument to start with and using it thereafter with care and discipline to assure trustworthy and reliable readings.

Using Experience as Data

The most obvious source of information for the making of inferences is our own experience. We each have been intimately involved in the growth and development of at least one person. This is important data, and its proper use can add immeasurably to our understanding of others. Even the suffering we have endured can help us understand and sympathize with others who suffer. This effect, however, is not automatic. One can observe in the lives of friends and acquaintances how hardship, isolation, or tragedy have made some people angry, hostile, and closed off from others, whereas other people seem to have become increasingly warm, gentle, and understanding as a consequence of what they have been through. What seems to make the difference is the individual's ability to accept or be open to experience. Those who have been deeply hurt often build walls around themselves for self protection. Such walls protect individuals from interaction with others but, unfortunately, also prevent getting through to them.

Intimate experiences wherein one has an opportunity to communicate with others deeply and meaningfully, add much to the capacity of an individual to act sympathetically with others. These experiences provide the raw material from which understanding is built. Research evidence shows that people who have not been loved are incapable of loving and that acceptance of others is related to acceptance of self. Apparently, one needs to have experienced a feeling in order to be able to truly grasp its meaning for another. This does not mean that it is necessary to have experienced the same event that another person has. That, of course, is impossible. What *can* be experienced are the meanings of events, feelings, attitudes, beliefs, or understandings. Because the authors are males, they cannot experience childbirth. They can and have, however, experienced with their wives the joys, anxieties, fears, and fulfillment of childbirth, to say nothing of their common experience of the problems of parenthood.

It is probable that any peak experience in which one is living and participating "to the hilt" contributes something significant to one's capacity to interact with life and with others. Having felt the glory of a sunset, one can know much better what it means to another. Winning, losing, loving, hating, suffering disillusionment, or triumphing over adversity—these qualities of living can make one more alive. Intimate experiences wherein one is able to communicate heart to heart with another, for no matter how short a period, extend and increase one's capacity for understanding.

Postponing Personal Need

Developing sensitivity requires willingness to postpone immediate need satisfactions in the interests of another. This is often difficult. Our own ways of perceiving and thinking have such a feeling of "goodness" or "rightness" and the tendency to impose our own structure on events is so strong that a conscious effort is required to set them aside for even a little while. An outstanding teacher of our acquaintance once illustrated this. The evening before class she spent hours working out a new project. The next day she waited for an appropriate moment to tell her students about the exciting project she had worked out for them. They were busy and interested in what they were doing, and for a long time she had no opportunity to break in. Finally, she started telling them about the new project, but no one paid any heed! After several attempts to capture their attention, she said with some irritation, "I guess you just don't want to hear what I have arranged for you!" This brought no response. The students continued with the projects they were already engaged in except for one lad, who could always be counted on for some kind of comment. He replied, "Not today, Mrs. Smith." She told us some time later, "You know, I was really kind of hurt. I thought it was a wonderful idea and I had worked so hard getting it ready! Somehow, though, my good sense managed to prevail and I set my own idea aside for a later occasion." It often takes a real wrench to break loose from our own predilections to follow the thinking and needs of others.

Freud observed that we seldom recognize a problem in others that we have not wrestled with ourselves. Psychiatrists and clinical psychologists, presumably well trained in making careful diagnoses, have been known to describe their clients as having the psychiatrist's or psychologist's own problems. The personal discipline required for the development of sensitivity is greatly facilitated by the possession of a deep conviction that "I, too, could be wrong." Nothing gets in the way of empathy more than the bland assumption of infallibility. It is helpful to understand that there is literally nothing a person (including one's self) might not do if exposed to the right combination of unhappy circumstances. Uncomfortable as it may be, belief in one's own fallibility makes the development of empathy with others much easier.

Sensitivity to others is a difficult skill to display in the absence of positive personal satisfactions. The capacity to set one's own needs aside in the interest of someone else is a quality of people achieving some measure of self-actualization. Inadequate and threatened people must be so continuously on guard against the world that there is little time or inclination remaining to be concerned about others. Only a free self can give of itself. An important prerequisite for the development of sensitivity, therefore, is the opportunity for fulfilling experiences in the life of the helper.

Notes and References

1. See note 9 of Chapter Two.
2. C. R. Rogers, "The Characteristics of a Helping Relationship," *Personnel and Guidance Journal* 37 (1958):6–16.
3. P. W. Jackson, *Life in Classrooms* (New York: Holt, Rinehart and Winston, 1968).
4. For example, see H. G. Ginott, *Between Parent and Child* (New York: Macmillan, 1965) and T. Gordon, *Parent Effectiveness Training* (New York: Peter H. Wyden, 1970).
5. Anne F. Kilguss, "Using Soap Operas as a Therapeutic Tool," *Social Casework* 55 (November 1974):525–530.

ELEVEN

THE SIGNIFICANCE OF COMMUNICATION

Learning always has two aspects: exposure to new experience and the discovery of its meaning. The new experience may occur as a consequence of the interaction of a person with some aspect of the physical world. Of far more importance to most of us, however, are those experiences that occur as a result of trying to communicate with other people. Although everyone engages in these attempts with varying degrees of success, the processes of communication are especially important for the helping professions. They are the primary tools of the trade. What happens in the interactions of teacher and pupil, counselor and client, priest and parishioner, supervisor and worker depends largely on the communication skills of the helper.

COMMUNICATION: A FUNCTION OF COMMON MEANINGS

Communication is much more than a matter of words. The development of language is a great human accomplishment and facilitates more effective communication of meanings. But even as we admire this accomplishment, we must keep in mind that words are no more than symbols. In themselves, without their underlying meanings, they lack the impact to produce the changes in meanings necessary for modifications in behavior. We are all familiar with the fact that the behavior of many of our friends and acquaintances is often vastly different from the words they speak.

Communication is a function of common meanings, the overlapping of the perceptual fields of the communicator and the person who receives the communication. It is a matter of acquiring common "maps," so that the meaning existing for one person may exist for others as well. Successful communication depends only partly on what is said or happening outside the individual. More importantly, comprehension is determined by what goes on inside the person, in the peculiar world of meaning that makes up her or his perceptual fields.

When meanings overlap we have the feeling of understanding or of being understood. When meanings fail to overlap, communication breaks down and misunderstandings occur. A teachers' college dropped the designation "probationer" for students who were getting practical field experience when it discovered that some people in the communities the students served thought the students were just out of jail! Breakdowns are also amusingly illustrated in the faux pas that children make on test papers or in reporting their experiences. We are amused when a child tells us, "God's name is Harold," because in Sunday school he prayed, "Harold be Thy name." Or when he tells us he sang in church about "the consecrated cross-eyed bear!" Failures of common meanings that leave us standing on a freezing street corner for a half hour because the friend we were supposed to meet thought we said 2:45 instead of 2:15 are much less amusing. They can even be disastrous for the world when nations misunderstand one another so badly that they go to war.

What Is Communicated?

What is communicated is not what is intended but what is comprehended. Here, for example, is what one child comprehended from the Pledge of Allegiance. When asked to explain the pledge word by word, it came out something like this:

"I give a lot of money to the old soldiers for the flag of the United States and the flag holder on which it stands, one country under God, that you can't take apart, where you do as you please—just you and me and for everybody else!"

The fact that words do not mean the same things to all people is a common observation. This fact is so important in human affairs as to have resulted in the science of semantics, which was developed to provide us with a better understanding of the importance and use of words. A well-known semanticist, S. I. Hayakawa,[1] points out that words differ not only in the *content* of their meaning but also in their accompanying *emotional impact.* Such words as pretty and ugly not only describe an objective quality of appearance, but they also carry connotations of goodness or badness, of attraction or repulsion. Descriptive words like Democrat and Republican are always associated with shades of feeling, which are likely to be far more important than the factual circumstances they describe. Even the simplest words we use in daily life have emotional attachments, especially when the words are concerned with belief, values, attitudes, or feelings. The meanings attached to words do not remain static; they shift with changing times and places. The connotations of words like moon, grass, gay, and black are notorious examples of how word meanings have changed.

To be unaware of changes in meanings can create serious misunderstandings. One of us witnessed a heated argument between two young lovers because of the failure of one to recognize that a common word had taken on a new meaning. The word was *commitment.* Traditionally, this word has meant something one has to do against one's will. Recently, the word has come to mean that one is dedicated to a cause, has devoted himself, body and soul, to some idea or person. The quarrel began because the young man had assimilated this new connotation, whereas the young lady still interpreted the word as meaning an obligation, a task one was forced to do. Consequently, when the young man said he was committed to his love, she flew at him indignantly, asking, "What do you mean you're committed? I'm not going to force you into anything!" And a serious argument began.

The concomitant meanings attached to words have sometimes been known as "incidental" learnings. They often create annoying problems for research workers because they introduce factors into experiments that cannot be easily controlled by the experimenter. For the professional helper the "incidental" aspects of words will often be far more significant than the words themselves. In some helping situations the words used between helper and helpee may even be of no consequence whatever. The act of engaging in a human interaction with another person may in itself be the important facet of the helping relationship. Humans are intensely social animals and often very lonely ones, even when surrounded by thousands of other people. Accordingly, the very fact of being able to get through to someone may fill an important need. This is especially true for those who are afflicted with deep feelings of alienation. Almost everyone has had the experience of sitting next to a stranger on a train or plane and being surprised at the depths and extent of feelings communicated by a seatmate. In such instances the stranger is not interested in any advice you have for him. He has chosen to talk precisely because he will not have to listen to advice. What the stranger seeks is the experience of release in telling his story to someone—anyone! All he needs is a willing listener.

The slightest confusion in a conversation can lead to miscommunication. One of us was inadvertently involved in an amusing situation in which such confusion prevailed. The principals were two graduate students—one a female and the other a male. They had the same major professor, whose name was Don. This was also the name of the lady's husband. The two students met one afternoon and a conversation began:

"Hey, Julie, how you doin'?"
"Hey, Mike, just fine."
"Have you seen Don today?"
"Yes, I saw him this morning." (Julie's husband was sometimes out of town, so she thought nothing of the question.)
"Is he going to the AHE conference?"
"Yes, we're going together. We have a room at the _____ motel."
"You guys are staying in the same room?"
"Sure, we always do."
"Wow, I didn't know you two were so close!"

There was a pause in the conversation, and then they both turned red with embarrassment and broke out laughing, for they realized that she had been talking about her husband and he had been talking about their adviser. It is with such miscommunication that vicious rumors often start.

Nonverbal Communication

Because of the importance of language in daily life, most of us are keenly aware of our verbal exchanges. But communication also occurs without words. While growing up, people learn to interpret various types of behavior that act as clues to help them understand the motives and actions of others. Some nonverbal behaviors, like certain facial expressions and attitudes of fright, anger, or hostility, are common enough to be easily read by everyone. Some are restricted to members of the same culture, subculture, occupation, or locality. Others are highly individual, so characteristic of a particular personality that friends and acquaintances know at once what the person is thinking and feeling. Even from a great distance we can spot our friends by the way they walk or the gestures they make. Who has not spoken to a friend by a look? Shrugged his shoulders in resignation? Made a face at an enemy? Conveyed concern by a touch of the hand? These nonverbal communications are often far more powerful means of conveying meanings than a book full of words.

While traveling to Washington with a friend, one of the authors experienced a nonverbal, deeply meaningful communication with a total stranger that occurred in the twinkling of an eye. As the author was walking down the aisle after the plane had landed, he glanced at a young woman seated next to the window, holding her baby. She was moving her nose back and forth slowly through her baby's hair. As the author passed, she glanced up, met his eye, and instantly they shared an eloquent experience. As they descended the steps from the plane, the friend asked the author, "Do you know that woman?"

"Never saw her in my life," the author replied.

"Well! She certainly talked to you!" exclaimed the friend.

"Yes, and I talked to her too!" said the author.

The young woman was caught in the act of smelling her baby's head, a meaningless gesture to most of the passengers debarking. But she was thoroughly enjoying the experience, for there is something special about the smell of a baby's head. It is a sensuous, loving experience that the author too had known with babies of his own. So in an instant two strangers shared a deeply meaningful experience and never a word was spoken.

Helpers need to be aware of the nonverbal messages they convey, for these messages play an important part in the kinds of relationships helpers establish and affect success or failure of those interactions. Nonverbal statements may even disclose to others purposes not clearly perceived by the behaver. This fact was clearly brought home to one of us in the following incident: During the course of a workshop the author spent some time sitting with various groups. Coming to one group, he picked up a chair, carried it to the circle, turned it backwards, and sat down, straddling the chair with his arms across the back. After a minute or two the leader of the group asked the author, "Why don't you join our group?" To this the author replied, "I thought I was." "Look at the way you are sitting," said the group leader.

"How come you have that fence between you and us?" The author was taken aback. He thought to himself, "I am sitting this way because I want to be kind of informal." Thinking about the matter still further, however, he had to admit to himself that he really did not want to join the group; he really wanted to hold himself aloof. His nonverbal behavior betrayed his true feelings to others even when they were not clear to the author himself.

Someone once wanted to know what characteristics of counselors their clients found irritating. So the researcher interviewed a large number of individuals who were or had been in counseling and asked them this question. Quite a list of behaviors was catalogued, but the interviewers placed near the top of their list that one of the most aggravating things counselors do is pick their noses. We can't imagine that someone would pick his or her nose while at the delicate business of sorting out the life of another, yet it was identified by the subjects of this study with a high enough frequency to suggest that it occurs quite often. No wonder so many counselor educators are enthralled by the use of video recorders in counselor training!

Responsibility for Communication

When understanding fails to come about in human interaction, it is common to blame the other person. If he does not understand, it is easy to point out, "We told him what to do!" This neatly places the responsibility for communication on the receiver. In a helping relationship it also absolves the helper of blame. She can wash her hands of the affair and continue to feel successful no matter how great a disaster she has produced for her client. Communication, to be sure, is always an interaction, but in a helping relationship the responsibility for its breakdown must lie with the person assuming the helping role. One who assumes the role of helper has the obligation to deliver; responsibility for communication lies with the communicator, not the receiver.

If we are acting as helpers and others do not understand us, that is our fault, not theirs. If you the reader do not understand what we the authors are saying, then we haven't said it well enough. If the person in the receiving role accepts some responsibility for listening carefully or trying to understand what is being conveyed, that, of course, facilitates a meaningful exchange. It cannot, however, be demanded or even expected by the helper. A major goal of helping is freeing people so that they will be able to enter into effective dialogue. It is unfair to expect the student or client to already have achieved the very goals the helping process is designed to produce!

COMMUNICATION MUST BE RELATED TO NEED

How well helpers are understood is ordinarily a function of the following three major factors:

1.   The relationship of information to need
2.   The relationship to existing information already in the field
3.   The openness of the field at the moment of communication

Earlier we observed the effects of need on perception. Other things being equal, we perceive those events we need to perceive. Ads for new cars are bypassed until we begin to feel that the old car is getting a bit shabby. We don't worry about health aids unless we are sick. People take in the information they need. The rest, if they perceive it at all, is likely to leave them unmoved. This creates a great problem for educators, who must provide information and experience for students who may not need that information for years to come. Teaching people what they want to know is comparatively easy, but it takes real genius to communicate when need is not patently evident. Professors of education know well that it is much easier to work with in-service teachers than with student teachers. The veterans know what they need and are grateful for any help they can get!

A major portion of the time and efforts of good teachers is devoted to creating needs even before information is provided. This is what the first-grade teacher does when he sets up a store in his classroom. In the course of running the store the children need to know about money and arithmetic because they have to make change. Spelling is important because they have to make a sign. They must know how to read to understand the label on a bottle. The need to know how to get along with others and how to run a store and sell its goods requires cooperation. Some people who do not know any better regard such teaching activities with suspicion because they're too much fun. Although it may look like play to outsiders, what is really going on is an ingenious way of creating problems for children, the crucial first step in learning. In higher grade levels the creation of need may be accomplished through involving students in planning their own educational experiences, operating their own student governments, or designing procedures to enable them to use their own resources, with ever-increasing opportunities for self-direction.

The importance of the relevance principle for communication can also be observed in other helping professions. A person who is given a psychological test that she or he has not requested, for example, is likely to have little or no interest in the valuable information or advice the counselor would like to give. Social workers know that giving a client information he sees no need for will cause the worker to be regarded by the client as ignorant or annoying. Dietitians are often frustrated because, despite the vast quantities of information they have about proper nutrition, the people they want to help frequently ignore the information and continue eating what they like. A common complaint of clergy everywhere is that those who need sermons the most are the ones who never come to church. Donald Snygg, a friend of ours, once pointed out that "there is nothing in this world so useless as answers we do not have problems for!" The attempt to provide such answers frequently results in failures of communication in all aspects of the helping professions.

Information and Censorship

People need information in order to deal with life. If they cannot get information when they need it, they may be plunged even deeper into the problems they face. If they do not have access to accurate information, they may have to make adjustments to life on the basis of distorted or inaccurate data. Thus there is no place for censorship in effective helping processes. Rather, the process requires that clients receive help in obtaining whatever information is needed with the greatest possible dispatch. The failure to give adequate information is one of the major causes of lack of communication between older and younger generations.

Members of older generations often think they are protecting young people by not giving them information or by distorting the facts. Such a pity, for it is only by obtaining as much relevant and accurate information as possible that people will be able to deal with life adequately. Confusion arises and mistakes are made when ignorance prevails, not when one is well informed. One of us came on a perfect example of this, in an encounter with a fourteen-year-old girl. She was having intimate relations with her boyfriend but was experiencing no trepidation about the consequences of her behavior. Why? Because she did not yet know how one got pregnant! Whoever was responsible for keeping this information from her was surely doing her a disservice, not a favor. We have confronted children as young as ten or eleven who had already become involved in such things as sexual intimacy and drug abuse. Ignorance will not save these children; only TLC and the best, most honest, and most accurate information we can give them will!

Helpers also may have to decide what information to provide a student or client. Should a child be told her intelligence test scores, for example? Applying the principle that "there is no information about self that a person ought not have," the answer would seem to be unequivocably "yes." The problem of communication, however, involves more than simply providing information. It is a question of meaning. To provide people with test scores they do not understand may actually have the effect of providing them with false information. The helper who supplies information, therefore, has an additional responsibility to ensure that it is understood. This may be such a difficult, time-consuming task that a helper may prefer not to give the information in the first place. The time required to assure adequate understanding (granting the competence of the helper to do so) may be so large a factor as to warrant withholding information—not on the grounds of whether or not it is good for the student but whether or not the helper has the time and energy available for the necessary clarification or the wish to engage in the discussion.

The methods helpers use to relate information to need are extraordinarily varied. Many counselors, for example, have learned to wait for their clients to express a need to know. They do this because they know that information given before need is often fruitless and may even be destructive to the helping relationship. Consequently, they rely on a client's own drives for health,

recognizing that if they are successful in helping the client search for meaning, sooner or later the client will become aware of her or his lack of important information. Then the counselor can help the client get it whichever way
is most appropriate at the time. For example, the father who has finally
reached the conclusion that his child needs special care can then be helped to
find the appropriate agency. If the same information had been given when
the father first came for aid, he might have received the impression that the
helper was not interested in the case and was trying to pass the problem on to
another helper. Or, he might have felt guilty and frustrated at being unable
to care for the child himself. Admitting that one has failed with one's own
child is not an easy matter. Information about where and how to send one's
child to an agency or institution must be preceded by the question of
whether to send the child at all. Even that can only be dealt with when one
has come to terms with one's own inadequacies. Giving people information
they cannot use is an exercise in futility.

Teachers have discovered by experience that self-direction is an effective
way of helping students relate information to need. Students will search out
information they need with ingenuity and vigor. What is more, knowledge
acquired through such research is far more likely to be permanent and pertinent to future needs. Accordingly, modern educators devote much time and
attention to getting students involved in the learning process and to creating needs they never knew they had. This makes the learning process
more efficient and the presentation of information more meaningful for
the student.

Social workers have learned in practice the value of "confrontation with
reality"—that is, the importance of permitting a client to come face to face
with problems, to accept the consequences of his or her own behavior. A po-
tent source of information for everyone is the feedback one gets from one's
own behavior. Protecting a person from such information may constitute a
kind of censorship wherein the individual is robbed of experience that could
be significant in a return to health. The delinquent, continuously excused for
his misbehavior, for example, may thus be led to *expect* to escape responsibility for his actions and so may not perceive the necessity for better kinds of
adjustment. One of the most successful forms of treatment used with delinquents, reality therapy, is based on this premise.[2]

INFORMATION MUST BE RELEVANT
TO IMMEDIATE NEED

It is not enough that information should seem important to the receiver;
if it is to be effective, it must also be related to current problems or interests.
Immediate needs are always more pressing and pertinent than those at a distance. Long-term goals initiate and direct behavior, but they do not sustain it.
If one's behavior is to be maintained along a path toward the attainment of a

major goal, the process must be enhancing and reinforcing along the way or one will not continue. People go to college to get a degree, but that goal alone will not keep them there. The nature of day-to-day experiences will determine whether or not they will continue. If the process of becoming "educated" proves to be satisfying, people will remain until they take a degree and perhaps continue to work toward higher degrees. If the process is not satisfying, they will drop out to pursue some other more satisfying course. Long-term goals are significant only as they can be translated into more immediate steps for action. Almost anyone can observe in other people how far-off goals, no matter how explicitly stated, are frequently belied by short-term actions. The student who loudly protests that she wants to be a doctor more than anything in the world, even while failing required courses for entrance into medical school, is a common example.

INFORMATION MUST BE RELATED TO EXISTING MEANINGS

The Importance of Fit

Whether information can be truly communicated depends on the readiness of the receiver to absorb it. Only as a person discovers the relationship of new experience to that which is already in existence can it be comprehended. A great many frustrations in communication come about because communicators have not successfully helped their clientele perceive the place of new information in their existing fields of awareness. This failure to relate the new data to the old results Festinger has called *cognitive dissonance.*[3] He points out how difficult it is to absorb new ideas when they cannot be brought into harmony with those already present. Piaget also emphasized this fact in his descriptions of growth in children's reasoning.[4] He called it the *problem of the match.* Prescott Lecky talked of the individual's need for *self-consistency* and pointed out that the acquisition of meaning was a consequence of a person's attempts to achieve order in his experience.[5] The principle also operates when we find ourselves in a social situation in which our usual expectancies do not fit, as, for example, when we go to an unfamiliar church with a friend and find ourselves confused about how to behave in this new setting.

Speed and Pacing

Communication takes time. Although information can be transmitted from one person to another with great speed, comprehension is another matter. It requires a searching of the field, matching and adjustment of new understandings into the total gestalt. One of the most common destroyers of communication is the impatience of the communicator. Experienced lecturers know that it is a rare audience that can be expected to carry away more than one or two new ideas.

Every experienced teacher or counselor is familiar with and every every inexperienced teacher or counselor is frightened of what is called the *pregnant pause.* Many times during a teaching or counseling session a helper will make a statement, hoping to evoke a response from a student or client—but nothing happens; there is absolute silence. To an inexperienced helper this can be terrifying. Like the stand-up comic who tells a favorite joke and receives little or no response from his audience, the helper feels like he or she has just bombed out, laid an egg, feels the proverbial lump in the throat and knot in the stomach.

The experienced helper, however, comes to learn that this may be a "moment of truth," a pause full of significance. During such pauses many helpees are actually thinking deeply, experiencing perceptual reorganization, or collecting their thoughts. Such pauses are difficult, to be sure. If one feels responsible for making things happen, a moment can seem like forever. But if one lets the moment run its course, one often finds that it leads to important communicative breakthroughs.

Time spent in making certain that meanings are conveyed is not time wasted. People in the helping professions often destroy their own effectiveness because they fail to recognize the time required for communication. They become so preoccupied with "covering the subject," "getting on with the discussion," or "coming to a decision" that clients or students are lost in the race. People do not put up with this for long. They have more important things to do, so they "turn the speaker off," fall asleep, or amuse themselves in the best ways they can. One's own behavior when listening to a boring speaker provides a familiar example. Many speakers are lucky that most people are well mannered. On the other hand, the quality of speaking might be improved if audiences expressed their displeasure and speakers had to accept the full consequences of their behavior.

Although communication may often fail because the receiver is not yet ready to comprehend the information being communicated, it can also be rendered ineffective or useless when the receiver is long past the readiness point. Who has not passed a dull hour listening to a speaker relate what is already known? Many a helper has made himself unproductive by providing information his student, client, or patient already has or has long since passed beyond.

Boredom is one of the major problems in education. There has been a lot of concern about the dropping scores on college entrance exams and the lack of basic skills among college students. Although this may be true, we are not sure what it means. Anyone who is really worried about our youth going to the dogs hasn't recently stood before a group of teenagers in high school or twenty-year-olds in college. It is becoming more difficult to do a good job of teaching precisely because our young people know so much more and want to be much more actively involved in the learning process than ever before!

The Value of Simplicity

Other things being equal, the simpler the material, the more likely it is to be comprehended. What is simple, however, is a highly individual matter. What is easy for the student of calculus will seem difficult for the person struggling with basic multiplication. The importance of simplicity seems obvious but is frequently violated in practice. Some helpers honestly believe that it is good for people to be confronted with terribly difficult and complex tasks. They operate on the principle "the harder, the better." To be sure, an individual does need to confront problems, but information that is complex beyond her or his readiness to grasp it can result only in discouragement.

Some communicators make themselves ineffective because they are more interested in the impression they are making than in communicating. So graduate students and learned scholars are often dreadful writers. They really don't care what they communicate so long as they display their own erudition. They write to impress their colleagues or their bosses. Whether anyone else comprehends is a minor concern. Indeed, if others don't understand them, they may take this as further proof of their intellectual superiority.

One of us, while an undergraduate student, had this point made by a professor. Like many college students, the author was in awe of anything in print. Reading an article his instructor had given him, he was dismayed to find that he couldn't understand a word. He became overwhelmed with a sense of inadequacy and began to doubt whether he had the capacity to fulfill his dream of going to graduate school. He went privately to his professor by way of making a confession. "Sir, I'm sorry, but I can't analyze this thing in class. I have read and reread the article, and it just doesn't make any sense to me. I can't understand a word the author is saying!"

"You feel pretty bad about it," the professor said.

"Yes."

About that time the professor broke out laughing and said, "Don't feel bad, young man. It doesn't make any sense to me either, because the writer didn't say anything. It's included in the articles I asked you to read as an example of the worst kind of writing, reporting, and research I could find. If that guy said anything in that article, we are both pretty dumb."

People who really want to communicate do not regard simplicity as unscholarly. They recognize simplicity as a factor that affects comprehension and use it to make communication more successful. A goal of science is to make things comprehensible by reducing events to the simplest possible terms. This is known as the *law of parsimony*.

Principles and Details in Communication

A variation of the need for simplicity in communication can be observed in the general or specific character of information. There is almost no end to the number of details one can find in a given body of information. Helpers are more likely to facilitate changes in meaning by emphasizing general principles than by concentrating on details. This fact led Bruner and others to emphasize the importance of the "structure" of knowledge rather than the facts of knowledge.[6] They point out that general principles are much more likely to find translation into the existing field of information than are details, and they advocate that education orient teaching to emphasize principles rather than details. Unfortunately, many information providers emphasize the opposite; they focus attention on details rather than structure. Professors, for example, frequently fill their lectures with details, test their students on details in objective examinations, and concentrate so exclusively on the students' handling of details that students soon get the message: It is the details that are important. These they try to memorize. Because unrelated facts are difficult to fit into already existing information without the unifying principles that give them meaning, they are quickly lost. Effective communication depends on the sensitivity of the communicator to what is going on in the listener. Good communicators continuously search the feedback they get from their audiences and adjust their own behavior accordingly to assure maximum impact.

Many of the principles discussed earlier can be observed in operation in the behavior of effective public speakers. An interesting example of this is the famous speech made years ago by Russell Conwell, who traveled the Chautauqua circuit giving a speech entitled "Acres of Diamonds." This single speech was so immensely successful that Conwell amassed a fortune, which he later used to found Temple University. The structure of this speech is simple: A basic thought is stated in the simplest possible terms and is then illustrated in ways that enable the hearer to fit the principle to his or her own need and daily experience. The pattern is repeated throughout the address.

Communicating within the System

Communication between helper and helpee comes first. But there is another major problem in the helping professions: the difficulty of communication between helpers. Even though all who are involved in helping processes may agree that their purpose is helping students or clients, the methods used to accomplish this purpose may be a matter of far less agreement. So counselor and client may have different conceptions of what ought to be going on in the counseling hour, and students, teachers, parents, administrators, and professors of education may all have different conceptions of what should be happening in a schoolroom. Sometimes arguments about these differences in the perception of desirable goals can become heated, and helpers may find themselves confronted with conflicting demands and expectations. Here are a few examples pertaining to a hospital patient:

A nurse wants a patient to walk, the approval of the other nurses, and the personal gratification of solving the problem.

The patient wants to avoid pain, stay in bed, be loved and cared for, and avoid embarrassment and humiliation.

The hospital wants the patient out as soon as possible. So do the patient's relatives. The physician wants the patient to walk, and the nurse wants to get the job done. Everyone wants the patient well. Everyone also has differing conceptions of how this is to be brought about, to say nothing of personal goals that are unrelated to the patient's welfare. All these purposes must somehow be resolved in the process of helping the patient get well.

Sometimes two or more helpers need to work together with a particular student or client. Without a clear understanding of commonalities, effectiveness can easily be destroyed. For a student or client to find himself caught in a cross fire of helpers at war with one another is a disaster. In a team or institutional setting it is important that helpers recognize and appreciate their common goals and purposes. Unhappily, this is often not the case. Teachers and counselors, for example, sometimes deal with each other as antagonists rather than as co-workers. Some counselors delight in gossiping about the terrible things that parents and teachers have done to the children they are working with. And some teachers regard the work of counselors as unwarranted invasions of their prerogatives and speak of them with disdain. Such attitudes are not only bad for those in need of help, but they also seriously undermine the esprit de corps of the institution. Helpers who treat one another with disdain are unlikely to work together effectively. They are themselves in need of help.

Those in the helping professions need to be keenly aware of the distorting effects of their own self-concepts. Helping people is a heady business and can sometimes result in exaggerated views of one's personal power or indispensability. One's own activities naturally seem to be right and important. What others do may then seem less important or valuable because it is less understood. Carried to extremes this can result in a kind of cult, with firm beliefs that its practitioners are "the chosen ones." These attitudes may be further institutionalized with elaborate entrance ceremonies designed to maintain the "purity" of the profession. People in the helping professions must understand the basic commonality of their tasks and appreciate the work of other professions with sympathy and understanding. The goals of helping are so great that no branch of the profession can hope to make the helping process its exclusive prerogative. The helping professions must work in concert.

The helper's task is to provide the conditions that will free the client's own need for self-fulfillment. This is a process of problem solving and learning in which the helper serves as catalyst (to set events in motion) and teacher or guide (to assure the process has maximum opportunities for producing positive growth). The specific ways in which this is brought about will differ from one branch of the helping professions to another, but whatever the branch the moral responsibility of the helper is the same: to assist clients in the quickest, most effective ways possible. To permit people to suffer a lack of fulfillment any longer than absolutely necessary is cruel and inhuman. Helpers must always, therefore, use the most efficient ways possible to help their clients achieve maximum growth and health. For helpers "to do their own thing" because it is their thing to do is not enough; they must be keenly aware of their personal assets and limitations as well as those of the particular branch of the helping professions with which they are identified. This is essential for all helpers, especially for those working with clients in trouble or suffering deprivation.

The responsibility of helpers goes further. To understand one's self and one's branch of the profession is not enough. Helpers must see themselves and their professional efforts in the broad perspective of the whole helping process, including a proper appreciation of the contributions of other branches. Clinical files bulge with unfortunate cases of people who did not get the help they needed because the helpers they chose were either too enamored of their own special competencies or too ignorant of the possibilities inherent in other aspects of the professions to use them. For each person in the helping professions to be competent in all others is clearly impossible. The truly effective practitioner is aware of community resources and is free to use them. Among those resources are the other helping professions. In addition to their own specialties it is necessary that helpers have an understanding of and an appreciation for the potentialities of other professionals and the will to make maximum use of them.

Focus on Similarities

Professional helpers should focus on their similarities, not their differences, if they are to be of maximum benefit to their clients, students, or patients. As we have said, the primary purpose of helping is client self-fulfillment. This goal is the same for every helping profession whether it be counseling, social work, pastoral care, nursing, teaching, group work, or any of the dozens of other specialties recognized in the field. Although practitioners may behave in different ways to assist people in achieving self-fulfillment, the primary goal remains the same.

In a study of the beliefs of psychotherapists, F. E. Fiedler found that experienced psychotherapists—no matter what school of thought they were working in—were closer together in what they believed constituted a good helping relationship than were beginning therapists and expert therapists in the same school of thought.[7] Apparently, as they became more expert in their professions, they grew closer together. This seems to suggest that there is probably a "good" helping relationship toward which people move as they become more expert. Even more intriguing, Fiedler found that the "man in the street" could describe the good helping relationship about as well as the experts![8] Apparently, there is a "good" helping condition that all of us are vaguely aware of even if that is not our primary business.

In a similar experiment R. W. Heine concluded that there is probably only one basic psychotherapy and that all therapists approach this common principle to some degree.[9] Other studies show that the belief systems of good counselors, teachers, resident advisers, school psychologists—even good politicians and Episcopal priests—are basically alike.[10] Such findings should not surprise us. After all, if the basic nature of people and the laws of behavior are stable, one would expect applications of these basic principles to show in common practice. Because they arise from common bases, the principles governing the operation of effective helping relationships *ought* to be similar.

Helping as Learning and Teaching

The process of helping is a process in problem solving governed by our knowledge of learning dynamics. Helping people discover more effective and satisfying relationships between themselves and the world is an exercise in learning. In that sense all helpers are fundamentally teachers. Some helpers will no doubt recoil from the thought of helpers as teachers. What they do seems so different from the kinds of teaching they have observed or experienced. This is probably because they are accustomed to thinking of teaching as "telling." The techniques used by helpers in the one-to-one relationships of counseling, for example, seem a far cry from such procedures as lecturing, assigning, evaluating, rewarding, and punishing. Teaching seems to them synonymous with controlling, directing, and even coercing people. Such practices are used by some teachers. Many modern teachers, however, regard them just as distastefully as do their colleagues in other helping professions.

There is little reason to suppose that classroom learning is basically different from that occurring in the varied relationships of any of the other helping professions. All are concerned with learning, and all must devise ways of operating from the same basic concepts about the nature of learning and how it is brought about. Each hopes to assist the student or client to learn new and better ways of dealing with himself and the world around him. The best teachers today are a far cry from the forbidding, authoritarian stereotypes characteristic of a generation ago. Helping people learn is the basic problem of the helping professions, and helping people learn is precisely what we mean by teaching. In a very real sense, then, every therapist is a teacher and every teacher is, to some degree, a therapist.

In the early days of the development of the helping professions, various branches sometimes sought to establish exclusive domain over the right to practice in one aspect or another. For example, at one time some people hoped to define the practice of psychotherapy so as to make it the exclusive prerogative of the medical profession. After years of effort it became apparent that counseling and psychotherapy cannot be defined in ways that do not involve what thousands of others in the helping professions do or even what some people generally do in daily life. If warm, friendly talk or the giving of advice were made the exclusive property of a particular profession, few of us, whether professional or not, could long remain out of jail! *There is no place for competitive activities between helpers in the helping professions.*

OPENNESS AND COMMUNICATION

A major factor in determining the success of communication is the condition of the receiver. In Chapter Five we saw how the experience of threat interferes with the individual's perceptions by creating tunnel vision and self-defense mechanisms. Both these phenomena interfere with communication. Every human being has an insatiable drive toward enhancing self. To do this, one must also defend one's self against humiliation and degradation. No organism can deal with everything simultaneously. Selection is necessary. People take in what they need and defend themselves against what seems disruptive or destructive. Highly self-actualized people are maximally open to the world; deeply threatened ones are surrounded by walls that isolate them from human intercourse.

Barriers established in response to the experience of threat are even more important for communication because of the threat–counterthreat spiral. These cyclic effects have the potential to destroy communication and even, in their extremes, to result in destruction of the communicators themselves. Once begun, the experience of threat may bounce back and forth from one communicator to another, spiraling upward to increased intensity and increased interference with communication. Barriers to communication are brought about by attempts at self-defense and by retaliatory attacks (also a kind of defense) of one against the other. Once embarked on a threat–counterthreat spiral, it is difficult to stop, and communication is likely to get worse unless the experience of threat can somehow be reduced and the channels of communication, reopened.

Breaking the deadly threat–counterthreat cycle calls for some combination of the following:

1. *Attention to the feelings involved in the process of dialogue* Preoccupation of the participants with action (who did what to whom and what is to be done in retaliation) inflames the threat–counterthreat cycle. It obscures the causes of difficulty and turns the attention of the dialogue from the sources of cure. To resolve a threat, one or both parties must become concerned with the feeling aspect. In the helping professions this is a major task of helpers and is expressed in almost everything they do.

2. *Absorbing or draining off feelings of threat* If one or both parties can find a way to respond with less threat than they receive, the vicious circle can be interrupted and hostility can be given opportunity to decrease. The helper can do this by absorbing the threat, as the teacher does when he lets a child work off her anger in some harmless fashion, or as the counselor does by staying calm and not expressing shock at what her client has to tell her.

3. *Contributing to the personal feelings of security in participants* Positive feelings about self make possible greater toleration of threat and less need for self-defense. Helpers accomplish this goal by helping clients to achieve greater feelings of self-actualization, either through their own interac-

tions with their clients or through the manipulation of external events to this end.

4. *Adjusting the interchange to the tolerance levels of the reactors*   Matters are consciously arranged to assure that communications have as little inflammability as possible. The helper cannot do this for the client. She can, however, control her own responses or set an example by her own behavior. To do this requires a great deal of sensitivity and a high degree of self-discipline.

5. *Recognition of difference*   Appreciation of difference and its value in human affairs will, of itself, help to lower the temperature of interactions. It contributes to the feeling that "it is all right to be me" and acceptance of a similar right in others. For this reason much of the work of helpers revolves around the recognition and acceptance of difference expressed in innumerable ways in the various branches of these professions.

6. *Resolving the attack–appease dilemma*   To deal with threatening situations, many people behave as though there were but two possible solutions: to attack or appease. Such a dichotomy, however, presents a person with two unpalatable choices. Appeasement requires giving in, surrendering one's own interests, or, worse still, yielding to blackmail. Attack has equally unacceptable connotations. Although we are willing to defend ourselves with vigor and determination, to attack others without provocation is as repugnant in one direction as appeasement is in the other. We are essentially a peace-loving people. Attack seems the method of the bully or the despot, and its use seems morally indefensible.

There is an alternative to appeasement and attack, an approach that social scientists have discovered is basic to good human relationships everywhere. It is not so much an alternative to attack or appeasement, since it approaches the problems of threat and counterthreat on a different axis altogether. It is a position that says: "I am a person of dignity and integrity. I stand foursquare in the security of my fundamental convictions. I have no need to attack you, nor will I permit you to attack me. I do not fear you, and I will give you no cause to fear me." This position is neither attack nor appeasement. It is not concerned with winning or losing. It is concerned solely with maintaining the dignity and integrity of people and with preserving their freedom to grow and develop.

Appeasement destroys the dignity of the appeaser. Attack violates the integrity of others. The alternative maintains the dignity and integrity of the helper without violating the rights of others or relinquishing one's own in the process. It is a position of strength and security that stands *for* something as well as against something. It is equally applicable to relationships in the various helping professions: to the internal operations of schools, classrooms, and institutions; and to international affairs.

Just as threat interferes with communication, challenge tends to improve it. Each human being is a neatly balanced system that continuously seeks fulfillment. This drive keeps pushing the person forward, but each individual also contains her own checks and balances—her accelerators, brakes, and safety valves. How far and how fast she will go depends on how she sees herself and the situations in which she is involved. Because her drive is insatiable, she must move if the way seems open to her and within her capacities. But the drive for fulfillment will also not permit her to behave in ways that seem likely to destroy her self-realization.

Effective helpers learn to work with people's checks and balances rather than against them. They learn to follow the lead of their students, clients, or parishioners. They know that their clients will confront what they need to when they can, so helpers devote their attention to creating the conditions that will make this possible.

Authority and Communication

An interesting illustration of the effects of challenge and threat on communication may be observed in people's responses to unearned authority. Unearned authority is that prestige and status that a helper or leader has when she first confronts the people she seeks to help. The group leader, for example, comes to the meeting with built-in status and authority because she is the leader, perhaps also because she has a doctor's degree, wrote a book, or has a reputation in the community. This authority is unearned because it was not given to her by the people she now seeks to communicate with. She may have earned it elsewhere but not with these people. Over a period she may earn authority with them, as group members discover for themselves what the leader has to offer. Each member invests the leader with more or less authority, depending on the individual's experience of the leader as a person; as a knower, speaker, demonstrator; and as a sensitive or insensitive human being.

Unearned authority, for most people, is likely to be threatening. Accordingly, all the effects of threat discussed in Chapter Five are likely to accompany the interaction and get in the way of effective communication. It is a common observation that students and clients simply do not hear teachers and group leaders in the first sessions. Instructions given, advice proffered, information outlined—all have a low incidence of comprehension and must almost always be repeated in more or less detail later on.

With increased experience on the part of clients, students, parishioners, or group members, the leader is given more or less positive or negative authority. If the earned authority is positive, the leader's words are likely to be received as challenging and enhancing. These effects may be so pervasive as to cancel out such ordinary drawbacks as lack of experience and the like. Herman Wessels wrote of a young first-year teacher he had known:

> When he left last June for further study there was an astounding outpouring of affection on the part of his students, and this surprised him. For he had come to us shy and not too sure of himself, and he had found his steadfast purpose through these bright, seeking youngsters whom he taught. He

emerged as a person who carried the authority not of age and life experience, but the authority of commitment and true caring.[11]

Communication is immensely increased by positive earned authority, so much so that some of the usual crutches to aid communication may no longer be necessary. When unearned authority is high, for example, the college student takes notes. In the case of negative earned authority, this happens because the student has discovered that what the teacher has to say is unimportant. When there is a high degree of positive earned authority, however, note taking may slacken off for a different reason, because people are less likely to forget what important people say.

Notes and References

1. S. I. Hayakawa, *Language in Thought and Action* (New York: Harcourt, Brace and World, 1964).
2. W. Glasser, *Reality Therapy: A New Approach to Psychiatry* (New York: Harper & Row, 1965).
3. L. Festinger, "Cognitive Dissonance," *Scientific American* 207 (1964):93–107.
4. J. Piaget, *Judgment and Reasoning in the Child*, trans. M. Worden (Totowa, N.J.: Littlefield, Adams, 1959).
5. P. Lecky, *Self-Consistency: A Theory of Personality* (New York: Island Press, 1945).
6. J. S. Bruner, *Toward a Theory of Instruction* (New York: W.W. Norton, 1966).
7. F. E. Fiedler, "A Comparison of Therapeutic Relationships in Psychoanalytic, Non-Directive and Adlerian Therapy," *Journal of Consulting Psychology* 14 (1950):436–445.
8. F. E. Fiedler, "The Concept of an Ideal Therapeutic Relationship," *Journal of Consulting Psychology* 14 (1950):239–245.
9. R. W. Heine, "A Comparison of Patient's Reports on Psychotherapeutic Experience with Psychotherapeutic, Non-Directive and Adlerian Therapists," *Journal of Psychotherapy* 7 (1953):16–23.
10. A. W. Combs, *A Personal Approach to Teaching: Beliefs That Make A Difference* (Boston: Allyn and Bacon, 1982).
11. H. M. Wessels, "Four Teachers I Have Known," *Saturday Review of Literature*, June 7, 1961.

TWELVE

MODES OF HELPING

This chapter concerns itself with the circumstances within which the helper must carry out his tasks. These include such factors as the limits of time and place in which the helper works, the numbers he must deal with, and the particular definitions of role and function demanded by the position he holds. From the helper's personal "mix" of all these elements will come decisions of how best to use himself as an effective instrument for helping.

SOME POSSIBLE MODES OF HELPING

Some of the more general roles helpers may perform are as follows:

As *authority figures,* directing the processes of helping toward the achievement of clear-cut goals. This may include a vast array of control techniques ranging from gentle persuasion to open manipulation focused on the process of helping or on the helpees themselves.

As *mentors,* teaching students and clients things they ought or need to know. The need may arise from outside the helpee in the requirements of others or may be formulated out of the helpee's own interests or aspirations. Helpers in the teaching role may vary from highly authoritarian task masters or "fountainheads of knowledge" to friendly representatives of society, or those who practice modern conceptions of teaching, whose functions are practically indistinguishable from the functions of counselors and psychotherapists.

As *facilitators, aids, assistants,* or *counselors,* helping students or clients discover new meanings about themselves and the world. Helpers in these roles operate from an open-system orientation, concentrating on creating conditions that facilitate self-discovery for those they work with. The group includes a number of "schools" in counseling, psychotherapy, social work, and humanistic education.

As *consultants,* working with and through other people. In these roles helpers exert their influence as third parties, contributing to the work of other helping persons rather than directly to helpees. Examples of such roles might be school psychologists helping teachers find more effective ways to help difficult children, or human relations consultants aiding people in schools, industry, or public office to carry out their functions more effectively.

As *private individuals* or *citizens*. Helpers are not always professional people. They live and work and play like everyone else in families, institutions, and society, and the ways they function in these settings determine their personal happiness and fulfillment on one hand and the kind of contributions they make to the welfare of other citizens and to the communities in which they live on the other.

Changing the Environment

All helpers at one time or another are called on to influence the environment of those they seek to help. Sometimes this influence is direct. At other times it is occasional or fortuitous. For some helpers it represents the primary way in which they work with other people; for others it is a device used only on occasion. In the broadest sense all forms of helping are accomplished through effecting some kind of change in the helpee's environment. Changing parents' attitudes changes the environment for their child. Even the changes produced in psychotherapy by the most person-centered counselor are brought about by the relationship created by the therapist's presence and behavior, which is a form of modifying the client's environment.

The physical world is the place in which we live, and it provides us with the physical needs for growth and survival. Whatever can be done to make it more productive, healthful, and beautiful must be a primary goal to everyone interested in the welfare of humanity. It is also a major social problem of our times, and no matter what a helper does in a professional role, exerting influence as a private citizen to create a better environment for all must remain a major responsibility. When students and clients can be helped by environmental means, these may be the best and most efficient ways of helping. If a child's school difficulties can be solved simply by changing teachers, for example, it may be better to take that action, if it can be arranged. Helping, after all, ought to be done in the quickest possible ways.

Major changes in environment can effect monumental changes in peoples' lives. We are familiar with one such success story. A friend of ours was born and raised in one of the seedier areas of Los Angeles. At age ten he was drinking, smoking, stealing, and running with a gang. By age seventeen he had a reputation as a "bad boy" and had been jailed twice. By the end of the eleventh grade he had been absent from high school more than eighty days and was suspected of being involved in various delinquent behaviors. His parents were at their wits' end and almost everyone was sure that it wouldn't be long before he would be in serious trouble. As a matter of fact, before too many years had passed, several of his close friends did just that, being incarcerated for things like drug dealing, rape, and even murder.

One of the major reasons this particular youth's behavior had been tolerated for so long was his athletic ability. Being talented in sports, he had always been given the benefit of the doubt. His high school principal finally decided that it was time to put a halt to things, however, and in a conference with him and his parents gave the boy an ultimatum. The principal did not think the young man was without redeeming qualities, so rather than directly lowering the boom, he gave the boy three choices: He could shape up, go into military service, or go to a correctional institution for youthful offenders. The boy selected the service, and that choice may literally have saved his life.

For one thing, his decision removed him from his negative environment. It brought new people into his life who saw the world quite differently than his former associates. He began to take on different, more positive values and to see opportunities he had never dreamed of. And, most important, he met and married a beautiful lady, who gave him love, purpose, and responsibility. Because of this major change in course he did not wind up in jail or in some dark alley as predicted but is a psychology professor at a major university.

But such radical changes in environment are more often fortuitous than not, and controlling the environment is not always feasible for professional helpers. What, for example, can the school nurse do about the family of a child who feels unloved or unwanted, with his parents on the brink of divorce? What can a teacher do about a brutal or alcoholic father, or an immature, overanxious mother? A physician may know that smoking is dangerous for a patient but may be unable to prevent her from doing it.

Generally speaking, the older an individual gets, the more difficult it becomes to affect behavior by controlling his or her environment. The world of a helpless infant is small, composed for the most part of parents and the home. But as the child grows older, the world to which it responds grows ever larger and infinitely more complex. By the time a child reaches adulthood, the possibilities of controlling behavior by attempting to control his world are slim, if not impossible. Parents can easily move dangerous objects beyond the reach of a toddler, but imagine the problems involved in preventing a grown-up from finding the means to commit suicide if he really wants to do it. Relatives of alcoholics know only too well the impossibility of keeping liquor from their loved ones who have become addicted to the substance. For most people, attempting to affect behavior through control of the environment loses its value as an effective tool for the helping professions by the time they reach adolescence. After that some other means to help must be found. If the environment surrounding clients is to be changed, more often than not it will have to be changed by the clients themselves, and helpers will need to exert their primary efforts toward helping clients change their perceptions about themselves and the world.

One-to-One Relationships

Some helpers, like counselors and nurses, work almost exclusively with individuals. But every helper must at one time or another, whether superficially or in depth, carry out some part of his or her function in a face-to-face relationship with one other person. Helping people in one-to-one relationships might be thought of as a continuum of purpose—from interviews (*getting* information from the client) through advising (*giving* information or guidance) to counseling and psychotherapy (*facilitating* personal discovery of meaning at deeper and deeper levels).

Many of the needs people have for help can be satisfied by simply providing information. More difficult and personal problems, however, are likely to be moral ones—matters of decision, desire, hope, frustration, or deprivation. People who come for such assistance already have most of the information they need. Modern practices in counseling and psychotherapy, therefore, are much less concerned with giving people information and much more concerned with developing relationships designed to help people explore and discover new and more effective ways of perceiving.

Early in the history of counseling it was assumed that the advice given by counselors made the difference. Later on, improvements in the client's health were thought to be a function of the *methods* that counselors used, and practitioners argued at great length about whether directive or nondirective methods were most efficient. More recently, the *relationship* between counselor and client has come to be regarded as the most significant aspect. At first, this came about because counselors focused on the facilitating effect of the relationship on the exploration of meaning. Now, we are beginning to understand that the relationship does much more than simply facilitate; it teaches as well.

Helping Through Groups

Through the use of group sessions the number of people who can be helped has increased enormously. As a consequence, those in the helping professions are experimenting in various ways with the use of groups for human growth and fulfillment. Major considerations in education, for example, are how to group children for most effective learning and how to use group discussion as a tool of teaching. Social workers are experimenting with family therapy groups and community action programs. Counselors and psychologists are concerned with the use of groups for the advancement of mental health. Occupational and recreational therapy have become important branches of the healing arts, and human relations experts are concerned with the problems and resolution of group conflict. The kinds of group experiences constructed by helpers to achieve these ends may vary widely from groups that are little more than pleasant pastimes to intensely therapeutic ones.

Discovery groups   In the past thirty or forty years special types of groups have been developed by various branches of the helping professions to aid students, clients, and patients explore new and more adequate understandings of themselves and their relationships to the world. Leaders of such groups generally concentrate more on the group process than on specific outcomes. Emphasis is on the experience of participating in the group and what the individual can make of it. Such groups are widely used in many aspects of the helping professions and generally serve three purposes:

1. *Sensitivity training*   Group experiences are used to help participants develop increased sensitivity to themselves and to others. Some forms of these groups are called encounter groups or confrontation sessions. Sensitivity groups have been particularly popular in the training of workers in the helping professions, in the training of executives in industry, and in public relations.

2. *Group therapy*   Groups are used for their therapeutic value, especially in assisting patients or clients with personality problems. Such techniques have been widely used, for example, with prison inmates, potential juvenile delinquents, marital partners, and parent education.

3. *Learning groups*   Group techniques are used to assist students in the exploration and discovery of the meaning of ideas in many content fields. Learning groups have recently been used especially in humanistically oriented school programs, like open classrooms, values clarification, role playing, class discussions, and in a wide variety of techniques for involving students in decision making and responsibility for their own learning.

The Helper as Consultant

Helping is often conceived almost exclusively as dialogue or encounter between a helper and one or more helpees. But helpers in any branch of the professions find it necessary from time to time to work with and through other people. So teachers seek to help children through parents; school psychologists seek to help children by conferring with teachers; social workers may meet with judges or city councils to help the people they serve in their home communities.

People who are good at their jobs are notorious for getting promoted to administrative or supervisory roles. Therefore, expert counselors or teachers often find themselves in positions in which they no longer work directly with clients or children. Instead, they must use their expertise through influence on counselors and teachers. Helping effects must be produced at second or third hand. The specific techniques required for operating in such fashion will frequently differ from those used when working more directly, but the basic dynamics do not change. The fundamental principles guiding the supervisor's or consultant's relationships are the same as those that guide the teacher, social worker, or counselor.

Among the special problems of helping indirectly is the frustration of having to rely on others to get things done. This is especially true if plans must be formulated at some distance from the scene of action. When one is away from the pressures of immediate events, appropriate paths for action can often be seen with greater clarity. For helpers at the front line who are inescapably immersed in the problems, matters may be perceived very differently. Patience and understanding are even more essential when it is necessary to work with and through other people. Effective helping from more remote levels of operation depends on open communication. Many otherwise good programs have disintegrated because of failure to recognize and deal with the importance of this question. The farther away the helper must work from the scene of direct involvement, the more difficult it is to keep the lines of communication open.

Who Is the Client?

Many a helper, forced to work in consulting roles, makes herself ineffective because of confusion about who the client is. The client is always the person with whom the helper is immediately in touch. For example, a teacher asks the school psychologist for help in working with a difficult child. If the psychologist sees her role primarily as one of working face-to-face with a child, at the time of the teacher's complaint she is likely to reply: "Very well, Mr. Atwood, send him down to my office and I'll see what I can do with him." In making this response the psychologist has lost a valuable opportunity to be of assistance. The proper client for a consultant is *whomever the consultant is confronting.* The school psychologist who sees herself in this broader role does not make the mistake of sending her primary client away. Instead, she tells Mr. Atwood, "I can see how difficult it must be for you to work with him. Sit down and let's talk about it." She begins her work by trying to help the teacher. She recognizes that helping the child involves helping the teacher deal with the child more effectively. Because the teacher is the person who is in daily intimate contact with the child, success will most likely be reached with and through the teacher. As the psychologist helps the teacher deal with his frustrations, she contributes directly to his strength and capacity to carry out his job, and he is better able to deal with the child who is his current problem.

When school psychologists work this way they frequently do not have to work with the child at all. Sometimes the opportunity to discuss the problem works therapeutically and is enough to give the teacher new courage to try again and insight to try new approaches. Even if this does not occur, at the end of the session with a teacher the psychologist can still arrange to see the child and talk some more with the teacher on another occasion.

An additional complication for helpers working in consultant, administrative, or supervisory roles is created by the authority associated with such positions. Generally speaking, the greater the authority of the administrator or supervisor, the greater the anxiety and fear of encounter with her. This is likely to hinder creativity, create resistance, and impede communication between first- and second-level helpers. In earlier chapters we discussed the importance of "visibility" in fostering helping relationships. It is especially important for helpers who are working at remoter levels, therefore, to give high priority to keeping open lines of communication with those they must work through.

SOME MANAGEMENT ASPECTS OF HELPING

Management and Manipulation

Methods of helping through control and direction of students, clients, or patients are often impatiently rejected by some workers in the helping professions, and the words "manipulation" and "management" have sometimes been regarded as synonymous with evil. It is, of course, true that behavioristic approaches to helping may become mechanistic and dehumanizing. But this must be so only if they are used without a guiding philosophy. When used in a humane context, behavioristic principles, techniques, and methods can help people be more successful, lead to self-enhancement, and change self-concepts.[1] Having stated a set of goals, one may select many procedures for achieving those ends. The only time helpers are forced to reject a particular way of achieving goals is when it violates their primary frame of reference.

We have stated the perceptual principle, that behavior changes when people change their perceptions of themselves and the world. A change in environment, however, can also result in changed perceptions and behavior. If people are moved to new, more positive environments in which they begin to have reinforcing experiences, receive more rewards, and are treated better by those around them, their perceptions will almost certainly change. As we have seen, there is no such thing as a good or right method of helping. The principle applies to manipulation. Of itself, it is neither good nor bad. It has acquired a bad name because it seems undemocratic to some helpers, a kind of violation of the dignity and integrity of the individual, or perhaps because it is not appropriate or effective for the kinds of problems some helpers deal with. But nothing is inherently wrong with manipulation per se. All helpers manipulate something—the environment, the client, themselves—to create a helping relationship. Like any other method, it may be used appropriately or inappropriately, positively or negatively, depending on the skill and understanding of the helper, the goals being sought, and the helper's own frame of reference for approaching the helping task.

Reinforcement

The kinds of relationships established by helpers will largely determine what they reinforce. One of the oldest psychological principles is that people tend to learn those things that result in some kind of reward. Everyone has a need for self-enhancement, and what is experienced as enhancing will likely be sought on other occasions. The professional helper, whether teacher, counselor, social worker, or supervisor, is important by virtue of her position.

What she rewards, consequently, has special significance for those with whom she works.

The helper may use reinforcement openly, so that both she and her client are aware of what is happening; for example, a teacher might say: "That's right, Jimmy," or "That's the way! You're doing well." On the other hand, what a helper reinforces may be so subtle that it is not apparent to the helper herself. Many a counselor has had the unhappy experience of reassuring a client, with the intent of strengthening his confidence, only to find she has produced a transference and made a client dependent on her. To avoid this kind of error, helpers need to be deeply sensitive to the meaning of their own behavior as seen through the eyes of clients. Otherwise, they may find themselves structuring the encounter in ways they had not bargained for.

Positive and negative reinforcement   The principle of positive reinforcement maintains that most learning depends on the presence or absence of reinforcement at the time behavior occurs. If a person's behavior is reinforced at the time of behaving, the probability of that behavior recurring is increased. When an infant utters a sound a mother will often give the child something pleasing, like a drink of milk, a bit of food, or a kiss. Thus that particular bit of behavior, the utterance, is positively reinforced and will most likely occur again. The same thing is true for helping relationships. Authority figures, such as teachers, nurses, and lawyers, are powerful reinforcers. Behavior manifested in helping relationships will greatly depend on what helpers do and do not reinforce by their words and nonverbal behavior.

The principle of negative reinforcement holds that a person's desired behavior will increase when noxious or irritating stimuli are removed. In other words, with positive reinforcement desired behavior is increased by adding something to the situation. With negative reinforcement, desired behavior is increased by taking something away from the situation. Both are intended to have positive results.

Reinforcement and feedback   One of the greatest assets of reinforcement is the opportunity it presents for feedback. Learners need continuous opportunities to observe the consequences of their acts, to see the results of perceptions, and to correct faulty assumptions. Perhaps even more important, feedback frequently has the effect of raising new problems to be solved. An act that does not produce the expected results immediately confronts the learner with a new problem. Without feedback the learner will not know whether his thinking needs further modification or not.

Effective learning, whether it be in connection with shooting on a rifle range, selling a product, raising a child, solving arithmetic problems, or making love, requires knowledge of results. Because this is so, much of the time and energy of helpers is devoted to helping students or clients discover and deal with the consequences of their decisions. Sometimes helpers may do this by providing real opportunities to test out new meanings—as when a coach provides an opponent for a young boxer to test his new stance. Sometimes helpers can only wait while a client makes her own tests in the world she lives in. On occasion this may mean that the counselor or teacher sits quietly while the helpee tries a solution that the helper knows will probably not work.

Reinforcement schedules   Whether in teaching, counseling, or some other helping relationship, varying the time, amount, and number of reinforcements is more effective than continuous reinforcement. In most helping relationships, reinforcement will happen on a variable schedule naturally, because most helpers do not deliberately or systematically pay attention to when they are or are not reinforcing a helpee's behavior. However, by systematically and intentionally varying the reinforcement, results can often be achieved much more quickly than if the variability is occurring simply by chance.

Those responses that a helper seeks to reinforce will depend on the frame of reference from which the helper approaches the task. Operating from a closed system, the helper attempts to reinforce a student's or client's behavior or those intermediate steps a client takes toward the achievement of objectives. Operating from an open system, the helper's reinforcements will be directed toward the conditions or processes of helping. That is, reinforcement is used to teach the student or client where to look for the most efficient discovery of new meaning.

Reinforcement in counseling   One way counselors assist clients to explore personal meaning is to hold significant factors up for examination. Out of the mass of facts, feelings, description, comment, and explanation, the counselor responds to the feelings expressed by his client. This technique is sometimes called "recognition and acceptance of feeling." It could well be called recognition and acceptance of personal meaning. The technique focuses the client's attention on personal meanings rather than on factual material expressed. By continual response to personal meaning the counselor reinforces the client's behavior, and before long the client begins to turn attention increasingly to personal meanings, often without need for further reinforcement from the counselor.

Reading the protocols of almost any counseling session will reveal this process of reinforcement in action. In the following excerpt from a counseling case, note how the counselor bypasses the factual content of what his client is saying to respond to the personal meaning she is expressing. The young woman in the case came for help because of her deep distress over a shriveled hand, which was a birth defect.

Y.W.:   I thought that—well, what I am trying to say is that I would try to push it off and I found that I couldn't.

C.:   You found that that was impossible.

Y.W.:   I thought that they were just being sorry and were trying to make up by giving me things.

C.:   They were sorry—

Y.W.:   (cutting in) That was no good. It did no one any good.

C.:   You don't want people to feel sorry for you.

Y.W.:   Never! I never want that!

C.:   I see. Although you didn't want people to feel sorry for you, you felt you got it anyhow.

Y.W.:   Yes, people didn't say anything but I could feel it. I used to wonder what would happen in a group if someone actually said something about it. It frightened me so. I think that I wouldn't know what to do. I am afraid of what they might do. I would rather not have my parents know what happens sometimes. Better that I know it just myself than all three of us.

C.:   You prefer that they not know about it.

Y.W.:   They must have known when I was little. In those days it didn't matter to me. I remember one instance when I went home from school—the only instance that I ever told them how I really felt. That was the time when I packed up here at school and took a train home. I just couldn't stand it any longer and called them up and told them I was coming home. I should never have done it. Some of the girls said something, and it got worse and worse until I couldn't stand it any more. So I went, and I was sorry I did.

C.:   You feel that that was a mistake.

Y.W.:   I don't know what happened. When I was on the train—I remember I called them and told them I was coming home and then on the train I decided that I would not tell them anything. I'd make up some other story about something else. I was riding home from the train in the car when Mother said, "Is it about your hand?" And then I told her about it. I just broke down and told her. That was the only time.

C.:   M-hm.

Y.W.:   Afterwards I told them I wanted something done. Something just had to be done! I had an appliance made, but it didn't work. I gave it up after a while and never mentioned it again. They didn't either. They didn't know the other times. I don't think there is anything to be gained now by telling them.

C.:   So this has been a kind of secret that everybody knew, but nobody talked about?[2]

Pointing the Way in Adult–Child Relationships

Haim Ginott, in a delightful book for parents, has recommended a similar technique to improve communication between parents and children. Here is a conversation he reports between a child and his mother.

> When a child comes home with a host of complaints about a friend or a teacher or about his life, it is best to respond to his feeling tone, instead of trying to ascertain facts to verify incidents.
> Ten-year-old Harold came home cranky and complaining.

Harold:	What a miserable life! The teacher called me a liar, just because I told her that I forgot the homework. And she yelled; my goodness, did she yell! She said she'll write you a note.
Mother:	You had a very rough day.
Harold:	You can say that again.
Mother:	It must have been terribly embarrassing to be called a liar in front of the whole class.
Harold:	It sure was.
Mother:	I bet inside yourself you wished her a few things!
Harold:	Oh, yes! But how did you know?
Mother:	That's what we usually do when someone hurts us.
Harold:	That's a relief.[3]

Pointing the Way in School

Teachers accomplish a similar kind of focus with reinforcing comments like the following:

"Billy, I can see that you feel very angry at Jimmy. I can understand how you might feel that way, but you're not allowed to hit him."
"How do you feel about the poem, Helen?"
"Do you think the court was justified in the ruling?"
"What do you think is the purpose of the procedure?"

Extinction

Extinction is another behavioral principle that is useful for the professional helper. It is based on the old adage that if you ignore someone or something it will go away. Stated in behavioristic terms, if reinforcement is not present or is removed, behavior will extinguish, disappear. Behavior that does not result in some form of feedback is soon discarded, as many parents and teachers have discovered. Expert teachers, for example, handle many behavior problems by simply ignoring them. They know that without some reinforcement the behavior is likely to spend itself quickly. Similarly, many problems between parents and children could easily be avoided if the child's misbehavior were calmly ignored.

As a significant other, whatever the helper does or does not do conveys some sort of message to the student or client. The choices that helpers make in reacting to clients or students are important. Helpers communicate meanings whether they want to or not. They are the data from which helpees learn about self and subtly express the approved or disapproved uses of the relationship. If helpers are unaware of interactions and their meanings, they run the risk of behaving irresponsibly and of making helping processes fortuitous. To meet the obligations they have assumed as helpers and to raise techniques above the level of mere accident, helpers must be keenly aware of the impact they have on their clients. This is even true when, as in the case of extinction, they do nothing at all.

Token Economies

Token economies are "little societies" based on the principles of operant conditioning. A group, say a public school class, earns tokens for performing specified tasks. In an elementary school class, children might be given tokens for being neat, doing their schoolwork, and cooperating. The tokens can be accumulated and exchanged later for something the student desires, such as free time, candy, and trinkets. The purpose is not to bribe children for learning or working. It is hoped that the behavior they are learning will become intrinsically rewarding, and the tokens will eventually be replaced by more abstract reinforcements. When tokens are given they are usually associated with social rewards, like praise. The goal is to replace the tokens with the intrinsic pleasure of learning and with social reinforcers.

Precision Teaching and Charting Behavior

Precision teaching is also an outgrowth of operant conditioning. It has been so fully developed and refined, however, that it may be considered a procedure on its own. Although it has been developed mainly for use in educational settings, some of the techniques growing out of its development are applicable in other helping relationships. For example, charting may be used to record the progress of any behavior change program. So in precision teaching students are sometimes asked to carry out a self-improvement program designed to change almost any kind of behavior, including such things as decreasing smoking, losing weight, increasing sexual activity, and extinguishing tics. Charting begins by establishing what is called the base rate of ongoing behavior (for example, the number of cigarettes smoked in a given period) when the program begins. Sometimes a behavior like smoking will decrease simply from learning what the actual frequency is. Generally, however, some type of consequence has to be added to bring about a change. With smoking, a person could be charged a dime for every cigarette he smoked or would have to decrease the amount of time he could engage in another desired behavior. One could also increase the amount of desired behavior for every decrease in the amount of undesirable behavior, which would be more humanistic. In any case, behavior continues to be charted, and a graphic measure of the effects of intervention is established. Observers, whether observing their own or someone else's behavior, know precisely how their efforts are affecting behavior. Once the basic technique has been learned, it can be used by any lay person or professional helper to change his own or another's behavior.[4]

SOME MANAGEMENT TECHNIQUES OF LIMITED VALUE FOR HELPING

Punishment

It is commonly assumed that punishment is a highly valued technique in behavioral approaches to helping. As a matter of fact, most proponents of operant conditioning stress the importance of positive consequences for facilitating change in behavior. B. F. Skinner has repeatedly expressed his reasons for rejecting the use of punishment as a device for producing significant change in human beings. One of his papers on punishment is subtitled, "A Questionable Technique."[5] There is little place for punishment in helping relationships, and helpers of many persuasions, humanists and behaviorists alike, have expressed grave doubts about its appropriateness as a technique for at least two major reasons. First, there is reason to doubt that punishment works in anything more than temporary and superficial fashion; and second, the technique often causes side effects whose negative consequences far outweigh positive results.

In examining the question of punishment it is necessary to differentiate between punishment in a physical context (a child burnt by a hot stove) and punishment in a social context (punishment by an angry parent). In the physical context, when a child touches a hot stove the consequences are usually no more than some slightly burnt little fingers. This is an objective, unemotional encounter with life, with causes and consequences clear even to a young child. A person, unless he is very ill, cannot remain angry or hold a grudge for long against a stove, and he certainly can't gain revenge on the punisher with much satisfaction.

Punishment inflicted on one human by another is something else. That involves much subjectivity and emotion. Furthermore, the reasons for the punishment are seldom clearly understood, the justification is usually questioned, and retribution is a likely possibility. Punishment in a social context is a questionable technique indeed.

The effect of punishment, more often than not, is temporary; in most instances it has only short-term effects. At the time punishment is administered, the culprit may stop what he is doing, especially if he is a young child being physically restrained by an adult. But there is every reason to believe, both in terms of scientific research and common observation, that the behavior will manifest itself again.

The most significant arguments against the use of punishment, we believe, are not in regard to whether it works, but in connection with the side effects that accompany its use. The following are samples of many such side effects.

1. *Punishment of any kind generates negative responses.* Persons who are punished become fearful, anxious, and hostile and because of these feelings often engage in "displacement"—that is, striking out at others in retaliation for the pain and embarrassment they have suffered. The results are seldom any better for the administrator of the punishment. Punishment is a vengeful human response, and it often snowballs. The more a person is punished, the more frustrated and hostile he becomes. This causes him to strike back even more forcefully, thereby causing the punisher to become more frustrated and angry and to punish harder and with greater furor—hardly a pleasant or fruitful human experience.

2. *Associating punishment with the undesirable behavior rather than with the self is often difficult, especially for young children.* It is easy for a child to mistake badness in the self rather than in the act for which she is being punished. To believe that it is "me" and not my behavior that is bad is a simple thing. This is likely to happen particularly when the punishment for a single act is prolonged over a period of time, as when someone is given the "silent treatment" for long periods after committing an undesirable act, or when a child is told, "Wait till your father gets home. You'll get it then!"

3. *Punished behavior can generalize to desirable behavior.* Without realizing the consequences, behavior that is inappropriate at a certain age or time is often punished, even though the same behavior will be desirable at another age or time. The result is that individuals inadvertently are made incapable of performing highly desirable and, in many cases, absolutely necessary human acts. The following is a specific example. One Christmas some parents decided that a nice gift for their three children would be a set of illustrated Bible stories. The set was beautiful, elaborate, expensive, and contained twenty-four volumes. It was accompanied by a wooden bookcase. The thought behind the gift was commendable, and the gift was a fine one indeed—but not for these children, at the time the set was given. All three children were much too young to appreciate it and were unable to care for it and use it appropriately. Nevertheless, on Christmas Day the children were shown the set, told it was theirs, and then were told they were not to handle it! If they wanted to use it or see some of the pictures, they would have to call on one of the parents.

One can guess what happened. It was too much to expect that a child could understand how he could own something and yet not be allowed to touch it. So time and again one child or the other attempted to take a book from the case, and each time they did so, the mother or father would punish the child.

Thus for a period of from one to three years, depending on which child was involved, his major encounter with books and religious material occurred under the stress and emotional turmoil of a situation in which he was yelled at, smacked, and generally dominated by an angry, reprimanding parent.

This kind of association may be the direct result of punishment for behavior that is bad at one time but good at another. Sex training, for example, is one area in which this frequently occurs. For years we punish, condemn, or manifest embarrassment at every response children make that has the slightest sexual connotation. Then, when they reach some magical age or join in marriage, they are expected spontaneously to be accomplished lovers.

The use of punishment for controlling misbehavior is inevitable at times. Sometimes the consequences of the act that a person is about to perform are so dire that there may be no time for another alternative. Sometimes certain behaviors must be stopped in the quickest way possible. As a tool for the helping professions, however, punishment generally leaves much to be desired. Although it may, on occasion, be necessary to use it, helpers need to be fully aware of the dynamics involved in its use and especially of the meanings it creates in the experience of the subject, lest helpers destroy with the left hand what the right hand is trying to build.

Competition

Most of us assume that competition is an excellent device for motivating people to extend themselves in athletic events, business affairs, or getting an education. People do indeed appear to be highly motivated by competitive effort, if one examines the behavior of successful competitors. Examining the matter in larger perspective, especially from the point of view of the behaver, the value of competition looks quite different.

When someone wins there have to be losers. For most people, competition is not a useful, nor even a healthy, technique. In discussing the matter David Johnson identifies three ways in which learning activities can be structured: cooperative, competitive, and individualistic.[6] He says that the first establishes a positive relationship between learners; the second, a negative relationship; and the third, neither a positive nor a negative one. He also reviews some of the literature comparing the effects of these three structures. His conclusions are overwhelming. He points out that cooperative structures, when compared to competitive and individual structures, promote:

- More effective communication and exchange of information among learners
- Greater facilitation of one another's achievement
- More tutoring and showing of resources among students
- Greater trust among other pupils and emotional involvement in and commitment to learning

- Higher utilization of the resources of other students, higher achievement motivation, and less fear of failure
- More divergent and risk-taking thinking.

And as if that wasn't enough, Johnson goes on to say that cooperative learning results in "stronger beliefs that one is liked, supported, and accepted by other students, and that other students care about how much one learns and they want to help one learn."[7]

After conducting their own research and completing a review similar to Johnson's, Carole and Russell Ames reached these conclusions about competition.[8] They say that competitive reward structures have more negative than positive implications for behavior and that the consequences of any failure are negative, but the impact of failure in competitive situations appears to be rather devastating to one's self-image. And because competition is a failure-oriented system even the self-esteem of a person with high self-concepts must suffer some damage.

We are impressed by the competitive features of our society and like to think of ourselves as essentially a competitive people. Yet we are thoroughly and completely dependent on the goodwill and cooperation of our fellow citizens at every moment of our lives. In turn, other people depend on us. We are indeed "our brothers' keepers" as never before in history. Although we occasionally compete with others, competition is not the rule of life but the exception. One needs but reflect on the past twenty-four hours to discover how overwhelmingly one's behavior has been cooperative and how seldom competitive. When understood in terms of the effects of challenge and threat, competition turns out to be a motivating force of limited value for some and downright destructive for others.

Examined in the light of our understanding of challenge and threat, three things become apparent about the effects of competition:

1. *Competition has motivating force only for those who believe they have a chance of winning.* That is to say, it motivates those for whom competition is perceived as challenge. People do not work for things they believe they cannot achieve; they work only for things that seem within their grasp.

2. *People who are forced to compete and who do not believe they have a chance of success are not motivated by the experience; they are threatened by it.* Far from motivating people, competition, under these circumstances, is quite likely to result in disillusionment and discouragement. Those who do not see much chance of success cannot be inveigled into making an effort. They avoid competition whenever they can. Any teacher knows that a child who works for scholastic honors thinks he or she has a possibility of winning. The competitors work like crazy, while the noncompetitors go about more important business of their own.

Whether or not competition is challenging or threatening depends on how the situation seems to the competitor—not how it seems to an outsider. Left to themselves, people will compete only rarely, and then only when they think they have a chance of success. Forcing people to compete can result only in discouragement or rebellion. When the cards are stacked against us we give up playing or start a fight with the people who are responsible for the stacking. Forced to compete, people may simply go through the motions in a dispirited, listless manner or revolt against the oppressors.

3. *When competition becomes too important any means becomes justified to achieve the ends.* Winning is the aim of competition, and the temptation is to win at any cost. Although competition begins with the laudable aim of encouraging production, it quickly breaks down to a struggle to win at any price. When winning is not crucial, as in casual sports and games, competition can add excitement and fun and so serve a useful and satisfying function. Competition as a way of life is a different matter. The means we use to achieve our ends are always bought at a price. When victory becomes too important, students cheat on exams, athletic teams begin to "play dirty," and business executives lie to their customers. Price tags must be read not only in dollars and cents but also in terms of human values—broken bodies, broken spirits, and disheartened and disillusioned people who do not appear in the winner's circle, on the sports page, or as guests of honor at the testimonial banquet.

Competition encourages lone-wolf endeavors, and lone wolves can be dangerous to a cooperative society. We need to be able to count on other people to seek our best interests along with their own. In the headlong rush to win, competition too easily loses sight of this responsibility. It values aggression, hostility, and scorn. "Dog eat dog" becomes its philosophy. Too often the degree of glory involved for the victor is in direct proportion to the abasement and degradation of the loser.

Notes and References

1. For more detailed discussions of how a reconciliation may be brought about between humanism and behaviorism, see Donald Avila and William W. Purkey, "Intrinsic and Extrinsic Motivations: A Regrettable Distinction," *Psychology in the Schools* 3 (1966):206–208, and "Self-Theory and Behaviorism: A Rapprochement," *Psychology in the Schools* (1972):124–126.

2. "Case of Edith Moore" by Arthur W. Combs, from *Casebook of Non-Directive Counseling*, edited by William Snyder, copyright © 1947, renewed 1974 by Houghton Mifflin Company. Used with permission.

3. From H. Ginott, *Between Parent and Child* (New York: Macmillan, 1965). Reprinted by permission.

4. Interested readers may find more detailed descriptions of charting and its uses in M. A. Koorland and M. Mitchell, *Elementary Principles and Procedures of the Standard Behavior Chart* (Gainesville, Fla.: Learning Environments, 1975).

5. B. F. Skinner, *Science and Human Behavior* (New York: Macmillan, 1953).

6. D. W. Johnson, "Student-Student Interaction: The Neglected Variable in Education," *Educational Researcher* 10 (1981):5–10.

7. Ibid., p. 7.

8. Carole Ames and Russell Ames, "The Thrill of Victory and the Agony of Defeat: Children's Self and Interpersonal Evaluations in Competitive and Noncompetitive Learning Environments," *Journal of Research and Development in Education* 12 (1978):79–87.

THIRTEEN

BEING AND BECOMING HELPERS

The helper's self is the primary tool with which the helper works. As we have seen, every human being has tremendous possibilities, and there is almost no limit to what a self may become. Understanding the self and learning to use it well is a lifelong process of personal discovery. Because every helper is unique, no universal rules, regulations, or procedures can be required for such explorations. Facilitating the growth of helpers is in itself a helping process, however, and the principles we have been discussing throughout this book apply to aspiring helpers and professional training programs as well. Such concepts cannot be expressed as clear-cut do's and don't's. They can, however, serve as suggestions for personal growth and as hypotheses or guideposts for effective practice.

BECOMING HELPERS

Becoming Begins from Acceptance

Research demonstrates that self-acceptance is closely related to acceptance of others. People willing and able to confront who they are with clarity and honesty are much more likely to be able to do this with those with whom they interact. Acceptance is a major characteristic of adequate personalities, and it is also a basic requirement for helping relationships. Becoming an effective professional worker is not a matter of trading in one's old self for a new one. Rather, it is a matter of learning how to use the self one has and of improving it slowly over a period of time. A good place to start is with the principle of acceptance, to begin with the declaration, "It's all right to be me!"

In any group of beginners the range of background, experience, attitudes, knowledge, maturity, and motivation varies widely. Some people are farther along at the beginning of a program than others will be at the end. Helpers also vary greatly in the speed with which they can grow, and the needs that students have for various kinds of experience are seldom the same. The student-helper must learn to appreciate her own uniqueness and exhibit a readiness to confront whatever is needed for her own next steps in development, irrespective of where others in the process may be. Setting unreasonable goals and making invidious comparisons with others only distort the focus of effort and result in anxiety.

Expert helpers do not develop overnight. *Techniques* of helping, like changes of costume, can sometimes be quickly put on. The development of an effective "self as instrument," however, is not achieved by using gadgets or gimmicks. There are few substitutes for experience in the helping professions. The growth of helpers is a product of increasingly differentiated perceptions, of maturing beliefs, values, and understandings. This takes time, and many an otherwise likely candidate has destroyed effectiveness by impatience or lack of self-acceptance. Sudden changes rarely take place in students, clients, or patients. Nor do they occur any more frequently in helpers.

Exploring Personal Meaning

Learning to use one's self effectively is a highly personal matter. Growth of self can occur only with the cooperation of learners and a willingness to commit self in the processes of growth. It follows that the development of helpers must be predicated on high levels of self-direction and acceptance of primary responsibility for their own learning by aspiring helpers. Responsibility and self-direction are learned. They must be acquired from experience, from being given opportunities to be self-directing and responsible. You cannot learn to be self-directing if no one lets you try. Human capacities are strengthened by use but atrophy with disuse. Autonomy, responsibility, and independence are the products of being willing to look and eager to try.

Changing the Self

Many assume that to help people change, the thing to do is to have them analyze themselves, decide what needs to be done, and then go do it. Some training programs, therefore, spend a great deal of time having young helpers indulge in self-examination, evaluating themselves and their behavior against long lists of the characteristics of "good" teachers, counselors, social workers, or whatever. Such approaches to changing self are rarely helpful. The self-concept is an organization of meanings that cannot be changed by simply *deciding* to be different or concentrating attention on behavior. People discover who they are and what they are from the feedback they get in their interactions with the world and with others or through the exploration of personal meanings. Intensive self-analysis often results in little more than maudlin self-indulgence. Having people examine themselves with great intensity concentrates attention on behavior rather than on the meanings producing behavior.

Our own clients in psychotherapy do not get better when they examine themselves or their behavior. They get better when they look at their personal meanings, at how they feel about their wives, husbands, kids, jobs or the people they are working with. For example, let us suppose that Mary

Johnson would like to make herself more lovable. To make herself more lovable, one thing she ought *not* do is sit around and think about her lovableness! She may, however, become more lovable by thinking about how she feels about other people—her friends, husband, parents, people she works with—or by thinking about minority groups, social problems, and what she values and cares about. As a consequence of this exploration, she may come to feel better about these people and events. Feeling better toward them, her behavior will mirror her better feeling. Other people, reacting to her new behavior, will then respond by treating Mary nicer. In turn, as Mary perceives this new reaction of others, she may discover she has become more lovable.

The extensive, internally consistent organization of beliefs characteristic of effective helpers is achieved only after long and frequent confrontations with ideas. Helpers acquire personal understandings in the same ways their students, clients, or patients do—through a continuous, step-by-step process of exploration. Belief systems are the products of discussing, debating, trying, thinking, experimenting, making mistakes, and starting again in never-ending inquiry. All this takes time and a wholehearted commitment to the process. It cannot be rushed. Nor is it simply a matter of acquiring new information. If it were true that people changed simply by knowledge about what ought to be done, then education professors would be by far the best teachers; psychologists and psychiatrists, the best adjusted; nurses and doctors, the healthiest; and ministers, the most serene. But everyone knows that this is not so.

Earlier in the discussion of the principles of learning we observed that there is a vast difference between knowing and behaving. Effective learning comes about as a consequence of discovery of personal meaning. It is not enough simply to know; helpers must understand so deeply and personally that knowledge will affect behavior.

Practitioner–Scholar Dilemma

Most students entering programs for the helping professions begin with a quest for information. All their previous school experience has been primarily academic, emphasizing the acquisition of information. Their success has been evaluated by tests designed to measure the degree to which information was acquired, and success or failure was demonstrated by grades intended to reward or punish performance in the approved academic competition. As a consequence, aspiring helpers come to training programs believing that they are not learning anything unless someone is telling them something new. This is a great pity, for failure to understand the practitioner–scholar distinction often delays progress in their new professional life.

The major goal for the scholar is to learn *about* something, to understand its relationship to other ideas, and perhaps to teach it to someone else. To achieve this end, scholars seek out sources of information wherever they may be obtained, from lectures, reading, research, field trips, demonstrations, or discussions with experts. The problem of the practitioner is a different one. For professional workers it is not enough just to know—helpers have to *use* what they have learned. That goal requires a different educational experience. Practitioners must get involved. It may be enough for the educational psychologist to know about children as a group, for example; but teachers, counselors, or social workers need to understand a particular child. Understanding people as unique human beings is different from understanding them academically.

This fundamental difference in objectives is the basis for the misunderstandings that often occur between students and teachers in liberal arts colleges and students and teachers in professional schools. One group is concerned primarily with the acquisition of knowledge; the other, with professional performance. So the scholar observes the nurse, the teacher, the counselor, or clinical psychologist and exclaims, "Mickey Mouse stuff! How unscientific can you get?" Professional workers, on the other hand, look at the work of the scholar and exclaim, "What good is that? Imagine trying that with my patient!" (or student or client). Each observes the other through the glasses of his own values, beliefs, and decisions as to what is important, and each finds the other wanting. This breakdown of understanding between scholars and practitioners sometimes becomes very bitter.

Beginning students in the helping professions often complain that they aren't learning anything, because they spend many hours in observing and experimenting and in interminable talk. They do not understand that beliefs, values, and purposes are not acquired from information alone but from the personal discovery of the meaning of information. For example, to make operational the basic principle of democracy—"when people are free, they can find their own best ways"—does not require more information. For most of us, what is needed is a deeper understanding of the full meaning of that simple statement. Most people can glibly state the principle, but comparatively few have so deeply comprehended its meaning that they consistently behave in truly democratic fashion.

Confronting Ultimate Questions

One of the ways in which helpers can test the depth of their grasp of purposes and dynamics is to come face to face with "ultimate" questions. For example, counselors who espouse belief in the confidentiality of counseling may ask themselves how far they are willing to stick by the principle. Would the counselor refuse information to a client's parent who demanded to know what her daughter said in the counseling hour? Would the counselor refuse information to another counselor? Would he or she defy a court order to reveal what a client confided?

How far would a social worker go in permitting a client to make her own decision? So far as to make a decision that seemed basically wrong to the social worker? To choose an antisocial act? To make a decision harmful to herself?

How far would a teacher go in maintaining the democratic belief? So far as to let students elect the "wrong" fellow student to office? To let children make their own rules? Or revolt against an autocratic school regulation?

Experienced helpers behave from instant to instant, apparently without ever thinking about what they ought to do next or how to go about it. Their behavior is a smoothly flowing, spontaneous response to students or clients determined, almost automatically, by well-established, internally consistent belief systems. Beginners approach their tasks in a more tentative fashion because they do not have such clear-cut guidelines. An internally consistent set of beliefs about themselves, other people, and appropriate purposes and processes makes smooth, effective practice possible.

Creating the Need to Know

One of the few principles of learning about which there is universal agreement is that people learn best when they have a need to know. Despite this understanding, a great deal of teaching is designed with almost total disregard for the principle. When people need to know they go to extraordinary lengths to find out. Without a need to know the most magnificent presentation may fall on deaf ears. Helper-learners can sometimes generate need from within their own experience, but real confrontation with problems is far more likely to provide effective motives for learning. Personal meaning is best achieved through problem solving: confronting dilemmas, questions, and events and seeking appropriate resolutions. Such problems can sometimes be manufactured and presented to student-helpers as hypothetical situations in written form like case studies, in spoken directions as in role playing, or in some form of audiovisual presentation as in psychodrama, records, or television. Confrontation is far more effective, however, when problems faced are real and immediate.

The most vital source of problems for student-helpers is, of course, actual confrontation with students, clients, or patients. Once practice teaching, counseling practicums, and social work internships were provided at the end of professional programs as opportunities for the student-helper to practice what he had learned from his teacher-trainers. Many professional programs now regard such experience as far more valuable for aiding students to find out what the problems are. Consequently, practical experience is now often provided throughout the training program as a vehicle for creating needs to know.

Although few student-helpers are ever able to choose precisely the nature of their experiences, they can welcome and take advantage of opportunities for new and positive experience. When this is done, chances are that those experiences will lead to further possibilities. Successful experience contributes to positive feelings about self, and helpers can increase their chances for such experience by trying themselves to the limits of their capacities. The basic principle that good helping relationships are challenging without being threatening is also a useful guideline for the explorations of helpers themselves.

Methods and Becoming

Every helping profession has its special kinds of techniques and methods for carrying out its functions, and the most immediate focus of the beginning helper's attention is usually concentrated on acquiring useful methods. It is a frightening thing to be placed in a helping role unequipped to carry out one's responsibilities. In the face of such threats, beginners beg for "tricks of the trade." The questions asked are likely to be, "What shall I do? How shall I do it? What do I do if . . . ?" Such questions are understandable. Survival is at stake, and beginners need basic techniques with which to get started. Searching for "right" methods in the helping professions, however, is a blind alley.

Helping relationships are human interactions, and the people who are involved in this process are unique human beings. The search for common methods to cope with uniqueness is an exercise in futility. The task of the helper-learner is a matter of finding methods that fit: fit the client, fit the student or patient, fit the problems to be dealt with, fit the situations in which helper and helpee are involved, fit the purposes and dynamics of the particular helping profession, and, of course, fit the nature and condition of the helper's self. The lack of right methods to be learned and practiced may be a disappointment to aspiring helpers. On the other hand, the uniqueness of methods means that no helper can be required to be like any other. Helpers can be who they are and what they are, and the methods they use can be their very own.

A common fallacy in some training programs is the belief that the methods of experts can be taught directly to beginners. As a matter of fact, many methods of the experts work only because they are expert. For example, expert teachers handle most disciplinary problems by ignoring them, hardly a method to be recommended to the neophyte! Similarly, many techniques of expert counselors, social workers, or pastors are effective because the background of experience, study, and assimilation of ideas have become so much a part of the effective worker as to make his interactions a smooth-flowing expression of his personal meanings. Exhorting beginners to model themselves after the experts can prove to be more discouraging than motivating. Even when beginners find themselves in what is ostensibly the same practical problem as the expert, they do not have the understanding or belief systems to make the method work. Beginning helpers need to find their own ways rather than adopt the ways of others. Helpers need experiences that make them stretch but at which they have a fighting chance of success. Setting goals too high can be discouraging and self-defeating. Setting them too low can result in apathy and boredom.

Painters speak of searching for their "idiom," by which they mean the peculiar style of painting that fits the individual artist and best expresses her message. In similar fashion, effective helpers engage in a continual search for ways to create helping relationships that best fit their own and their clients' needs. Effective helpers know that when their methods are authentic, the relationships they establish are more likely to be successful. As most of us know from our own experience in dealing with other people, those who try to pretend to be what they are not come across as phonies.

Special Experiences for Personal Growth

In addition to planned experiences provided by training programs and experiences sought out or contrived by helpers themselves, helper-learners can take advantage of a wide variety of opportunities especially designed to further personal growth and actualization. Some of these are in the very professions and practices for which helper-learners are preparing. Others may be found outside professional or academic settings. In Chapter Ten we mentioned some ways of increasing sensitivity and group experiences as aids to personal growth. Others may be found in modern techniques for expanding personal awareness and in various forms of counseling and psychotherapy.

Expanding Personal Awareness

A number of mind- or consciousness-expanding groups developed during the sixties, and many still exist. Some of these groups concentrate on aiding people to become more aware of their physical bodies. Others seek to free mental processes through various forms of meditation, through the use of hypnosis, or through the use of hallucinogenic drugs. Still others attempt to expand awareness in spiritual terms. Some of these attempts to expand awareness are very old, having deep roots in Oriental cultures, whereas others are comparatively new.

Some consciousness-expanding movements have evolved into religious cults, stoutly defended by adherents and accompanied by the trappings of religious ceremony. Others have been exploited for personal gain by self-anointed "masters" calling themselves psychologists, counselors, gurus, swamis, trainers, or any of a hundred other titles. Some movements, however, continue to grow and bid fair to make important contributions to human health and fulfillment. Some have even been the subjects of empirical research and so have established themselves on more than testimonial grounds. Among these latter are several forms of meditation.

Doctor Heal Thyself

Beginning helpers sometimes hesitate to seek professional help for themselves because they regard such actions as indications of personal weakness, which may be regarded as lack of fitness for the profession. Such attitudes are not only unfortunate, but they are also downright destructive to personal growth. The assumption that helpers must be extraordinary people of vastly superior character is totally out of line with the basic nature of helping professions. Effective helpers are human beings like everyone else, and they suffer problems and frustrations like all other members of the human race. Being an effective helper does not require that one be totally without problems, only that the problems be sufficiently resolved to assure minimum interference in the work of helping others. Many successful helpers have personally experienced pain and suffering and periods of inadequacy. It may even be true that many people have been initially attracted to the helping professions because they felt a need for personal help. After all, if one has problems, it is an intelligent thing to seek help in solving them.

Helping relationships are only the application of the best we know about healthy human interaction, refined and concentrated for the needs of particular students, clients, or patients. As such, they have value for all people. Growth is a continuous process, and whatever helps it occur ought to be available to the largest possible number of people. The authors have frequently sought the help of colleagues in the helping professions to explore and discover more adequate ways of seeing themselves and the world. Sometimes we have done this because we confronted personal problems. We have also made frequent use of such services simply for their value in clarifying thinking and stimulating personal growth. So have most other professional helpers with whom we are acquainted.

Even if these reasons for using the services of professional helpers were not enough, such services have important value for helper-learners for two other reasons: (1) Those entering the helping professions should demonstrate their faith in the processes they advocate for others; (2) being in the helpee's role is in itself an important learning experience for the aspiring helper. Sensitivity to others and the ability to perceive the world from another's frame of reference are vital skills for the helping professions. One important way in which the helper can sharpen these skills is through the experience of being a student-client, "on the other side" of the helping relationship.

THE HELPER'S OWN SELF-ACTUALIZATION

Helping relationships require that helpers either postpone their own immediate needs for fulfillment or find important satisfactions in being of service to their clients. To do this, helpers need to be well-disciplined. Self-discipline, however, is not an easy thing to maintain unless helpers themselves are achieving a significant degree of personal self-actualization. Deeply deprived people find it difficult or impossible to be much concerned about fulfilling the needs of others. Their own needs are far too pressing.

Helpers need to have themselves well in hand. Otherwise, the question of who is helping whom is likely to become confused. A complete reversal of roles for helper and helpee is not uncommon in teaching and counseling. This can easily happen with a resistant student or client who has learned to keep outsiders from approaching her private feelings by asking them questions about their lives and experiences. The unwary helper can be seduced by this gambit. He responds to the questions, assuming that the client really wants to know. This eases the conversation and seems to contribute to rapport. Unless he is aware of what is going on, he may soon discover that he is doing all the talking and using the experience to ventilate his own feelings.

Self-discipline can sometimes cover up the effects of mild deprivation, but even with the most rigorous personal discipline it is probably impossible for highly inadequate people to completely overcome that handicap to becoming an effective helper. All helping relationships require personal discipline. But self-discipline, no matter how strenuously applied, can rarely substitute sufficiently for positive feelings about self. Positive feelings about self make strenuous efforts at self-discipline less necessary.

Helpers do not have to be perfect. If they did, there would be few in the profession. What is necessary is an accurate, realistic view of themselves, their assets, and their limitations. People engaged in the helping professions must be responsible. In accepting a request for help, helpers assume the responsibility not to exceed their competence. To hold out a hope to someone that cannot be delivered is cruel and inhuman. Worse still, because a client can only judge the value of a helping relationship by her experience of it, a bad experience may prevent the client from ever getting the help she needs because of loss of faith in the process. Good helpers do not exceed their competence. The greater the self-actualization of the helper, the greater the degree of freedom within which he or she can operate effectively. Whatever their level of personal fulfillment, however, professional helpers must have clear understandings of themselves, their talents, and their limitations.

The Personal Self and Professional Self

Beginners in the helping professions sometimes cause themselves and others much unhappiness by confusing their roles as people and professional workers. A person's self and role are not the same. The self consists of a person's personal belief systems, his peculiar ways of seeing himself, and his relationship to the world. In contrast, the professional role defines a set of proper responsibilities and appropriate ways of behaving. These two concepts are related, but they are by no means identical. Although the self must be expressed authentically in the professional role, the professional role does not have to pervade the private life of the helper. One can live the *philosophy* of helping and apply it to one's own life. Attempting to live the *practice* of the various forms of the helping professionals, however, may only serve to complicate relationships in private life.

The relationships one has with spouse, friends, and co-workers do not call for the person's professional role but for authentic behavior as wife, friend, and colleague. The helper who seeks to be teacher or counselor to husband, friends, and colleagues may succeed only in frustrating and antagonizing them. What they are likely to experience is a hidden agenda—a feeling of being tolerated, used, or manipulated. Beginning counselors, for example, often make themselves obnoxious by "treating" everyone they come in contact with. Treating a person who has not asked for it, or teaching a person who does not want such a relationship, can be a blatant lack of acceptance. It imposes a relationship and so robs others of their right to choose for themselves.

Helpers are not immune to the effects of the self-concept on perception and may even be blinded by their professional roles. Pediatricians, concerned about a child's physical health, have been known to strap a child's arm to a board so that he could not bend his elbow and put his thumb in his mouth, without thinking about what this frustration does to the mental health of the child. Public health nurses and social workers often complain about people who live in shacks but nevertheless own television sets. They forget that if they lived in such squalid conditions, they too might wish to have what little joy and beauty a television set could bring them. Psychologists, deeply concerned about a client's behavior, have been known to overlook the evidence of brain damage in clients. Pastors may be so deeply concerned with the problem of a parishioner's sins that instead of helping, they "cast the first stone." Roles must be appropriate for the relationship in which they are used. It is important for helpers to keep perspectives clear.

The intense concentration of effort involved in many of the helping professions is most exhausting. In addition, the rigorous self-discipline required to carry out some of these relationships effectively requires setting one's self aside in the interests of other people. Even the healthiest self must still seek fulfillment, and this search cannot long be denied. Successful performance in the helping professions may in itself be a form of self-fulfillment, but the self is more than "professional." It is also personal, man or woman, husband or wife, citizen, friend, or any of a thousand other definitions. These too require care and feeding. It is important, therefore, that those who are engaged in the helping professions avail themselves of opportunities to engage in activities that are less demanding and more directly fulfilling of personal needs. The old adage that "all work and no play makes Jack a dull boy" has relevance for the helping professions. The most effective teachers, counselors, nurses, and psychologists known to us are people who do not work at their professional roles full time.

THE HELPER AS PERSON AND CITIZEN

The Helper's Own Economy

People in the helping professions are likely to have many demands made on them, especially if they are good at their jobs. The number of those needing help is great, and the number of professional helpers is small. As a consequence, the demands for aid directed toward people in the helping professions are often overwhelming. This raises difficult problems for helpers. Helpers usually enter the profession because they sincerely want to help other people. When the number of requests so far outnumbers their capacity to deliver, helpers may become discouraged, disillusioned, or embittered.

People in need of help can be terribly demanding of those who are in positions to assist them. This is especially true in those professions dealing with problems of mental health. Desperate people have little time to think of the problems of others. They are likely to be extraordinarily sensitive to slights and demand attention from helpers. To deal with such people requires great patience, a capacity to absorb hostility, and a depth of concern sufficient to carry the helper through long periods of little or no apparent progress.

The effectiveness of helpers depends on how they choose to use themselves as instruments. Some of these decisions will be predetermined by the titles they bear or the accepted practices defined by their places of employment. But even in the most rigidly prescribed settings, there are still many decisions to be made about whom to work with, how to use time, and how to go about the helping task. A helper's success at coping with varied demands depends on her understanding of clients, the nature of the helping task, the extent of the helper's compassion, and the depth of personal resources.

In deciding how to use themselves, helpers will inevitably make mistakes. Mistakes must be expected. They must also be forgiven. The compassion helpers advocate for others must be applied to themselves as well. The helper consumed by guilt or asking too much of himself may end up making himself ineffective.

Helpers are people too and must be permitted the privileges of being human. There may even be times when helpers will have to say "no" to requests that are made of them. This may be an anguished decision for helpers, accompanied by the feeling that they have somehow betrayed their trust. Like everyone else, however, helpers have limitations, and because of those limitations or constraints imposed by outside events, it will sometimes be necessary to reject requests for help. Indeed, not to do so may even result in compounding problems. Counselors, for example, who take on too many clients may end up teaching their clients that the process has little to offer. Teachers who cannot bear to hurt a child by saying "no" when they should may lead their pupils to greater disillusionment and a sense of betrayal at a later date.

Beware the Super Helper

Not recognizing one's limitations is self-destructive. It can rapidly lead to what many consider the number one health problem among professional helpers—*burnout*. In discussing the "super teacher," Elaine G. Wangberg says: "Teachers often think it is possible to do all that is asked of them—and to do it perfectly. This is an impossible standard to live up to. Given the number of roles teachers are called on to play and the number of interactions they enter into each day, there is no way they can always be successful!"[1] These words are generalizable to all helpers, and to paraphrase Wangberg, all helpers must get rid of the myth of the super helper "and begin to focus on and feel satisfied with the successes they do have." Wangberg also stresses that we must legitimize "taking" in the helping professions, even if we find the idea distasteful. By this she means that helpers must learn to take time for themselves, so that they may be replenished. A totally "used up" professional is of no use to anyone!

A Word about Burnout[2]

Burnout is a reality. Many people in the helping professions today are experiencing dissatisfaction with their jobs, boredom, physical and mental exhaustion, frustration, low self-esteem, and other symptoms associated with the term. But just how bad is it? A number of observers say that not only is it rampant in the helping professions but also inevitable. They say that the burden of dealing, day in and day out, with the problems of others is simply too heavy for any person to carry for an extended period. But we really don't know the true extent of the problem.

Little research has been done on burnout. Most of what has been written and said about it is based on little more than small, loosely controlled studies and hearsay. We do know, however, that recent reports[3] are beginning to challenge its magnitude. Much more research will have to be done before we can answer this question. We also know that attempting to be a super-helper—all things to all people all the time—guarantees burnout, and that it is a potential hazard for any helper who does not take time for his or her self.

The Helper as Citizen

The professional role of helpers demands a special responsibility for assisting individuals to achieve greater fulfillment. This in itself is an important contribution to society, but the responsibility of helpers does not stop there. They were citizens before they were teachers, counselors, social workers, or nurses, and the responsibilities of citizenship cannot be set aside by anyone. People in the helping professions, like everyone else, must come to some kind of terms with the world they live in. Their responsibility as citizens requires more than repairing the casualties of the system, as counselors might, or preventing future failures, as teachers may. Responsibility as citizens also requires contributing to the construction of a truly fulfilling society.

Professional helpers have several advantages in this, for their professions were established primarily to meet human needs. The successful completion of professional tasks leads directly to the enhancement of individuals and hence to the improvement of society. Both their professional training and job responsibilities provide helpers with opportunities to affect the social structure directly. Participation in the helping professions keeps one closely in touch with the basic emotions and perceptions of which human personality is composed. This insight and understanding of people and behavior can be of immense value for understanding the dynamics of society and contributing to its improvement.

A change in a person inevitably affects society as well. Helpers can make important contributions to social change by sharing their knowledge and by committing themselves to action wherever their special talents can be used. How they do this, of course, is an individual matter, depending on the helper's self, the situation, and the degree of involvement chosen.

The Helper as Agent of Change

Perhaps the most frequently heard excuse for personal inaction is the one that begins, "They won't let me." "They" may be bosses, parents, teachers, principals, supervisors, politicians, almost anybody. The implication is that one could do so much if only these nefarious influences were not in the way. The majority of reasons given by teachers, for example, for the failure of students to learn lie almost anywhere except with the teacher—the children were unmotivated, improperly prepared last year, and lazy and came from bad home situations. The tendency to place the blame for failure on others is by no means confined to teachers. It is a common excuse for inaction used by helpers in all the professions.

Sometimes supervisors, administrators, or others do impose restrictions on freedom. Equally as often these obstructions exist only in the minds of the complainants. When the accuracy of the "they won't let me" explanation for inaction is investigated, "they" are often amazed to hear of the roadblocks "they" are presumed to have placed in the way of progress. Obstructions to change do not have to be real. If someone thinks they exist, that is enough. Rosenthal and others have called this the "self-fulfilling prophecy" and demonstrated that when people believe a thing is so, they are likely to behave in ways that make it so.[4] Counselors who believe that their clients are resisting are likely to create resistance, and social workers who are convinced that nothing can be done do not make much of an effort to try and so increase the likelihood that nothing will be done.

Major changes often frighten people, especially if they are widely advertised in advance. This creates its own resistance. The same changes can often be brought about without opposition if they are instituted as "normal" procedures minus trumpets and fanfare. In every life situation there is always room to maneuver, a degree of slack that permits a certain amount of movement. The helper who systematically takes up this slack soon finds still more room to maneuver because people get used to events. They assume it is normal, relax attention, and so provide a little more room to wriggle. Operating over a period of time by a continuous process of "taking up the slack," considerable change may be brought about. Later, because the matter never became an issue, no one is quite sure how it happened. Meanwhile, it has become well established and, if successful, will probably be continued.

In the interest of maximum impact, behavior may sometimes have to be expressed less drastically than belief. At first glance such a statement may sound like a denial of the authenticity we spoke of earlier. Not at all. People may *believe* whatever they wish. Behavior, however, because it directly interacts with others, must be relevant and responsible. A man who believes he must be honest may speak out forcefully against racism, knowing full well it will be threatening to his hearers, because he *intends* to force a distasteful confrontation. The same honest man may "pull punches" when his sister inquires how he likes her hat, because he is also kind and loves his sister—values that are more important at that moment than being impeccably honest.

Because they behave in terms of their perceptions, those who hope to change behavior must be concerned with the relationship between the *meaning* of their actions in the experience of the people they seek to influence. To be unconcerned with the consequences of one's behavior is to be little more than self-indulgent. Maximum change is likely to be produced when we successfully find ways to challenge people without threatening them. One reason for the ineffectiveness of many who take a radical position for social change is their insistence on behaving in the full measure of belief without regard for its effects on others. In the process they often make themselves so threatening to those they would like to change that they leave these people no alternative but outright rejection.

Without compromising beliefs or abandoning eventual goals, helpers may achieve more by adjusting demands to realistic appraisals of what is currently possible. There may be times and places when radical or revolutionary concepts are in order. Radicals can and have had stunning effects on human affairs in the course of history. People who choose this way of forcing confrontation do so at the risk of destroying themselves in the process—but on occasion even that may be deemed a price well worth paying. Some social causes are so important that personal considerations need to be sacrificed for larger goals.

As members of the social order, people in the helping professions need to have a proper perspective of what can honestly be expected from society. Helpers sometimes think that they are not properly appreciated by the institutions they are involved in or the people they work with. Social workers bewail the fact that they are often misunderstood by the communities they are trying to help; teachers complain about the lack of public interest in the problems of the schools; counselors are shocked at the ingratitude of clients; and nurses are hurt that their patients forget them so quickly. Actually, this is a common fate of all workers in our society.

A democratic society *expects* each person to do his job. An interdependent society can exist only that way. This is especially true for the helping professions established expressly to serve other people. Society takes for granted that they will do their jobs. It also reserves the right to protest, complain, and accuse if it does not believe the job is being done. This is the democratic way, and professional helpers who think that they are not appreciated by society need only ask themselves, "When was the last time I dropped in at the police station to tell them what a good job they are doing?" "When did I last call up the sewage disposal works to express my appreciation for what they are doing?" or for that matter, "When was the last time you told your spouse how much you appreciate her or him?"

Conflicting Demands on Helpers

The professional role of helpers makes them responsible for aiding individuals to reach their maximum fulfillment. The personal role of helpers requires them to behave as citizens in ways that protect and enhance society. Fortunately, these goals are generally congruent, but at times they may come into conflict with one another. For example, a child caught in a disapproved act may beg his teacher not to inform his parents. A client tells his counselor that he has been shoplifting or his social worker that he plans to commit suicide. The problems created by such confrontations must be met by helpers. Solutions are not simple. They are further complicated by the fact that helpers probably would not have the information in the first place had they not successfully created an atmosphere in which the student or client felt safe in talking about such matters.

Similar conflicts come about when some social agency attempts to impose on helpers requirements that are contrary to their conception of the professional role. This situation arose when teachers were told they could not teach evolution or were required to lead children in daily prayers (an act that has been declared unconstitutional). It might occur too when a counselor or nurse is requested by an authority to divulge what a client or patient has said.

Matters like these raise difficult problems for the professional and citizenship roles of the helper. The resolution of such problems, for helpers confronted with them for the first time, is likely to involve a good deal of anguish. Pat answers seldom suffice. Each helper must think matters through for himself and arrive at his own decisions. After that he must be willing to take the consequences, whatever they may be. Making such decisions is painful. The pain is by no means worthless, however; it is precisely by wrestling with such problems that vision becomes clear, understandings are sharpened, philosophies are made more consistent, and further growth of the helper is achieved.

THE PROFESSIONAL HELPER AND ACCOUNTABILITY[5]

One hears a great deal about accountability in the helping professions, and helpers surely must be accountable. But what can they truly be held accountable for? Can helpers be held accountable for the behavior of their clients? To answer that question we need to answer a prior one: To what extent can *any* person, helper or not, be held accountable for another person's behavior?

Because complex behavior is never the exclusive product of any one stimulus or set of stimuli provided by another person, it follows that no human being can be held responsible for the behavior of another, except under three possible conditions:

1. *If the other person is too weak or too sick to be responsible for himself* Adults have to be responsible for some aspects of children's behavior, especially acts that might prove harmful to the child or to others. The same rule applies to those who are too sick to care for themselves and who need the help of others. Acceptance of the responsibility to aid such people has long been a basic tenet of Judeo-Christian philosophy. Such conditions of responsibility are comparatively short-lived, however, existing only until the individual can care for himself. Generally speaking, the older a child becomes, the more necessary it is for him to assume responsibility for himself. The principle is clearly recognized in the courts. It is also the goal of human development, as the organism strives for freedom, autonomy, and self-actualization. It ought to be the goal of helpers as well.

2. *If one person makes another person dependent on her* Whoever assumes the responsibility of making decisions for another person also assumes responsibility for his behavior. A person who, for whatever reason, induces or seduces another to surrender his autonomy at the same time assumes responsibility for his actions. This may occur in the case of physicians who accept the principle of "total responsibility for the patient." It may also occur in the case of the psychotherapist who permits her client to develop a deep transference, or in the case of a teacher who seeks to assume the role of a child's mother. Such dependent relationships may be desirable in the doctor–patient relationship. In most of the other helping professions, which are not depending on the helper *doing* something to his client, the development of such dependency is generally regarded as unfortunate and undesirable. The development of dependency runs counter to the basic objective of helping professions, which is the production of intelligent people who are capable of acting autonomously and freely with full responsibility for themselves.

3. *If responsibility is demanded by role definition* Sometimes responsibility for another may be imposed on a person by virtue of peculiarly assigned roles. An example might be the responsibility of the prison guard to make certain that prisoners do not escape. Such role-defined responsibilities for the behavior of others, however, are ordinarily extremely limited and generally restricted to preventive kinds of activities. So a teacher, by reason of his role, might be held responsible for keeping two children from fighting with each other. Holding the teacher responsible for whether or not a child does his homework is quite another question. One cannot, after all, be held responsible for events not truly within one's control, and few of us have much direct control over even the simplest behaviors of others.

But what of professional responsibility? For what can helpers be held accountable simply because they are helpers?

Helpers can and should be held accountable for behaving professionally. A profession is a vocation requiring some special knowledge or skill. The factor that distinguishes it from more mechanical occupations, however, is its dependence on the professional worker as a thinking, problem-solving human being who has learned how to use self, knowledge, and skills effectively and efficiently to carry out personal, professional, and social purposes. Professional helpers can properly be held accountable for at least five things:

1. They can be held accountable for being informed in their field of expertise. This is so self-evident as to need no further discussion.

2. Professional responsibility requires concern for the people involved in the process, and such concern can and should be demanded of helpers.

3. Helpers can also be held professionally responsible for their understanding of human beings and how they behave. Because people behave in terms of their beliefs, the beliefs that helpers hold about what clients are like and how and why they behave as they do play a crucial role in their performance. Professional helpers need the most accurate, sensitive, effective understandings about people and their behavior that it is possible to acquire.

4. Helpers may be held professionally responsible for the purposes they seek to carry out. Human behavior is purposive. Each helper behaves in terms of what he believes is the purpose of society, of its institutions, of his branch of the helping professions and, most especially, in terms of his own personal needs and goals. The purposes held by helpers play a vital role in determining what happens to clients. They provide the basic dynamics from which practices are evolved. They determine the nature of what goes on in the helping relationship.

5. Professional helpers can be held responsible for the methods they use in carrying out their own and society's purposes. This does not mean that they must be required to use some previously determined "right" kinds of methods. Methods in themselves are neither good nor bad. They can be judged only in terms of the purposes they were used to advance and the impact they had on those who were subject to them. The methods that helpers use must fit the helper, the student, or the client, as well as the circumstances in which they are employed. The essence of good professional work calls for thinking practitioners who can confront problems and find effective solutions. These solutions may be highly unique and personal.

Professional responsibility does not demand a prescribed way of behaving but rather that whatever methods are used have reasonable expectations of being good for the client. The emphasis is not on guaranteed outcomes but on the defensible character of what is done. Doctors, for example, are not held responsible for a patient's death. What they are held responsible for is being able to defend in the eyes of their peers that whatever they did had the presumption of being helpful when applied. Other helpers too must be prepared to stand this kind of professional scrutiny of their information, beliefs, and purposes and the adequacy of the techniques they use. Their actions should be based on good and sufficient reasons, defensible in terms of rational thought or as a consequence of informal or empirical research.

HELPING PROFESSIONS: A TWO-WAY STREET

Successful participation in helping relationships is in itself an experience in fulfillment. In earlier chapters we observed that whatever is experienced is experienced forever. We have also seen how the self may expand to include others. The helper's encounters with clients, students, or patients expand her own experience and influence. One of our friends once pointed out to us the three sources of immortality available to everyone. One kind, he said, is the immortality we achieve through our bloodlines. This, however, is a tenuous foothold. Hereditary links are easily broken by the failure of our children or descendants to reproduce. A second kind of immortality, he pointed out, is that promised us in the tenets of religion. Such concepts are comforting thoughts, but they could, conceivably, be wrong. The only kind of immortality we can all be sure of, he maintained, is that which we achieve as a consequence of our impact on the people in the world we live in. So the helper affects the client, and the client affects the helper, and each leaves the interaction changed in some way because of the experience. All future contacts will be affected because of this significant experience. "This," said our friend, "is a kind of immortality we can all be sure of. If in time we achieve the others also, that's like icing on the cake."

Helpers are warm-blooded, living, human beings with their own needs, capacities, hopes, fears, loves, and aspirations. In addition to these characteristics, which they share in common with all other human beings, helpers have assumed, or have had thrust on them, the responsibility for creating relationships that are helpful for others. How effectively helpers carry out this task will depend on how well they have learned to use their particular talents and personality for the realization of their own and society's purposes.

When helpers perform effectively, clients, patients, or students are not the only ones who profit. The increased humanity and sensitivity to others that is a result of intimate interaction with others is also one of the fringe benefits for workers in the helping professions. Helping others is a two-way street. One cannot successfully enter deeply and meaningfully into the life of another person without having that experience affect one's self as well.

Fred Richards has expressed, as well as we have ever seen it, the reciprocal nature of the relationship between helper and helpee. We would like to end this book with some of his statements about the way he sees the helping relationship. He is speaking about psychotherapy, but his words could well serve as a "code of practice" for all professional helpers:

> The path of psychotherapy is a journey in which two or more persons seek to discover one another and share one another's personal truth. To do this we will learn to risk disclosing who we are, to reach out to one another, to experience ourselves for who we are at the moment.

I cannot force you to change and grow. I will not tell you how to live. I will, however, invite you to grow, to become more aware, more loving, more able to live a richer, fuller life for which you accept responsibility.

Again, I will neither take responsibility for your life nor protect you from the pain and suffering of living. I will help you in your effort to change the perceptions and behaviors contributing to the unnecessary pain and suffering in your life. In regard to the pain and suffering that comes with simply living, I will help you to face it, accept it, and use it to grow. Sharing this effort with you will most likely help me to more creatively deal with the pain and suffering in my life.

I will be present with you. I will be as honest, genuine, and real as I can muster the insight and courage to be. I will exert my will to not hide from you, even when, feeling helpless, confused, and afraid, I feel an urge to do so.

I will be with you as long as I see you trying to grow. When I experience you as no longer trying to grow, I will share this with you. I will tell you my time left in life is precious to me and that I choose not to be with you. It is possible that for you my usefulness has ended and you perhaps need to seek help to grow elsewhere. We will talk about this impasse and hopefully not diminish our relationship when deciding whether or not to continue on the journey together.

I will not meet with you to help you become what is called a normal, adjusted, self-satisfied person. Nor will I help you to whine and wallow in the misery of your own making. I, too, have a tendency to do both of the above, so I will lovingly provoke you to share with me the effort to be more. I will help you to take charge of your life and to reinvent it if necessary.

I will invite you to tell your story, as honestly and truly as you are capable of telling it now, perhaps more intimately than you have ever disclosed it to another human being. I will not share your story with others unless you request I do so. I may decide to tell you part of my story when I believe it is appropriate and helpful to do so.

I will say hello to you as honestly as I know how, but my commitment is to encounter you in such a way that you will someday decide to say goodbye. It is my hope we will say hello and goodbye as authentically and humanly as persons like ourselves are capable of.

In a sense, I will help you to die, to leave behind outgrown and worn out ways of being, believing, and behaving in order that you can renew yourself and become a new person. To surrender and let go of the old and embrace the new is often a painful and joyful experience. I will not run away from the fullness of either your pain or joy.

I have myself learned that much of our suffering and misery, when seen and understood, can evoke laughter. There are times I may laugh at both you and myself. There are times when you may laugh at me and yourself. Hopefully there will be times we can laugh together. If we can share this laughter, there's a chance we will help one another free ourselves to grow and live.[6]

We know of no better set of guidelines for professional helpers, for those aspiring to enter one of the helping professions, or, for that matter, as a framework for daily living.

Notes and References

1. E. G. Wangberg, "Helping Teachers Cope with Stress," *Educational Leadership* 39 (1982): 452–454.

2. For a thorough treatment of the subject, see D. Welch, D. Madeiros, and G. Tate, *Beyond Burnout: How to Enjoy Your Job Again When You Have Just Had Enough* (Englewood Cliffs, N.J.: Prentice-Hall, 1982).

3. See, for example, L. C. Falkenstein, "Portland Teachers Defy Some Common Misconceptions of Educators," and F. C. Feitler and E. Tokar, "Getting a Handle on Teacher Stress: How Bad Is the Problem," *Educational Leadership* 39 (1982):454, 456–458.

4. R. Rosenthal and L. F. Jacobson, *Pygmalion in the Classroom* (New York: Holt, Rinehart, and Winston, 1968).

5. This section is adapted from a more extensive discussion in A. W. Combs, *Educational Accountability: Beyond Behavioral Objectives* (Washington, D.C.: Association for Supervision and Curriculum Development, 1972).

6. F. Richards, "Psychotherapy: A Loving Relationship" (unpublished paper). Reprinted with permission of the author.

INDEX